APPLIED FACILITIES
MANAGEMENT
FOR THE HOSPITALITY INDUSTRY

JOHN E. EDWARDS

cognella
San Diego, CA

Bassim Hamadeh, Publisher
Michael Simpson, Vice President of Acquisitions
Christopher Foster, Vice President of Marketing
Jessica Knott, Managing Editor
Stephen Milano, Creative Director
Kevin Fahey, Cognella Marketing Program Manager
Rose Tawy, Acquisitions Editor
Jamie Giganti, Project Editor
Brian Fahey, Licensing Associate

First published in the United States of America in 2012 by University Readers, Inc.

Trademark Notice: Product or corporate names may be trademarks or registered trademarks, and are used only for identification and explanation without intent to infringe.

16 15 14 13 12   1 2 3 4 5

Printed in the United States of America

ISBN: 978-1-60927-812-0

www.cognella.com 800.200.3908

ACKNOWLEDGEMENTS

I have been greatly aided in the composition of this book by the support and proofreading of my wife, Josephine, and I admire her patience and efforts to help me in this and all other parts of my life. I also am extremely grateful to David Bartl who corrected my punctuation and grammar as he helped me to focus my thoughts into a teachable format. Thanks are also due to Dr. Lynn Huffman who had the confidence to allow a facilities manager the opportunity to become a teacher.

I dedicate this work to all of those general managers in the hospitality industry who are not really sure what facilities managers do or how they do it. I hope that the principles, thoughts, and ideas in this book will help current and future general managers to understand the complex functions and responsibilities of the facilities manager.

CONTENTS

CHAPTER ONE
THE PRACTICE OF FACILITIES MANAGEMENT

CHAPTER LEARNING OBJECTIVES

After reading this chapter, the student should be able to:

1. Describe the role(s) of the facility manager as the responsible custodian of a property.
2. Describe a clear definition of "effective" facilities management.
3. Describe the volume of tasks that must be completed for effective facilities management.
4. Explain the expansion and increasing complexity of facilities management issues with the passage of time and future projections.
5. Understand and discuss the ethical responsibilities of a facility manager.
6. Understand and describe the concept of facilities management as a profit center rather than an operational cost burden.
7. Describe the training and education requirements to obtain the professional credentials for effective facilities management.

THE ROLE OF A FACILITY MANAGER

The position of facility manager exists in every business that has a physical location. In the hospitality industry this position has many titles such as "Chief Engineer," "Superintendent," "Property Manager," "Director of Engineering," or, in smaller operations, the position might simply be called "Maintenance Man" or even the "Owner." Whatever it is called, the role of this position remains the same. This position is responsible for maintaining the physical structure and operating systems of the establishment in a functional condition.

The physical structure of the building or property usually represents the largest capital investment for the business and establishes the corporate image of the firm. This includes the visual association of the building with the services or products provided. That means that the way the property looks, either by design or condition, provides the potential customer with a clear expectation of the nature or quality of the products or services that can be obtained and a reasonable idea of the price range involved. A customer does not go into a fast food restaurant to buy a lobster dinner and would not expect to find sushi available at a family-oriented, casual-dining restaurant. The facility itself creates an expectation and the facility manager is responsible to maintain that image. A customer may be interested in a "mom and pop" style small-town motel, but will pass it by if it seems to project a rundown or dilapidated appearance. In a similar fashion, the same customer may be attracted to the shiny and well-kept outward appearance of a chain hotel, but will form a lasting unfavorable impression of the quality of service if the hot water tap does not produce hot water. That impression would be applied to not only that particular accommodation but, in his mind, will also be associated with every hotel in the chain. The physical impression on the customer, good or bad, is a direct result of the efforts of the facility manager.

The facility manager maintains the factory for the products and services that the establishment sells. Just as an automobile manufacturer cannot build cars without a manufacturing facility, a hotel cannot sell rooms without a building and a restaurant cannot sell prepared food without a kitchen. The facility provides the physical location where a service or good is produced and the facility manager ensures that the structure or building meets the functional requirements for that production. The owner of the firm depends on the facility manager to do this as do all the other employees. Not only does the building represent the factory for production, it also provides a workplace for the employees. Therefore, they are depending on the facility manager to maintain the property in a condition that allows them to earn a living. All of the departments of the firm use the facility to support their activities and are therefore dependent on the skills and efforts of the facility manager.

Many people think that the facility manager makes sure that "things get fixed" if they fail or break, but this is only a minor part of the role. The facility manager has to concentrate on maintaining the property. Repair is only a small part of maintenance. In fact, repair can be viewed as the result of failed maintenance. If the facility manager could achieve perfect maintenance, then no system, component, or fixture would ever need repair because nothing would ever fail. This level of maintenance has never been achieved, but professional facility managers continue to try. The overall objective is to maintain the physical structure of the firm, not only to maintain the corporate image and the ability to produce services or goods, but also to allow for the growth of the firm. That growth may be a response to an increasing volume of business, but it will also be driven by the changing technology and progression of customer expectations. It is not enough for the facility manager to meet the business needs for the present. He or she must plan for the future of the property to allow for continued growth and expansion of the operation.

If the facility manager is successful, the customers' expectations will be met, the owner will realize a profit, and the business will grow. However, the customers and the owner will never consciously realize that their needs have been met. It is human nature to not notice the things that are going well, but to be concerned about the problems that are encountered. Therefore, if the structure is successfully maintained, very few people will notice. In fact, this author has often been amazed at the number of people who seem to believe that buildings are maintained by magical elves that come in at night to clean or repair everything before anybody gets up in the morning.

WHAT IS FACILITIES MANAGEMENT?

If maintenance is not done by magical elves in the middle of the night, then how is it accomplished? The answer that has developed over the past several centuries is that effective maintenance activities are provided by effective facilities management. Effective facilities management is defined as the actions and activities required to maintain a building or property in a suitable condition to allow operations to continue in a profitable environment. All available revenue and resources could be expended on a structure to keep it cleaned, maintained, and updated to the highest possible level, but if so many resources are being used that the business conducted in the structure does not show a profit, the entire enterprise will fail. Conversely, if no revenue or resources are expended to maintain the structure and it deteriorates to an unserviceable condition, the business will show a diminishing profit over time and ultimately fail as well. To prevent either situation the facility manager balances his efforts against costs to ensure that the firm continues to prosper. This balancing act means that some items in his activity list such as broken pipes and failed electrical circuits must be taken care of immediately, but items like wearing carpets or aging paint can be scheduled for more appropriate times. All of the tasks must be accomplished if the business is to continue to operate profitably, but the facility manager uses his management skills to complete requirements in a logical and managed sequence.

FACILITIES MANAGEMENT NEVER STOPS GROWING

Not too many years ago, facility management included making sure that the thatch roof didn't leak, the garbage was swept out of the common room downstairs, and not much else. In fact, it was a common practice in the inns of the original American colonies for customers to share beds. The fee that one paid to stay at the inn bought only a portion of a bed and if you wanted a discount rate, you could elect to curl up in a corner of the common room for the night. Buying a meal meant that you purchased a portion of whatever was in the pot over the fire and for an extra fee you could get a flagon of homemade beer in a dirty mug. The standards and practices of facility management matched the quality of the fare and board of the times. These conditions were the accepted level of accommodations of the period. Through the years, customers have come to demand a higher quality of service in their lodging and dining facilities and the industry has changed to meet those demands.

As the accommodations have changed to meet expanding and growing customer expectations, the requirements of facility management have expanded and grown to support the industry. As customers began to expect clean sheets, clean floors, glass windows, running water, modern sanitary equipment, and roofs that don't leak, the people taking care of the buildings had to develop more sophisticated skills and procedures to provide for those expectations. This growth has been accelerated by the advent of ever-increasing technology requirements. Not long after running water became more available, hot water was being demanded, causing the facility manager to learn how to maintain water heaters and fuel sources. Central heating systems led to the development of air conditioning. A formal postal system led to the development of the telegraph and then the telephone, followed by electronic mail and the internet. The customer has come to expect those services to become available very soon after they are developed. This meant that the facility manager had to either obtain the skills to support those services, or find a source of qualified technicians to install and maintain them.

While technology and customer expectations changed facilities, society itself also began to raise its standards of service. Regulatory bodies began to establish rules and regulations that did not exist before in areas such as fire safety and environmental impact. Other areas of general interest have also produced new requirements. The "green" movement and the resulting government controls on environmental concerns and regulation of resource use as well as the institution of equal opportunity laws and regulatory actions to support disabled persons or the special interests of children, elderly people, and any other identifiable category, all serve to increase the magnitude of building management. As various agencies and elements of authority write new laws and building codes, the facility manager must expand the expertise of his staff and the complexity of his procedures to ensure compliance. This trend toward complexity in regulation not only applies to customer expectations but also to employee expectations. The rules involving a safe and discrimination-free workplace have also increased the activities that the facility manager must perform to provide it.

Changing customer and employee expectations, changing technology, and expanding regulations are constant factors in the world of facility management. Interestingly, new regulations or technology do not often remove the requirements of old regulations or old technology that might still be present in a building. Therefore, the field of facility management continues to grow and modernize, but older requirements do not go away. Sometimes the older requirements have been replaced by newer ones. For example, very few hotels still maintain a stable to take care of customers' horses, but most are expected to have paved parking facilities available. Cutting and stacking firewood has been replaced by maintaining electrical heating, natural gas, and central heating systems. Every service that a hospitality firm adds to its menu to serve the customer will have a corresponding set of requirements that the facility manager must meet in order to provide that service. Since the progression and growth of the hospitality industry is expected to continue, it is reasonable to say that the field of facility management and the duties of the facility manager will continue to grow with it.

Continued growth and development not only expand the requirements for the facility manager, they also expand the number of management tools that are available to fill those requirements. Specifically in the area of systems and workload management, the progress of technology and information management systems has allowed facilities managers to index, manipulate, and manage a much larger volume of work. In addition, the new tools of Computerized Maintenance Management Systems (CMMS) and Computerized Facilities Management Systems (CFMS) also provide a much higher level of service to the occupants of a building. The Heating, Ventilation, and Air Conditioning (HVAC) control systems that are now available will maintain occupant comfort in an automatic mode with very little required input from the manager. New supply-handling systems coupled with maintenance management systems greatly improve the availability of replacement parts and materials to keep systems in service and simultaneously reduce the stockpiles that formerly were maintained by the engineering or facilities management department. These systems ensure that the right item is available at the right time with a greatly reduced down-time or out-of-service time for critical equipment. The management tools offered by Computerized Maintenance Management Systems (CMMS) and Computerized Facilities Management Systems (CFMS) protocols have improved staffing levels, reduced overtime requirements, reduced equipment and components costs, improved energy management, and have provided the facilities manager with the ability to provide a better-maintained facility at a lower cost to ensure continued profitability.

Using automatic data processing coupled with modern principles of facilities maintenance such as preventive maintenance, predictive maintenance, and reliability-based maintenance, facilities managers in the hospitality industry have developed and maintained building management systems that amplify the revenue-producing activities of an operation while reducing the maintenance cost to provide much better support to the profits of their establishments. As technology and research continue to expand the areas that a facilities manager must support, they will also allow the facilities manager to develop better tools to provide the required support. New materials, tools, equipment, and improved management efforts must all be incorporated into the daily operations of the facilities department. The facilities manager must constantly develop and research plans and improved management tools, allowing for future growth in all of his or her assigned or implied responsibilities and functions.

ETHICAL BEHAVIOR FOR FACILITIES MANAGERS

What do ethics have to do with facilities management? Doesn't facilities management deal with things? To the average building occupant, good facilities operations are invisible. As was stated earlier, some people seem to believe that magical elves take care of things overnight. Primarily for that reason the facilities manager must exhibit and require his staff to exhibit very high ethical standards. Very few people are watching them work and those who do notice their efforts usually do not have the technical expertise to discern that the work is being done correctly. Because of that, the only thing that binds the facilities manager and his technicians to produce good quality work is their own ethical values. It is easy to exhibit ethical behavior when someone is watching, but it can be difficult to control when activities are invisible.

The facilities manager is drawn in three different directions by his ethical responsibilities. First, he is ethically bound to provide the owner of the property with the best possible maintenance and facility support system. The system of building management that he devises must allow for the highest possible profit from the operation of the building. This means that costs must be reduced to the lowest possible level, but quality must be maintained to meet the operational and profit goals of the owner. The second element of the ethical dilemma for the facilities manager is his responsibility to meet the customers' expectations for quality of service, comfort, safety, and security. These expectations must be met regardless of the effect on the owner's goals, especially in the areas of safety and security. The facilities manager cannot take shortcuts or half-steps in providing a safe and secure environment for the customer. Occasionally, this will place the facilities manager in a conflict between the owner's goals and the customers' expectations. The third leg of the facilities manager's ethical dilemma is his responsibility to provide the employees with a safe, secure, and efficient workplace. Doing this involves ethical human resources management practices, balancing workloads, management of tool and materials requirements, and a myriad of other tasks and responsibilities that allow the employee to meet the requirements of the owner's goals and the customers' expectations. In a professionally managed operation, these three elements are not usually in conflict, but in some organizations, differing objectives or inefficient management can place the facilities manager in a three-way bind in making decisions.

The only way to solve such conflicts is to ensure that the owner or general manager is aware of the conflict. The facilities manager must tell his supervisor if a problem or situation is creating any difficulty in meeting the goals, objectives, or obligations in any or all of the three areas of his responsibility. Usually, priority adjustments or additional allocation of resources from the operations manager can resolve the problem. The facilities manager must keep the "Boss" informed of such problems to be ethically and professionally successful. This will often put the facilities manager in the role of the "bearer of bad news," but it is a measure of ethical performance that must be met head on.

If the facilities manager fails to behave ethically in any one of his three directions of responsibility, he will eventually fail in all three. Further, it is quite likely that his unethical behavior will also cause a loss of profits for the operation and possible failure of the business.

MAINTENANCE PRODUCES PROFIT

Accountants and general operations managers often identify maintenance requirements as an element of cost. Consequently, they are quite happy to reduce maintenance efforts in an attempt to reduce cost and therefore increase profits. This has often been a fatal mistake in management philosophy in the hospitality industry. Maintenance is actually a profit multiplier. Without proper maintenance of equipment and facilities, the efficiency of the operation will deteriorate and the ability to show profits will deteriorate with it. Every dollar that is spent on maintenance of the structure or systems in a building multiplies its profitability by increasing the quality and efficiency of the service that is provided.

Maintenance requirements generally use approximately 20% of the annual revenues of a hospitality establishment. This is sometimes viewed as a drain on profitability and for a very short period of time profits can be increased by reducing maintenance operations. Such managerial attitudes are connected to the belief that has already been discussed, that maintenance means repairing problems when, in fact, maintenance prevents problems and the need for repair. Equipment and building systems do not go out of service when they are not being used. They only fail or go out of service when they are engaged and needed. Therefore, a lack of maintenance will stop a profitable operation and turn it into a losing operation. A hospitality establishment is only paid for providing a service or a product. If the equipment fails while the product is being produced, the opportunity for profit is lost until repairs can be made.

The best example of the profit production of maintenance is the building's roof. The roof of a building is its most critical external surface. Without a roof, the tallest building in the world is just a fence that is open to the sky. The roof keeps out the rain. If the roof fails and allows a leak into a room or a dining room, the establishment not only loses the services of that room or an area of tables, but it also begins to suffer structural damage from the water, and the repair costs will continue to rise until the roof is repaired. Unfortunately, a roof cannot be repaired until the rain stops, so the loss of revenue from the lost service will continue to multiply. If the roof was properly maintained before it started raining, it would not leak and there would be no loss of revenue when the rain started. Therefore, profits are protected. Repair will not bring back the lost profits from a leak, but good maintenance will prevent the loss and ensure that profits continue.

All the structural and equipment systems in the establishment are critical and the facilities manager must schedule, direct, and control his efforts to protect all of them simultaneously. A pizza parlor will not suffer damage from rain if the roof is maintained, but if the pizza oven burns out because it was not properly cleaned, the restaurant is still going to be out of business. In like fashion, a loss of electrical power will close down the operation just as quickly as a collapsing roof. Failure of the air conditioning system will destroy the reputation of a hotel and a poorly maintained pump will cause a swimming pool to be unavailable on the hottest day of the year. A worn and torn carpet or a rickety chair presents the same threat of injury to a guest as a broken stairway step or an unlit hallway. A poorly cleaned kitchen or incorrect water temperatures in the dishwasher will cause food poisoning and close a restaurant just as quickly as a fire or a collapsing roof. All of these problems and countless more can and will destroy the profitable operation of any hospitality enterprise. Profits can only be realized and problems like these can only be prevented by systematic, repetitive, and carefully managed maintenance systems.

TRAINING FOR FACILITIES MANAGERS

The position of facilities manager requires an extensive and varied set of skills, both technical and managerial in nature. It is a popular stereotype that building superintendents, facilities managers, or maintenance managers are people who have been plumbers, carpenters, or handymen for twenty or thirty years and gradually moved up into that position. While that is true in some cases, it does not acknowledge the learning and experience that must be gained during the worker's career to produce the qualifications to be an effective and successful facilities manager. The image of an old man with greasy coveralls and a worn tool belt moving up to become a facilities manager is no more true than that of a truck driver becoming the CEO of a major truck manufacturer. While there are instances where such careers have occurred, the person who does this has to develop and learn a great number of additional skills and techniques along the way to become successful.

There are a few universities that are now offering facilities management as a major course of study. Universities that offer management and hospitality management majors include at least a familiarization course in facilities management or facilities as a required area of study. Professional organizations such as the Building Owners and Managers Association (BOMA), the American Hotel and Lodging Association (AHLA), the Association of Physical Plant Administrators (APPA), and others offer professional skill-development courses, seminars, and distance learning opportunities to help building managers and others working in facilities careers develop the knowledge and skills necessary to advance to

Figure 1.1. Facilities Manager Reponsiblities

- Equipment Selection
- Equipment Installation
- Maintenance Contracts
- Contractual Compliance
- Utilities Operations and Costs
- Waste Management
- Security
- Safety
- Staff Training
- Staff Hiring
- Staff Firing
- Quality Control
- Digital Information Systems
- Accounting and Cost Control
- Operations Coordination
- Scheduling
- Budget Development
- Parts Inventory and Control
- Emergency Planning
- Budget and Cost Control
- Corporate Reporting
- (anything else that comes up)

the management level. Community colleges, local trade schools, and university extension programs also present educational opportunities in this field. Many facilities managers have taken advantage of these educational opportunities and combined them with the curriculum of the universal school of hard knocks and hands-on experience to become very professional in their field. Recognition of this extra effort to develop management skills can be obtained by certification or credentials from the BOMI, the AHLA, and other professional organizations. Usually maintenance of these credentials requires participation in continuing education programs to ensure current skills and knowledge of the field.

The required credentials and certification to obtain a position as a facilities manager are not standard. A facilities manager with professional certification and a master's in business administration (MBA) has no greater guarantee for success than the individual who worked his way up from electrician's helper. However, all facilities managers who wish to be successful will need to obtain and develop skills that are not usually associated with the building trades. Such things as effective business correspondence, staff management, team organization, inventory management, human resources management, operational scheduling, contract administration, safety management, risk management, digital controls, basic accounting, information management, and many other areas must be added to the repertoire of the aspiring facilities manager's skills to ensure effective and successful facilities management. A partial list of the responsibilities of the facilities manager's position is presented in Figure 1.1, but it must be realized that this is not a complete list and often the job description of the facilities managers will have a final sentence that states, "other duties as assigned …" or a similar catch-all phrase to make sure that nothing is left out.

CHAPTER SUMMARY

In the role of facilities manager, an individual maintains not only the structure and systems of the building but also exercises oversight and support management for all of the activities within the building. The primary goal of all elements of an operation is to produce a profit. The facilities manager is responsible for ensuring that the physical location and structure of the establishment not only allows for profitable operations, but also is maintained in a suitable condition to sustain profitable operation into the future. To accomplish this, the facilities manager is occupied with an endless array of tasks stretching from routine and mundane such as removing trash and debris to the manipulation of complex automated data systems. The activities of the facilities manager are often invisible to the occupants of the building and they only notice when something does not happen as planned or a system goes out of service. Therefore, the only thing forcing a facilities manager to do things "right" is his or her own ethical values. No one is watching so only the facilities manager knows if the job is being done within prescribed codes or proper parameters. If the facilities manager is successful in maintaining the structure to established standards of condition or operation, then the occupying firm has a profitable environment in which to operate. Therefore it can be said that the facilities manager and his or her activities allow profits to be realized. This supports a statement that maintenance activities should be viewed as profit centers rather than elements of cost. The skills required to successfully maintain a modern building continue to expand as the complexity of technology continues to expand. These skills cannot all be learned "on the job" and formal training is necessary for a facilities manager to grow professionally. This training never really stops and professional organizations within the field of hospitality and facilities management have established qualification and certification standards to verify the attainment of required skills for the professional facilities manager.

GLOSSARY OF TERMS

Facilities Management
Those activities involved in maintaining the structural and physical condition of a building or property to meet the requirements of its intended purpose. In the hospitality industry, the focus of all facilities management actions is to support profitable operations.

Maintenance
The actions required to sustain the upkeep of a structure, building, or operational system in a serviceable condition. Any service failure is a reflection of failed maintenance. Therefore, repair is the action required to return something to serviceable condition and can be considered as a maintenance failure.

Computerized Maintenance Management Systems (CMMS)
Automated or digital management systems specifically designed to support the management of equipment or property maintenance activities.

Computerized Facility Management Systems (CFMS)
Automated or digital management systems designed to support and coordinate the management of operational and property maintenance activities.

Heating, Ventilation, and Air Conditioning (HVAC)
Utilities systems designed to control internal building environmental conditions to meet established standards for human comfort.

Ethics
This is the study of human values concerning the concepts of right and wrong in reference to human behavior.

Building System
An integrated element of a structure or building that can be addressed as distinctive entity within the property: electrical system, irrigation system, paint system, transportation system, HVAC system, etc.

STUDY QUESTIONS

1. Describe and define the primary role of the facility manager in a hospitality operation.
2. Describe and define the essential characteristics of "effective" facility management.
3. Discuss the progress of facilities management through history.
4. Will facilities management become simpler or more complex in the future? Explain your reasoning to support your answer.
5. Should facility management activities be considered as an overhead cost or a profit multiplier? Explain your reasoning to support your answer.
6. Describe the skills and knowledge that must be learned by the professional facilities manager. Where can these skills be obtained?

CHAPTER TWO
FACILITIES MANAGEMENT WITHIN AN ORGANIZATION

CHAPTER LEARNING OBJECTIVES

After reading this chapter, the student should be able to:

1. Discuss the significance of the facility manager as an integral member of the executive management team.
2. Describe the function of maintenance activities in retention of acceptable profitability rather than the preservation of a structure.
3. Describe the responsibilities of the facility manager in maintaining a functional environment to produce a profitable operation.
4. Describe effective relationships between the facility manager and other levels or areas of management.
5. Identify methods and tools used to establish mutual respect and cooperation between different management levels and areas.

THE EXECUTIVE MANAGEMENT TEAM

Some people, including a number of general managers, think of the facilities manager as a member of the lower-level staff of an organization. In fact, the stereotypical image is the handyman in coveralls and a tool belt, with an office consisting of a card table next to a boiler where he eats his lunch. Or, as was mentioned in Chapter 1, the contemplation of maintenance activities is so far removed from conscious thought that people seem to believe in the magical elves who fix things in the night. In fact, the facilities manager should be a member of the primary or executive staff of an efficiently managed hospitality enterprise. In the case of smaller family-run restaurants or motels, the owner, general manager, and facilities manager might all be the same person. In larger organizations, the distance between the boss and the facilities manager should not be greater than one step in the chain of control. A typical hotel staff organization is presented in Figure 2.1. Larger hotels might have more elements in their structure and smaller establishments might have fewer or have some of the functions combined under fewer managers, but in either case, the facilities manager needs to report directly to the general manager. The facilities manager is the only element of the executive staff who is required by circumstance and ethics to tell the general manager that something cannot be done. He or she is the one who knows if the physical structure of the property can support operations, special events, or new enterprises. Therefore, not only must the facilities manager be capable of carrying bad news to the general manager, he must also stop operations that will not be successful because of limited physical capacity or condition. To do this effectively, the facility manager needs to be in direct communication with the general manager and all other elements of the executive staff. Further, to support the many functions of the establishment, the facilities manager must also be able to coordinate and interact with other managers on an equal basis. He or she must understand the objectives that they are pursuing and advise them on any facility limitations or functional conflicts that must be overcome to achieve success. Specifically, the facilities manager must immediately inform the general manager of any function or operation that is not going to be profitable because of building or structure problems.

Conversely, the facilities manager is obligated to coordinate facility support for any current or new operation or function to make it profitable. To achieve this, the facility manager must be in a position on the staff that provides the earliest possible notification of upcoming events or anticipated operations. Thus, the facilities manager must be a primary staff member to effectively support the hospitality establishment. In many restaurant and hotel chains, the local facility manager can find support for his or her efforts at the corporation level. Corporations often include positions of "Regional Director of Property," "Vice-President for Facilities Support," or similar positions in their corporate management system. The corporate image is not presented to the public at the corporation level, but rather at the local level when the customer walks into a particular restaurant or hotel. Modern corporations are very interested in maintaining this image and have established the required upper-management elements to support their properties to remain profitable.

FIGURE 2.1: Hotel Staff Organization)

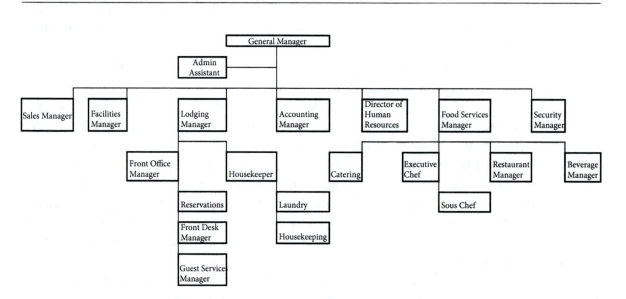

MAINTENANCE ACTIVITIES AS A PROFIT SOURCE

When a handyman-homeowner thinks of maintenance, they usually immediately move to thoughts of "fixing things." Further, they want things "fixed right!" Professional facilities managers don't think of maintenance in terms of repair of damaged or failing property elements of equipment. They think in terms of maintaining the function of the building in a profitable condition. From that standpoint they put less of their effort in "doing things right" and more into "doing the right things!" The technicians, plumbers, electricians, and other skilled workers who work for them are expected to "do things right," while the facilities manager is busy making sure that he is using the skills of those workers to the greatest advantage for the operations that depend on those facilities to make a profit. Repair of a broken or failed element of the property is not always the right thing to do at a particular time. Sometimes, those activities that keep other systems or elements from going out of service or getting a particular part of the property ready for an upcoming event will be of higher priority. Simultaneously, the repair requirements must be entered into the list of items to be completed so that whatever is broken or unserviceable can be returned to an operational status to contribute to profitable operations. Obviously, some immediate repairs must be made in the case of primary system failures, or emergency restoration of services but, because he or she will never have enough resources to do everything all the time, the facilities manager will be constantly juggling and adjusting the work schedule, not to "fix things," but rather to maintain a profitable operation.

Every building and every element of every building has a life cycle. The building starts out fresh and brand new with all working systems and as it starts to age, it will start to deteriorate if it is not maintained. The facility manager must establish the maintenance activities or system of maintenance functions to extend the life cycle of a building for the longest possible time. The duration of this life cycle is directly related to the profitability of the operation that occupies the building. Just maintaining the current systems or elements of the building will not extend its profitable life indefinitely. A hotel without running water might have been very profitable 150 years ago and it may have been kept in good condition for all 150 years of its existence. The wallpaper could be beautifully preserved, the carpet might be bright and clean, and the basins and jugs in the rooms are made of the best china available, but if it still does not have running water, the hotel will not turn a profit. Repairing broken kerosene lamps and repainting scraped banisters would not have been enough. To stay profitable the facility manager or the line of facility managers who worked there during the life of the hotel would have been required to update and install modern utility systems, including water, to meet customer expectations. In fact, modern hospitality establishments are in a constant cycle of renovation and restoration. This is required to meet the needs and expectations of their customers in the developing world. For example, a hotel that is only fifteen years old was probably built without automatic data communication systems installed. However, the same businessman who was a satisfied guest when it was new would not stay there now unless computer connections have been installed to allow him to conduct his business from his room. In fact, many customers now require "wireless" connections. To keep the building itself in a mode of profitable operations, the facility manager had to foresee the need for newer systems and have them installed in a timely manner.

FACILITY MANAGER RESPONSIBILITY FOR PROFIT

The business environment provided by the physical structure and grounds of a hospitality establishment is a combination of materials, equipment, and systems incorporated into the building and location in which it is located. A restaurant on the 25th floor of a skyscraper office building in Chicago would probably not provide a business opportunity for a casual family-dining format, but it lends itself very easily to a business-oriented lunch or dinner-club atmosphere. In either format, the (HVAC) system of the building must function effectively or the customers will be uncomfortable and dissatisfied with their dining experience. Although the general manager of the restaurant is expected to manage his enterprise to be successful and profitable, the facilities manager must accept responsibility for the upkeep and operation of the HVAC system and is, therefore, responsible for the maintenance of a profitable operation. The facilities manager is responsible for every physical element that supports the operation of any enterprise. Everything from painting the walls and resurfacing the roof to providing the electricity that runs the walk-in refrigerator and the gas that cooks the food falls within his or her area of responsibility. If any item of equipment or any structural system is not fully functional or threatens the safety and comfort of customers and employees, profitability is affected. Customers will be repulsed by peeling paint on the walls in the same way that a dead roach next to the hostess stand will cause some customers to select another restaurant. A formerly regular guest will not return to a hotel where the water heater no longer works well and the torn carpet can result in a liability suit from a customer's turned ankle. Anything and everything that a facilities manager does or fails to do can affect the profitability of the operations. Because of that fact, facilities activities are more closely related to profitability than they are to cost. If the structure is not maintained correctly or the equipment and systems do not operate effectively, then profits will suffer. Therefore, assets invested in facilities maintenance do not represent costs, but are actually contributions to increased or sustained profitability.

RELATIONSHIPS BETWEEN THE FACILITIES MANAGER AND OTHER MANAGERS

The facilities manager is the only member on the executive staff, other than the general manager, who must be very familiar with the needs, expectations, and procedures used by all of the other members' areas of responsibility. The facilities manager must coordinate his or her efforts to support the operations of all other departments of the organization. The support has to be constant, consistent, and oftentimes invisible to the supported department and their customers as well. To achieve this, the facilities manager must be aware of requirements, scheduling limitations, and operational needs for every aspect of the entire establishment. Every other department is a customer to the facilities manager and their needs must be met. A relationship must be established that allows the facilities manager to obtain and monitor information concerning customer department operations to enable the facilities department to provide effective support. This information should include not only physical information concerning utilities, operating systems, structural requirements, and other such items, but also operating schedules, upcoming events or problems, and special areas of concern. Departments will not provide this information automatically. The facilities manager has to train his customers to communicate their needs in a routine manner. Daily reports, distributed operations calendars, production performance data, and routine problem reports must be included in a standing system of communications exchange amongst the executive staff. In a like manner, the facilities manager must provide routine information regarding facilities capabilities, problems, and operations that may affect the customer departments and their operations. The supported operational departments need to understand what they must do to make sure that the facilities manager identifies their requirements. The customer and the provider need to work together to make sure that they are providing the best possible service to guests and customers of the establishment.

THE PRIMARY MANAGEMENT TOOL OF THE FACILITIES MANAGER

The management tool that the facilities manager uses to plan, control, coordinate, and complete his support of a profitable operation is actually a combination of many different activities, communications, and technical information. It is best described with the title of Facilities Management System (FMS). Regardless of the size of the operation, from small one-man operations to global chains of hotels and restaurants, the needs of the operation cannot be met and the myriad of required tasks that the facilities manager must complete cannot be accomplished without an organized system in place. Not only must the facilities activities be organized into a system to accomplish all of the required tasks in an appropriate manner to maintain safe, efficient, and profitable operations, but the managers of the other departments or management areas of the establishment must also know how to enter requirements into the system. Further, the established system must perform consistently and routinely. The only way to make that happen is to document the system so that it can be understood by all users and service providers. Written policies or standard operating procedures will greatly assist a facilities manager in communicating policies and procedures to his workforce and his customers by establishing routine expectations. The customers must have a good idea of the normal response that they can expect from the facilities manager and facilities technicians. A customer who knows what to expect can anticipate his or her own requirements and schedule their activities around an expected response from the facilities department. To ensure understanding of the facilities management system in place and the efficiency of its operations, the system must be designed to support the policies and management standards established by the operations manager. If the facilities manager is providing services and materials that do not match the needs of the operation then effectiveness, efficiency, and possibly even the safety of customers and employees will suffer. All occupants will respect and cooperate with a management system that provides them with dependable and timely service. Conversely, a facilities management system that does not meet their requirements, is slow in response, or lackadaisical in its maintenance quality or schedules will often be bypassed or circumvented by its customers. They will find a way to get their needs met either by self help or outside contractors, but often their solutions will be detrimental to the life or condition of the facility itself. Departments wiring their own computer systems or redesigning their own plumbing or lighting systems can disrupt normal building operations, create building code violations, and even threaten the safety of all building occupants.

Organizing the requirements of facility into a logical management system is the basis for mutual respect and cooperation with the other departments within an organization, but the customers must know how to use it and what role they play in the system. The facilities manager must keep them informed and trained through a consistent and continuous exchange of information. Providing copies of written policies or standard operating procedures is the first step, but the facilities manager must also explain how those procedures work and further, should inquire of the supported departments whether or not the written procedures will meet their needs. This personal inquiry is very important to establish communications. Many facilities departments have implemented a review or written evaluation of work or services provided to the customer departments, allowing them to comment and make suggestions for improvements. Such reviews can be very helpful in the training of technicians as well as identifying shortcomings in completed work. The facilities manager must redesign plans and procedures periodically to better meet the operational requirements of the organization and customer evaluations can be very helpful in improving the efficiency of operations. The facilities manager can also review current projects, problems, concerns, and achievements with the executive staff at staff meetings. This can help to produce an understanding amongst the other departments of the demands that are being met and work that is being completed, much of which they may not even see.

CHAPTER SUMMARY

To ensure successful operations in any hospitality establishment, the facilities manager must be an integral member of the primary staff or the executive management team. This allows the facilities manager to coordinate building requirements and available resources to provide the best available support for successful operation of the enterprise. The effective and efficient conduct of facilities maintenance activities is a primary contributor to the safe and profitable operation of any hospitality concern. Many general managers consider maintenance activities to be an element of overhead cost when, in fact, proper maintenance produces a longer and more efficient lifetime for profit-making equipment and structural systems. Whereas a lack of maintenance can reduce profits and expose building occupants, customers, and employees to unsafe and hazardous conditions, a properly maintained physical plant will produce profits at higher levels for a longer period of time with less risk of malfunctions. The facilities manager must establish effective means of exchanging operational information with all departments within the organization to ensure that each department has the best possible opportunity for successful operations. The facilities manager cannot assume that he or she inherently knows the needs of each department. A system of communication must be established so that facilities condition and preparation matches the requirements of the operating departments. The facilities manager must be viewed by all departments as an equal element of management. They must know how to make their needs known to the facilities manager and they must also trust that their requirements will be met in the most efficient manner possible. The continued safe, efficient, and profitable life of a hospitality enterprise depends on the efficient and effective management of its facilities manager.

GLOSSARY OF TERMS

Executive Management Team
This is the primary staff of an organization. Members of an executive management team report directly to the general manager or owner of the organization.

Physical Plant
This is the physical structure of the property. It includes the structure itself, its grounds, and all utilities systems contained therein. In local usage, some organizations refer to the facilities management department or engineering department as the "physical plant."

Building Life Cycle
The life cycle of a building starts from the date that it is first put into service until it can no longer be safely or profitably used for its intended purpose. This period of time can be extended by effective maintenance activities.

Renovation
The process of renewing and updating a property or item of equipment to offset the effect of age or extended use, to regain original levels of efficiency, or to meet changing requirements or operational functions.

Restoration
The process of completely gutting a space or building, or dismantling a piece of equipment and replacing all obsolete or outdated components, systems, or elements to bring it back to a level of acceptable functional use.

Facility Management System
A facility management system is an organized system of procedures, actions, and management efforts that coordinate the activities of occupants, technicians, and managers in the operation and maintenance of a structure or property.

Occupant
Any individual or agency that is housed or present within a physical structure or facility.

STUDY QUESTIONS

1. Why should the facilities manager be included as a member of the executive management team?
2. What are the responsibilities of the facilities manager as a member of the facilities management team?
3. Explain how a maintenance activity can be described as a profit source.
4. What should a facilities manager do to ensure that the needs of the other operational departments are being met? Please explain why this is important to the organization.
5. What is the primary tool of the facilities manager? Why?

CHAPTER THREE
FUNCTIONS AND RESPONSIBILITIES
OF A FACILITIES MANAGER

CHAPTER LEARNING OBJECTIVES

After reading this chapter, the student should be able to:

1. Identify specific areas of facility management responsibilities in systems and structures.
2. Describe the rules, regulations, and codes that affect facility management activities.
3. Describe the effect of conflicting responsibilities, obligations, and ethical considerations in facilities management activities.
4. Describe certification requirements in technical and professional areas.

In the first and second chapters of this book, the growing complexity and enormous scope of duties and responsibilities of facilities managers were referred to in general terms. In this chapter, those requirements will be further explained and reviewed from several different points of view. Some of these activities are driven by factors that are internal to the organization, while others are imposed by external agencies and authorities. Several responsibilities are affected by both internal and external policies, requirements, codes, and regulations. As development of the hospitality industry progresses in response to the changing and evolving expectations of the customer, the duties of the facilities manager are also changing and evolving. Some actually are simplified by the application of modern technology while others become more complex. Some changes result in additions to the overall workload while some lighten the burden, but all must be integrated into the facilities manager's list of responsibilities.

OPERATIONAL SYSTEMS

Because no single activity, item of equipment, or structural element stands alone in its function, the facilities manager must organize support of the structure, and the operations it houses, into related systems. All of these systems are grouped with a logical selection of directly related elements or activities, and each system in some way is connected to every other system either as a support factor or as a dependent operation. All of the systems combine to form the complete functional facility.

The physical components of the structure can be separated into systems with different characteristics and requirements. For example, the structural frame system may be steel, wood, reinforced concrete, a combination of all three, or some other material, all of which support the wall-covering system and the roof system and floor system. The exterior walls could be brick and masonry, concrete, wood, steel, or any of several other materials that must be maintained and protected by different methods and scheduled tasks. The interior walls might be constructed of painted sheetrock, plaster, fiberglass, vinyl, wood, concrete, or any of many other materials, and again, all of these will require different cleaning and maintenance activities. Between the exterior surface and the interior surface, modern construction practices call for the installation of a waterproof membrane called the moisture barrier. Together the exterior and interior walls' surfaces, with the moisture barrier in between them, form the structural wall system, which is sometimes referred to as the structural or building envelope.

This structural envelope supports the roof. The roof is considered a system because it can be made of many different materials or structural designs. It is generally considered to consist of three separate components: the decking, the insulation, and the weatherproof covering. In the traditional floodcoat roof, the decking could be wood, steel, or concrete and its purpose is to support the other two layers. On top of the decking, the insulation could be any material that provides a barrier to the exchange of heat through the roof. The insulation may also serve to provide slope to the roof to aid in the runoff of moisture. The floodcoat weatherproof covering consists of roof felt, which is sometimes called tar paper, and a moisture-proof membrane of melted bitumen tar spread over the surface. This floodcoat is held in place and protected against damage from ultraviolet sunlight by a coat of gravel or ballast. All of these elements together form a floodcoat roofing system. The variations available in roofing systems are numerous. They include terra cotta tile, asphalt shingles, slate, wood shakes, straw thatch, and hermetically sealed continuous vinyl membranes, to name a few. All of them are considered systems and each of them requires different maintenance processes to perform their protective function and reach their expected serviceable life.

Within the weatherproof shell formed by the roofing system and the building envelope, operational systems are installed to support the occupants and/or the intended function of the building. Electricity is provided by the electrical system. Fresh water is provided and waste water is removed from the building by the plumbing system. A comfortable environment for the occupants of the building is supported by the HVAC system and communication within the building is provided by the telephone system and the electronic information system. The building must have a fuel support system, a fire safety and alarm system, and some sort of emergency power system. Occupants are protected from harm and theft by the security system and they can see to do their work because of the lighting system. Multi-story structures usually have a vertical lift system such as freight or passenger elevators and escalators. The facilities manager attempts to control and support all of these systems through the use of a maintenance management system that is controlled either by paper forms or automated management systems.

The management of all the aforementioned systems would not be difficult if they could be separated and dealt with as stand-alone concerns. Unfortunately, that is impossible because they are intertwined throughout the building. The plumbing system depends on electrical pumps and is often controlled, or at least monitored, by the electronic information system. The heat generated by the electrical system is controlled by the HVAC system, which is also dependent on the plumbing system as well as the electrical system. The telephone system may carry the messages that control the HVAC system and the electrical system and is, in turn, dependent on the electrical system for power. The elevators require electricity, lighting, and electronic controls that are connected to the fire safety alarms. The security system depends on the integrity of the building envelope and roofing systems and the electronic communications system. Even the maintenance management system requires the support of the electrical, plumbing, HVAC, and all the rest of the systems to function effectively, and they all require the maintenance management system to keep them operating. The facilities manager must deal with all of these systems as an integrated co-dependent conglomeration of activities, materials, and requirements that is called a building.

As new configurations or improved capabilities are developed for any of these systems, the other systems must be adjusted or updated to accommodate or support the change. None of them is independent and the effective maintenance of each of them is critical to the systemic health of all of the others. Further, effective and coordinated maintenance support cannot be accomplished without an organized system that not only ensures the operation of the building systems, but also allows the profitable operation of the occupant activities.

RULES, REGULATIONS, AND CODES AFFECTING FACILITIES MANAGEMENT

Modern facilities are constructed, modified, maintained, and operated in accordance with a vast array of requirements imposed by governing authorities and professional organizations that prescribe performance standards for buildings and structures on international, national, state, and local levels. Some of these regulations are established in the interest of public safety or health. Other rules and codes are designed to improve and ensure efficiency in energy use or prevention of environmental damage. Most municipalities establish local standards to ensure the safety, health, business, or community life of their citizens. The facilities manager must maintain their property structure to conform to all of these mandates. None of them can be postponed or scheduled until other rules are met. Attention to all the requirements is demanded simultaneously. Fortunately, there are areas where the different codes overlap and meeting the requirements of one might also satisfy the stipulations of several others. The facilities manager must be aware of these common points but also realize that a single change in any code may remove the commonality and cause a function that was perfectly legal yesterday to be in violation of several standards today.

Just as the general managers of the hospitality industry must grow and adjust to the global influence of an international market, facilities managers must ensure that the structures and buildings under their control meet the requirements of international agreements and standards. The International Organization for Standardization (ISO) is the largest publisher of international standards in the world. This organization is formed by the national standards agencies of 157 countries. Although it is a nongovernmental organization, it has grown over the last sixty years to include more than fifty thousand experts from government, research, science, engineering, accreditation and certification agencies, industrial associations, and consumers. The published standards of this body include more than 17,000 voluntary standards covering such things as environmental management to medical instrument requirements and engineering practices. The facilities manager should be particularly aware of the 14000 series of standards that address environmental issues. This series of standards addresses most of the "green" issues that have captured public interest in the last three decades. Because of that public interest, many international tourists as well as local consumers have begun to choose their accommodations and dining establishments based on adherence to these international standards. The facilities manager must take steps to comply with these standards to support the profitability of the organization. These efforts can be seen in such activities as landscaping designs, building material selections, waste disposal procedures and recycling programs, as well as energy conservation and management efforts in hospitality enterprises.

The ISO has also been instrumental in the development of the Global Ecolabelling Network (GEN) beginning in 1994. This organization is a body of third-party certifying organizations. Ecolabelling is the process of performance certifying or labeling organizations, companies, or products as compliant with ISO standards. One of the participating bodies in the United States is Green Seal. Green Seal tests and certifies more than forty categories of materials including paints, floor care products, and chemical cleaning products. Green Seal also certifies lodging establishments as meeting standards in energy efficiency, water conservation, waste handling and minimization, purchasing policies, recycling, hazardous waste, and waste water management. These certifications can be very important in attracting environmentally conscious customers.

The International Facilities Management Association (IFMA) certifies facilities managers and chief engineers based on their expertise and skills in much the same way as professional organizations license and certify attorneys, architects, and engineers. The required training and academic credentials needed to obtain this certification provide assistance to employers by ensuring that the facilities manager understands the required standards for buildings as well as possessing the skills to maintain and care for the physical establishment.

The World Commission on the Environment and Development (WCED) has established the concept of sustainable development. Through their efforts a definition of sustainability in the environment is widely understood internationally. Its definition of sustainable development is "meeting the needs of the present without compromising the ability of future generations to meet their needs." Sustainability is much more than just an interest in the natural environment or conservation of natural resources. Under the influence of the WCED, the concept of sustainability has expanded to include eco-systems, economic development, food production, energy use, and social environment. Some authorities express this as a three-level approach that includes economics, environment, and equity, while others label the three manageable areas as profit, people, and planet. These headings are exactly the same but with different names. "Economic development" includes the concept of profitable operation. "Planet" addresses use of the environment without inflicting irrecoverable damage. "Equity" addresses the distribution of wealth in a healthy way to ensure the continuing financial welfare of the business community and its workers.

All three areas of concern increase the requirements on the facilities manager endeavoring to maintain a property to a profitable condition while trying to ensure the continued or sustainable health of the enterprise. The lodging establishment, obviously, must make a profit to remain in business, but the lasting beneficial effect on the business community and the environment are also very important. The business must not exploit any part of the community environment in the endeavor to make a profit, nor can it create a damaging effect on the natural environment of the future.

The Coalition for Environmentally Responsible Economies (CERES) was formed and developed its "Green Hotel Initiative" in 2001. CERES is composed of international corporations interested in sustaining national economies and the global economy while reducing detrimental impact on the natural environment. The Green Hotel Initiative is an attempt to encourage its corporate members to consider environmental factors and issues when making lodging decisions. This is a direct influence on international business travelers to frequent those hotels and resorts that are striving to reduce the environmental impact of their operations. Through this effort many corporate members have begun a practice of holding "green meetings" when they arrange for conventions, seminars, and corporate training meetings. These organizations often send a "Green Hotel Initiative Best Practice Survey" to establishments that are being considered as locations for such activities. Facilities managers who are not making an effort to reduce the environmental impact of their hospitality enterprise may find that they have missed significant opportunities for profitable activities when they submit the results of this survey to a prospective international customer.

The Montreal Protocol of 1987 established a schedule for the replacement of ozone-depleting refrigerants. It also produced other regulations and rules regarding the use of refrigerants and maintenance of refrigeration equipment. All of these measures were a response to the investigation by many scientists indicating that the Earth's atmospheric ozone layer is damaged by the uncontrolled release of chlorofluorocarbons (CFC), which were used as refrigerants prior to the protocol. The CFCs were initially replaced by hydrochlorofluorocarbons (HCFC), which seemed to have less effect on the atmosphere. Currently, the HCFCs are being replaced with hydrofluorocarbons (HFC), which have very little if any effect on the atmosphere. Many countries including the United States have signed the protocol and adopted its requirements as elements of law. Facilities managers have had to modify the HVAC in their buildings to comply with these laws. They also must consider these rules in the purchase and maintenance of new equipment and systems.

The World Travel and Tourism Council and the International Hotel and Restaurant Association have also introduced a large number of initiatives to increase awareness on reducing environmental impacts in the hospitality industry. As a result, facilities managers have received guidance training materials, technical assistance, and incentive programs to adopt accepted "best" practices to protect the environment while increasing the efficiency of their operations. Several large corporations have led the way in establishing programs to reduce the environmental impact of their properties in all sectors of the hospitality industry.

At the national level, several agencies including the Congress of the United States have authority to issue rules and regulations. The subjects that are regulated cover almost every area of facilities operations. The rules and regulations published and implemented by these agencies control and monitor facilities operations with established standards for virtually every aspect of building maintenance and operations.

One of the most influential nongovernment agencies affecting facilities management in the hospitality industry is the National Fire Protection Association (NFPA). The NFPA was originally formed in 1896 by a group of insurance-firm representatives to standardize requirements in risk management related to fire sprinkler systems that were then being introduced in buildings. This effort has grown to include safety factors involving electrical systems and now addresses all aspects of building design and construction. As a result of several fires in the 1980s involving lodging facilities such as the November 1980 fire in the MGM Grand Hotel and Casino fire in Las Vegas, Nevada, which killed 87 people, the Las Vegas Hilton fire in 1981, which killed 198 people, and the December 1986 fire at the Dupont Plaza Hotel and Casino in San Juan, Puerto Rico, which killed 97 guests, many hotels and lodging corporations have joined the NFPA. The NFPA now includes fire departments, insurance companies, lodging firms, manufacturing associations, labor unions, trade organizations, and even interested individuals in its membership. The NFPA maintains oversight for the development and maintenance of more than 300 codes and standards related to fire and construction safety. Many national, state, and local governments have incorporated these codes and standards into their own laws and regulations. Even if local authorities have not officially adopted NFPA standards, they are still recognized as the professional standard for fire safety and are therefore binding on facilities managers.

Regulations and required standards of construction and installation of electrical service in the United States are established and enforced by local governments. These rules are established as local codes and are based on the National Electric Code (NEC), which was developed and is updated by the NFPA. The provisions of these codes should be considered to be minimal standards for safety. They cover wiring practices, wire size and types, circuit loading, circuit capacity standards, and similar safety concerns. As older structures and buildings are renovated and upgraded, facilities managers must ensure that their establishments are also brought up to code. All new work must meet current codes even when done in buildings that were originally built to meet earlier code specifications. This can greatly increase the cost for some projects and maintenance activities. Safety factors for technicians and electricians maintaining electrical systems are also governed by the NFPA Code 70E "Electrical Safety in the Workplace."

Additional requirements regarding electrical systems and electrical safety concerns are addressed in the Occupational Safety and Health Act (OSHA). The rules provided by this act are extensive and include subjects such as design-safety standards for electrical systems, safety-related maintenance rules, safety-related work practices, and safety requirements for special equipment. Facilities managers must consider OSHA requirements and guidance when procedures and practices are developed for their properties. They should be established as minimum electrical safety standards during maintenance activities.

The National Safety Council (NSC) was founded in 1913 and was granted a congressional charter in 1953. It is an organization of members including more than 55,000 businesses, labor organizations, schools, public agencies, private groups, and individuals. This nonpolitical organization is dedicated to protecting life and promoting health. The NSC provides training and educational programs that facilities managers can use to support workplace and customer safety in their properties. This organization prevents injuries and deaths in the workplace, homes, and on the roadways by supporting research, education, and safe procedures and behavior. The results of these efforts contribute to OSHA rules and regulations.

One government agency whose effect on facilities operations is expanding is the Environmental Protection Agency (EPA). The EPA was established by an act of Congress in December of 1970. As more people, elements of government, and concerned citizens' groups have become interested in the protection of the natural environment, the EPA has expanded and now includes the offices and agencies listed in Figure 3.1.

EPA actions that have been directed at the hospitality industry have specifically addressed energy use and efficiency with programs such as the EPA Hospitality Benchmarking Service. This service allows hotels to compare their energy use with comparable properties and receive a relative numerical score. Those establishments achieving a high efficiency score are listed on the EPA Website for perusal by interested customers.

The energy efficiency thrust by the EPA also resulted in the U.S. Energy Policy Act (EPAct) of 1992. This act establishes minimum efficiency levels for electric motors and requires that inefficient motors be replaced by motors with a certified EPAct efficiency rating. This affects the purchasing decisions of facilities managers when they select replacement motors because of repair requirements or the upgrade or renovation of systems in their buildings.

Within the U.S., the EPA has also established drinking water potability standards with National Primary Drinking Water Regulations. These standards are upgraded as new information becomes available. Facilities managers must ensure that the water they provide for use in their properties meets these standards. However, it is not enough to meet EPA standards for potability: the facilities manager must investigate local codes and regulations in their municipalities because the National Standards allow local agencies to establish more stringent requirements.

Figure 3.1: Environmental Protection Agency Offices

EPA Offices

- Office of Administration and Resources
- Office of Air and Radiation
- Office of Enforcement and Compliance Assurance
- Office of Environmental Information
- Office of Environmental Justice
- Office of the Chief Financial Officer
- Office of General Counsel
- Office of Inspector General
- Office of International Affairs
- Office of Prevention, Pesticides, and Toxic Substances
- Office of Research and Development
- Office of Solid Waste and Emergency Response
- Office of Water
- Office of Chemical Safety & Pollution Prevention

Hazardous wastes are addressed by the EPA with the Resource Conservation and Recovery Act. This act defines hazardous waste as any substance exhibiting at least one of the following characteristics:

- *Ignitability*   Substances that can create fire under certain conditions, are spontaneously combustible, or have a flash point less than 60 degrees Centigrade or 140 degrees Fahrenheit.

- *Corrosivity*   Corrosive wastes are acids or bases (pH less than or equal to 2, or greater than or equal to 12.5) that are capable of corroding metal containers.

- *Reactivity*   Reactive wastes are unstable under normal conditions. They can cause explosions, toxic fumes, gases, or vapors when heated, compressed, or mixed with water.

- *Toxicity*   Toxic wastes are harmful or fatal when ingested or absorbed.

Untrained or uninformed managers and employees in restaurants and hotels often are not aware that they work with hazardous materials. The facilities manager must establish training programs and control systems to reduce the hazards presented by common chemicals and working materials in the hospitality industry. These can include detergents, paints, floor finishes, boiler chemicals, swimming pool chemicals, solvents, cleaners, and even unusable garbage. Waste materials that cannot be recycled, reused, or used for any other purpose are considered to be hazardous waste materials.

In 1971, the Occupational Safety and Health Administration (OSHA) was established in the United States with a charter to develop and enforce standards, procedures, and regulations to protect American workers. Lodging establishments have been required to comply with OSHA's Hazard Communication (HazCom) Standard, "29CFR,1910.1200" since 1988. This standard addresses the handling and storage of hazardous substances and chemicals. Hotels use many hazardous materials including aerosols, floor cleaners, flammable chemicals, carpet cleaning materials, detergents, furniture polish, bleach, fabric softeners, bathroom cleaners, pesticides, and many other chemically based materials. Facilities managers must be well versed in this standard to ensure that their facility is in compliance with this law. Facilities managers must set up programs to ensure that their establishment inventories all hazardous materials on their property. Every chemical or hazardous material in use must be addressed with a program that includes employee training in the use and storage of these materials, the proper labeling of all hazardous materials, and the provision and maintenance of Material Safety Data Sheets (MSDS) for employee use. An MSDS is published by the manufacturers of chemicals as required by law. The same law requires the facility manager to have an MSDS for every chemical present in a building and a copy must be kept on file. In addition, copies must be available to the employees of the organization at all times. The MSDS explains the properties of the chemical product, handling requirements, appropriate uses, storage requirements, flammability, specific ingredients, health hazards, and appropriate emergency procedures such as first aid for exposure as well proper fire and explosion responses. All of this must be included by the facilities manager in a formal hazardous materials program that incorporates training for employees and ensures that required protective equipment is available to employees using chemical products.

The American Gas Association (AGA) was founded in 1918 as a trade organization representing natural gas supply and production companies and includes organizations that manufacture gas appliances. More than 190 local energy utility companies delivering natural gas to 56 million homes, businesses, and industries throughout the United States are also members of the AGA. Facilities managers must ensure that gas appliances used in their buildings meet certification standards published by the AGA.

HVAC systems used in well-designed and -maintained facilities must meet standards and guidance published by the American Society of Heating, Refrigeration, and Air Conditioning Engineers (ASHRAE). ASHRAE is a technical society for those individuals and organizations interested in HVAC and refrigeration systems. Founded in 1894, ASHRAE develops, publishes, and updates a recognized series of standards for building codes as they relate to HVAC systems. The four-volume ASHRAE Handbook is consulted by engineers, mechanical contractors, architects, and government agencies for guidance and technical data and is considered as the accepted standard in the absence of coded requirements.

The Illuminating Engineers Society of North America (IES) was founded in 1906 with a stated mission to improve the lighted environment by bringing together those with lighting knowledge and by translating that knowledge into actions that benefit the public. Members of IES are regarded as the top professionals in their field and are globally respected. Membership includes engineers, lighting designers, consultants, lighting equipment manufacturers, electrical contractors, architects, researchers, and academic instructors. IES publications address recommended practices for a variety of lighting applications such as office, sports, outdoor lighting, healthcare facilities, and many others.

The National Sanitation Foundation (NSF) was founded in 1944 to standardize sanitation and food safety at a time when the United States had no national sanitation standards. It is a not-for-profit, nongovernmental organization that provides standards, development, product certification, auditing, education, and risk management for public health and safety. NSF certifies materials and products for a multitude of applications. One important field of NSF's interest is materials and products that come into contact with drinking water–systems components. NSF standards are generally accepted as minimum standards for a variety of public health-related industries and subject areas. These include drinking water treatment and contact materials, health and wellness supplements, food equipment manufacturing and composition, plumbing, refuse containers, and dishwashing equipment.

Serving the hospitality industry for nearly a century, the American Housing and Lodging Association (AH&LA) is the sole national association representing all sectors and stakeholders in the lodging industry, including individual hotel property members, hotel companies, student and faculty members, and industry suppliers. AH&LA provides members with public relations and image management, education, research and information, and other value-added services to provide bottom-line savings and ensure a positive business climate for the lodging industry. The standards established by this organization are essential for providing acceptable levels of service and facilities operations for the hospitality industry.

Facilities managers must accomplish their work through the efforts of others. Employees must be supervised effectively and efficiently. Many agencies and government bodies have established rules and laws to ensure that employees are provided a safe and fair place to work. Several of these agencies and their mandates are listed below. The successful facilities manager must have an awareness of these policies and regulations.

The Equal Employment Opportunity Office (EEO) is responsible for the management of the Equal Employment Opportunity Program (EEOP) in the United States. The program specifies that employers must provide equal opportunity for all employees without regard to race, color, religion, sex, age, national origin, sexual orientation, and physical or mental disability. The goal is to eliminate discrimination based on factors irrelevant to job performance. All facilities managers must be aware of this program when making any employment decision such as hiring, training selection, promotion, transfers, and any other personnel actions.

In 1964, the Civil Rights Act was a landmark legislation enacted by the Congress of the United States. This act outlaws major forms of discrimination against blacks and women, including racial segregation. This ended unequal application of voter registration requirements and racial discrimination in schools, at the workplace, and by all facilities that serve the general public. The act has since been expanded to include all citizens regardless of race or gender. The current trend in the business world is the pursuit of diversity. This concept requires the workforce of any establishment to reflect the demographics of its surrounding community environment.

The Fair Labor Standards Act of 1938 (FLSA) is a federal statute of the United States. It applies to all employees working for any enterprise engaged in commerce or the production of goods for commerce. The FLSA established a national minimum wage, established rules for the payment of overtime at a rate of time and a half in specific types of employment, and prohibited employment of minors in "oppressive child labor." Later amendments have updated the minimum wage and established additional standards. In 1963, the Equal Pay Act was added to the FLSA making it illegal to pay lower wages to workers based solely on the basis of gender. It does allow for unequal pay for equal work when wages are established by a seniority system, a merit system, or a system based on measured quantities of production. This particular amendment removed facilities maintenance skills and trades from a "men-only" status. FLSA was further amended in 1993 by the Family and Medical Leave Act, providing eligible employees up to twelve weeks of unpaid, but job-protected leave for family and medical reasons. Facilities managers must be aware of the stipulations of the FLSA.

In past years women could be released from employment if they became pregnant. The Pregnancy Discrimination Act of 1978 prohibits such personnel actions because of pregnancy. Discrimination occurs when women are fired, not hired, or otherwise handled differently from other employees based on their pregnancy or intention to become pregnant. Facilities managers must not discriminate against pregnant women and mothers because of the fear of lost productivity, because of absence or an inability to use temporary employees, or because they believe that the employee will require too many accommodations after she returns to work. Since 1978, employers are legally bound to provide the same insurance, leave pay, and additional support that would be allowed for any employee on medical leave or disability. This applies to enterprises with fifteen or more employees, including all employees, not just those in the engineering department.

The Americans with Disabilities Act of 1990 (ADA) requires that all commercial facilities and buildings change their physical surroundings and equipment to allow disabled persons to enter and use their facilities. Further, policies and procedures that denied access to disabled persons had to be revised. Of the five "Titles" or headings of the act, the one that has the most impact on hospitality enterprises is Title III. It addresses public accommodations and commercial facilities and covers all existing and future construction of lodging establishments, restaurants, entertainment, and recreational structures. Title III also requires that auxiliary aids must be available to disabled persons so that they may enjoy all the goods and services offered by an establishment. This affects all building systems. For example, fire alarm systems must have a visible signal as well as an audible signal, elevators or ramps must be installed to allow access to upper floors, and restroom or bath facilities must be modified for use by disabled persons. All of these modifications must be implemented by the facilities manager. Building and construction specifications and standards for these modifications can be found in the American Disabilities Act Accessibility Guidelines (ADAAG). All construction must comply with ADAAG and other building codes such as International Building Code (IBC), and American National Standards Institute (ANSI) standards that pertain to the disabled and removal of accessibility barriers.

FACILITIES AND FACILITIES MANAGEMENT CERTIFICATIONS

Systems and equipment used in buildings and structures must meet requirements and standards prescribed by many authorities and agencies. Testing and certification of appliances, equipment, and building systems is provided by several agencies and establishes the written credentials verifying that performance and safety standards have been met. Employees in specific skilled positions, including the facilities manager, may also be certified as meeting established standards of proficiency. Providing necessary training requires commitment, time, and money, but ensures that employees have the needed skills and knowledge to produce professional and profitable levels of facility and structural condition. This is especially important for individuals holding positions and performing tasks that require licensing and certifications such as electricians and plumbers.

Several independent testing organizations certify equipment as safely meeting its performance requirements and specifications. The Underwriters Laboratory (UL) tests many different categories of equipment, but is probably best known for the testing of electrical appliances. UL designs and conducts tests for normal operations and then tries to test equipment in dangerous situations that may occur in normal usage before products are released to the market. If facilities managers insist that only electrical products with a UL rating be purchased for use in their establishment, they will minimize the risks of equipment failure, electrocution, and fires.

In the United States, the most important environmental certifying body for the hospitality industry is the U.S. Green Building Council (USGBC) with its Leadership in Energy and Environmental Design (LEED) program. The USGBC is a nonprofit organization made up of members from the building industry. It is their purpose to promote the construction and renovation of buildings that are environmentally responsible, profitable, and healthy places to live and work. The LEED certification for a building is a nationally accepted standard for the design, construction, and operation of "green" buildings. For the facilities manager, identification and certification of a building for LEED may be the highest endorsement that can be achieved. It is recognized by many discerning customers and they prefer to support enterprises that meet the requirements of this certification. There is currently no category of LEED certification specifically designed for the hospitality industry, but all hotels and restaurants will fit within the category of "New Construction." Some facilities managers feel that the costs associated with pursuing a LEED certification are prohibitive. However, when one considers the increased revenue from an environmentally conscious clientele and the reduced operations cost because of improved efficiency of building energy use and systems performance, the attainment of a LEED certification is a good financial decision.

The United States government also provides environmentally related certifications under two partnership programs. The most well known is the Energy Star program. This program is co-sponsored by the EPA and the U.S. Department of Energy (DOE). Energy Star certifies products based on their energy efficiency such as lighting equipment, food service equipment, laundry appliances, heating and air conditioning units, and many others. The program expanded in 1999 to include commercial buildings and provides guidance and standards to building contractors and facilities managers to reduce energy use. Those buildings that exhibit efficient performance in the top 25% of buildings in the country are eligible for the designation of Energy Star. Increasing concern with the environment, fuel costs, and social responsibility in energy use is pushing facilities managers to pursue this certification for their properties.

The second partnership sponsored by the EPA is the Design for the Environment Program (DfE). The mission of DfE is to encourage equipment manufacturers and distributors to voluntarily reduce risks to people and the environment by reducing the pollution produced by their products. DfE focuses on reduction of chemical risks, and energy use. Its label on a product means that a DfE scientific review team has screened and approved the product for potential health hazards. The label certifies that the product has been made with the safest possible ingredients.

When looking for guidance in reducing the environmental impact of their properties, facilities managers can refer to many of the organizations listed in this chapter for publications and information. The International Business Leaders Forum's Tourism Partnership and the Center for Environmental Leadership in Business have published _Sustainable Hotel Siting, Design, and Construction_. This document provides a comprehensive overview of the issues governing sustainability and environmental impact for the hospitality industry, specifically addressing hotels.

The Building Owners and Managers Institute (BOMI), founded in 1970, is a not-for-profit educational institute that has earned a reputation as the trusted property and facility educational resource for top corporations, government agencies, property management firms, unions, trade associations, and individual facilities or building managers. The BOMI is recognized for its certified designations: Real Property Administrator (RPA), Facilities Management Administrator (FMA), Systems Maintenance Administrator (SMA), and Systems Maintenance Technician (SMT). These designations provide a credible reference in industry, ensuring employers that prospective and current employees are properly trained and have the knowledge to meet the highest level of performance in property and facilities management.

The American Hotel and Lodging Association (AH&LA) also has developed a certification program for facilities managers. The Certified Engineering Operations Executive designation links the profession to the hospitality industry by establishing an expected level of expertise for those individuals responsible for the care of structures and properties in the industry. It requires that individuals seeking the designation complete a mix of education and experience and that their expertise be exhibited by standardized examination. This program recognizes individuals possessing a specified combination of experience and knowledge in the field of facilities management.

One additional source of professional credentials for facilities managers is available through the Certified Facility Manager Program (CFM) of the International Facility Managers Association (IFMA). This program also requires a mix of experience and formal education requirements in facilities management and related fields. Formal examination and periodic re-examination are required to achieve this certification.

CHAPTER SUMMARY

A building is a complicated amalgamation of inter-related systems, all of which must be designed, constructed, and maintained in a specific manner to provide the occupant with the services and utilities needed for their activities. The facilities manager must develop policies, procedures, and systems that coordinate the maintenance and care of the building to ensure that the building can be operated in a profitable mode for its entire lifetime. The standards and requirements that must be met to achieve this level of performance are dictated by many agencies and organizations. The successful facility manager must comply with all of the published requirements simultaneously and continuously. The mission of the facility manager is to protect the commercial interests of the building owner, the safety of guests and occupants, and to provide the staff and workers with a safe and productive workplace. This mission is endangered if the facilities manager fails to meet any of the accepted or legally required standards and specifications for his property. Many organizations have established minimum levels of expertise for the certification of individuals, and professional facilities managers and the hospitality industry depend on these credentials to identify those professionals who can manage this complex system of needs, standards, specifications, rules, regulations, and requirements.

GLOSSARY OF TERMS

HVAC
Heating, Ventilation, and Air Conditioning

ISO
International Organization for Standardization

IFMA
International Facilities Management Association

WCED
World Commission on the Environment and Development

CERES
Coalition for Environmentally Responsible Economies

CFC
Refrigerants containing chlorofluorocarbons

HCFC
Refrigerants containing hydrochlorofluorocarbons

HFC
Refrigerants containing hydrofluorocarbons

NFPA
National Fire Protection Association

NEC
National Electric Code

OSHA
Occupational Safety and Health Act

NSC
National Safety Council

EPA
Environmental Protection Agency

EPAct
U.S. Energy Policy Act

MSDS
Material Safety Data Sheets

AGA
American Gas Association

ASHRAE
American Society of Heating, Refrigeration, and Air Conditioning Engineers

ADA
Americans with Disabilities Act

ADAAG
American Disabilities Act Accessibility Guidelines

IBC
International Building Code

ANSI
American National Standards Institute

IES
Illuminating Engineers Society
NSF
National Sanitation Foundation

AH&LA
American Housing and Lodging Association

EEO
Equal Employment Opportunity Office

EEOP
Equal Employment Opportunity Program

FLSA
Fair Labor Standards Act

UL
Underwriters Laboratory

USGBC
U.S. Green Building Council

LEED
Leadership in Energy and Environmental Design

DOE
U.S. Department of Energy

DfE
Design for Environment Program

BOMI

Building Owner's and Manager's Institute

RPA
Real Property Administrator

FMA
Facilities Management Administrator

SMA
System Maintenance Administrator

SMT
Systems Maintenance Technician

IFMA
International Facility Manager's Association

CFM
Certified Facility Manager

STUDY QUESTIONS

1. Discuss the interdependent relationship of building systems.
2. What is the subject of the ISO 14000 series of standards? Discuss their impact on the hospitality industry.
3. Which Title of the Americans with Disabilities Act (ADA) has the most impact on the hospitality industry? Where could a facilities manager find guidance to comply with this title?
4. Discuss the respective effect of chlorofluorocarbons (CFC), hydrochlorofluorocarbons (HCFC), and hydrofluorocarbons (HFC) on the Earth's atmosphere. What actions have been required as a result of the Montreal Protocol of 1987?
5. Discuss the activities of the National Fire Protection Association (NFPA). How do its activities affect the hospitality industry?
6. What act was passed as a result of the Environmental Protection Agency's energy efficiency efforts?
7. Discuss the effect of the Fair Labor Standards Act (FLSA) on the facilities manager.
8. What is the intended function of a Material Safety Data Sheet (MSDS)? Where should they be stored?
9. Why would an employer want to know if an applicant for the position of facilities manager has professional certification? What agencies provide such certification?
10. What is the highest endorsement that a building in the hospitality industry might achieve for energy management in the U.S.?

CHAPTER FOUR
INFORMATION MANAGEMENT IN FACILITIES OPERATIONS

CHAPTER LEARNING OBJECTIVES

After reading this chapter, the student should be able to:

1. Understand and describe the requirements for current and accurate management information.
2. Describe the increasing complexity and growing volume of available information.
3. Describe the need for recovering and processing information into useable categories and systems.
4. Describe the use of automatic data processing as a facility management tool.
5. Describe methods of using management information to facilitate and generate effective management decisions and actions.

All managers depend on accurate and timely information to support good management decisions. This information can come from a number of different sources including the news media, customer comment cards, employee reports, accounting data sheets, and many others. The facilities manager has the same need for information and derives needed data from all the same places as any manager and several sources that other managers don't have. The information sources for a facilities manager can include a large number of additional indicators that other managers don't see, such as equipment readouts, thermometers, pressure gauges, and even inanimate and static elements such as peeling paint, or unexplained grease stains in the hall wallpaper. Some of these sources produce information requiring immediate emergency actions such as a smoke detector alarm or a phone call from a guest reporting a water leak, while others give indications of ongoing maintenance requirements such as squeaking bearings or a slight variation in equipment performance. All sources must be monitored, categorized into appropriate levels of urgency, and met with effective maintenance or repair activity to ensure the continued profitable operation of the building enterprise.

It is important to realize that all of the indicators, gauges, and sources provide data. This data only become actionable information when the facilities manager has noted them and determined the meaning of the data. The first step in analyzing data is to decide which datum produces the most important information. Because the facilities manager cannot look at all data constantly and simultaneously, a system of key data or system indicators must be developed to allow urgent needs for action to be indentified rapidly while more routine needs are scheduled for appropriate action in a systematic and organized approach.

CRITICAL REQUIRED INFORMATION

To effectively manage a property involved in the hospitality industry, a facilities manager must derive information from many sources. In the past, operations managers gave very little consideration to including the facilities manager in the decision-making circle for management of the enterprise. In recent years the error of this practice is being recognized and the facilities manager must aggressively work to be included in the executive staff of the hospitality enterprise. Not only will this provide better management information to the operations manager, but it will also benefit the facilities manager and the property by assisting in the assignment of work priorities, project schedules, staffing requirements, and continued profitable operation of the facility.

In addition to being included in the executive staff level of the operation, the facilities manager must actively pursue information by asking questions and compiling data. Operational information and anticipated requirements need to be obtained from primary managers. Schedules of upcoming events, complaints of facility shortcomings, and desired improvements in structure and maintenance activities from other managers all help the facilities manager to provide the necessary support to ensure profitable operations. Comment cards from other employees at all levels and customer surveys can be very valuable sources of essential items of information. Forecast needs and strategic operational planning schedules can help the facilities manager to prepare the physical environment of the building to provide required services before upcoming events.

External information is essential to the management of a hospitality facility. Facilities and hospitality-related professional publications can keep the facilities manager aware of improved equipment, materials, and methods as well as provide industry statistics for comparison and evaluation of facilities performance. Awareness of current events locally, nationally, and globally will ensure that the facilities manager is prepared for upcoming events as well as trends in facilities operations. Threats to safety and security that have important implications for the hospitality industry are often revealed in news programs and newspapers and the facilities manager needs to be aware of these. Even weather broadcasts reveal important information needed for facilities preparation. Things as simple as bringing in the lawn furniture or turning off the sprinkler system can prevent loss through damage from wind and rain or loss of efficiency by using energy and water when it isn't needed. Facilities managers need external information to help them keep their property operations profitable. They cannot simply react to things going wrong or out of service. They must be proactive to protect their facility from impending problems and situations.

INFORMATION GROWTH

Some of the information monitored by the facilities manager has been considered important or critical in the past for obvious reasons. Two hundred years ago, a puddle on the floor was evidence of a roof leak. A puddle on the floor today indicates a water leak, either from the roof or some part of the plumbing systems. In both cases the facilities manager must take action in response to the information to prevent further damage to the structure or discomfort to the building occupants. All elements of the structure and its systems have become more complicated and integrated with the passage of time and the amount of data available to the facilities manager has grown exponentially. Several external elements and influences were discussed in Chapter 3 that require added information-gathering and processing. The internal requirements have also expanded with the increased sophistication of equipment and systems. A whole new range of required data to be considered has entered the facilities manager's area of responsibility. Such things as the following now must be monitored, recorded, and processed:

- Air quality
- Chemicals used in building materials production
- Recycling programs
- Asbestos abatement and encapsulation
- Hazardous waste disposal
- Radon emissions
- Lead contamination in water and building surfaces
- UPS systems
- Power generation, transmission, and distribution
- Disaster planning and recovery
- Fire and life-safety system design and operation
- Security system design and operation
- Suspended ceilings
- Refrigerant management

All of these subjects and many more have been added to the mix in facilities management. Because of this growth, the facility manager can be overwhelmed by raw data. A method must be devised to separate the data and analyze it into useable elements of information. Appropriate routines and operations must be designed to react to this information so that the facilities manager can effectively manage the property without loss of service in essential systems or deterioration of the overall physical condition of the building and the enterprise it houses.

ORGANIZING REQUIRED INFORMATION

Obviously, no single person can simultaneously watch and consciously react effectively to the enormous amount of available data. Therefore, the facilities manager depends on the facilities staff to respond to information within their respective areas of responsibility.

This does not mean that the facilities manager waits for his staff to report a problem, but it does mean that a team of people are employed to process required information as a team effort. The facilities manager must identify those specific items of critical information that provide accurate indications that the team and its functions are operating effectively. This is much the same approach that a doctor uses when examining a patient. Several critical factors are checked to indicate health or the need for further analysis. Most doctors start with checking the patient's weight to identify any drastic change since the last examination, followed by a check of body temperature and blood pressure to ensure that the patient is not suffering from infections or serious imbalances in current body functions. Next, almost all doctors will use a stethoscope to identify any abnormal heart or gastric sounds. Finally, the doctor will look at the patient and ask, "are you having any problems or pains?" or "how are you feeling?" All of these measurements and readings are items of critical information that provide the doctor with an indication of the overall health of the patient. In a similar manner, the facilities manager must develop indicators of critical information that provide an evaluation of the condition of the building or structure.

There are hundreds of measurements or readings that could be used to evaluate a facility, but each facilities manager must choose the ones that provide the best overall picture of the operational health of the property. This sometimes has been called the "Dashboard Approach to Management." If a driver is paying attention to his vehicle, the dashboard provides critical information to tell him the overall condition of the vehicle and data about its safe operation. Just like a building, there are many things in an automobile that could be monitored by a dashboard instrument. These include such things as transmission temperature, tire pressure, exhaust temperature, manifold vacuum, et cetera, but only a few critical elements are actually indicated on the dashboard. Most automobiles have gauges or warning lights on the dashboard to indicate vehicle speed, engine temperature, engine oil pressure, and electrical charging output. Some vehicles also have a tachometer to report revolutions per minute of the engine. Normally these few items of critical information ensure that the driver is aware that the vehicle is traveling at a safe speed for the conditions, the engine is not overheating, the lubrication system is operating correctly, and the vehicle battery is being maintained in a fully charged condition. The facilities manager must indentify a few such indicators that reflect the healthy operation and maintenance condition of the building. This does not mean that other things are not being measured or monitored. It just means that these few items give an instant evaluation of good health or immediate guidance to a manager's quickly identifying the source of an impending problem. As mentioned before, water standing in a puddle on the floor is a critical indicator of a problem. It does not reveal what the problem is, but it should cause the facilities manager to start an investigation to find the source of the water.

The critical items that the facilities manager chooses are the key to the development of an effective maintenance management system. Elements of such a system are discussed in other chapters, but without a methodical, systematic approach to the myriad of data and information available, the facilities manager would soon be overwhelmed. Each facilities manager must develop a means to have the selected elements of critical information measured and transmitted to his management "dashboard" to enable him to "drive" effectively and efficiently.

AUTOMATIC DATA PROCESSING SYSTEMS

The introduction of automatic data processing has many applications directly involving the facilities manager. When other managers consider information systems, automated operations, or automated information management, they view only the management uses of computer systems. The facilities manager must look at advancing technology in two ways. First, the facilities manager must consider computer-specific technology in comparison to workplace-specific technology and, secondly, he or she must consider computer technology that is used to support occupant operations versus computer technology used to support facilities activities.

Computer-specific support of management information includes automated systems used to support general management or direct use of computers by operations personnel and building occupants to control or manage their activities. It also includes automated systems used to support facilities management programs and projects or the direct use of computers by the facilities managers in their own management efforts. Workplace-specific support is the use of computers to control and manage the actual physical work environment of the building systems such as computerized control of HVAC systems, lighting schedules, or energy use.

Computer technology used to support occupant operations includes automated office systems in areas of accounting, payroll, marketing, sales, budgeting, personnel management, etc. A growing element is the support of telecommunications systems for voice, data, image, and fax transmissions, including such things as telephone systems, broadcast or closed circuit television programs, and/or microwave transmissions. All of these expanding systems must be supported and maintained within the physical building structure. This is a much greater challenge than most people realize. In the case of an established lodging operation in an aged property, the building that was constructed 75 years ago, or more, was never designed to support a telephone in every room and computer systems. All of the required infrastructure such as wiring, power, and access chases must be installed to accommodate the new systems. A newly constructed building must be designed from the onset to incorporate these systems and prepare for expanding technological advances in the future. In the old and the new building, space must be identified for the added necessary equipment to provide and maintain new or updated services and systems. Facilities personnel must be retrained or specifically trained technicians must be added to the staff to provide the necessary expertise to keep modern technology operating.

The facilities manager must also incorporate new technology and computerized operating systems into their own activities. This includes Computer-Aided Facilities Management Programs (CAFM), Computerized Maintenance Management Systems (CMMS), and Computerized Facilities Management Systems (CFMS) and their components such as computer-assisted design (CAD), asset tracking and bar coding for inventory, preventive maintenance, automated work control, etc. Facility master planning programs and strategic planning databases are valuable automated tools for budget control and growth management while building equipment and systems are managed with automated energy management systems and computerized control systems. Occupant safety is improved through the use of automated fire alarms, security systems, and life-safety systems, which in turn are managed by building automation systems under the control of the facilities manager.

It is immediately apparent that the operational side and the facilities support side of technologically automated systems overlap. The use of an automated tool by the operational side is supported by the facilities manager as a building system. The facilities manager must also use automated tools to manage the activities required to maintain the building and coordinate the support of the operational automated systems. Computers have become an integral factor in the management and decision-making process of the hospitality industry. Therefore, the facilities manager must add these systems to the list of equipment and functions that must be maintained. In doing that, he or she must also be a user of computer technology and incorporate it into facilities management as well as facility design, renovation, and future construction.

COMPUTERIZED FACILITIES MAINTENANCE MANAGEMENT SYSTEMS

Computerized Facilities Management Systems (CFMS) or Computerized Maintenance Management Systems (CMMS) in the hospitality industry provide the facilities manager with an entirely new toolbox of management information and actions to support a building and its hospitality operations functions. Not only can a computer control major systems like HVAC, but it can also balance and integrate the operations of several systems to provide overall guest comfort and safety. CFMS/CMMS can also provide the workforce with management tools to ensure efficient and timely maintenance and repair activities. These computers can replace production accounting, routine paperwork, and dispatch operations formerly handled by several different workers. Preventive, predictive, scheduled, and reactive maintenance work orders can all be created and monitored using automated data processing systems. The automated work orders can be electronically issued to the appropriate technician, establish inventory adjustments to account for the materials used, record expended man-hours for the labor expended, and establish a permanent work record for the equipment or system being maintained. These actions are usually done by a stand-alone CMMS but larger organizations are starting to incorporate these functions as a work and inventory module of a larger CFMS. In the larger systems, this integrated module provides required information to the operations side of the establishment, notifying appropriate staff elements of equipment or rooms that are *out of service* or *returned to service*, as well as giving fund-expenditure information and inventory-adjustment data to appropriate accounting departments.

Work requests or repair requirements can be entered into CFMS/CMMS by keyboard, handheld communicator units, automatic sensors, phone call, or preprogrammed schedules, depending on the procedures programmed into the system by the facilities management staff. Preprogrammed task packages can automatically issue required materials from inventory on receipt of recurring or scheduled work orders and automatically order replacement stocks. The work can be tracked from inception to completion with complete records and these records can be recovered by task, completed time period, recurring frequency, individual employee work productivity, or numerous other categories used to analyze the efficiency of operations. CFMS/CMMS therefore becomes not only a functioning work-control tool, but also a very effective information recovery system providing timely and accurate information to support facilities management decisions.

CFMS/CMMS can also be connected to remote management elements, materials suppliers, and labor contractors through the internet. The contracted material or labor supplier can receive a request for replenishment or a work order for action as a work request is being entered into the system. This not only accelerates response to needs, but also establishes a cost record and response time record for external vendors to support ongoing management decisions. The entire CFMS/CMMS can also be remotely monitored by higher corporation management offices, eliminating much of the paper reporting requirement previously handled by the facilities manager. This allows one management element to oversee the operations of several different properties from a central point or from a remote point. The facilities manager can adjust his systems and coordinate actions in response to timely and accurate information without actually being on the property. These systems will continue to develop and expand to become sharper and more powerful tools for the facilities manager.

MANAGEMENT DECISIONS

The expansion of information and automated data handling systems available to the facilities manager has made it possible for maintenance and facilities-condition information to influence facilities management decisions. By making better management decisions concerning the property itself, the facilities manager can exert an active and direct influence on the success of hospitality operations as well. This was often needed and wished for in earlier manual systems, but very seldom achieved. The use of automated information management systems in facilities management has redefined building operations by making all systems immediately visible on a single computer screen. This tool allows the facilities manager to successfully manage his property as an integrated system of related factors. Each separate factor and element of the system is available for study and the collective effect of all systems is available to monitor the overall health of the building. Comparing the condition of the property to the operational planning and external data gives the facilities manager the ability to make management decisions based on facts rather than guesswork.

Management decisions must be made by human managers. Facilities managers cannot expect their management information systems to make decisions for them. Even automated data processing systems that react to particular elements of information with a preprogrammed action are not making decisions. They are only following the instructions given them by the manager who designed the system. Decisions normally grow to take up the amount of time available to make them. Emergency actions are management decisions made in reaction to specific elements of information regarding an accident or system failure. They are made very quickly because there is no time available to look for additional information. In comparison, management decisions regarding future planning, equipment upgrades, facilities renovation or design, or reaction to future operations must be considered with all applicable information. A long-range decision should not be made until all the relevant facts and figures are considered. The facilities manager must design and maintain systems that provide data and information necessary for effective decision-making for both emergency and longer-range decisions.

CHAPTER SUMMARY

The availability of current and accurate information is an essential element of effective facility management in the hospitality industry. The facilities manager cannot depend on guesses and assumptions when making decisions that affect the physical condition, safety, or profitability of a property. As modern facilities systems have become more complex and sophisticated, the amount of information that is available to the facilities manager has expanded enormously. The need to process, categorize, and analyze this information to support effective decision making has also grown. Management information systems have been improved greatly through the use of automatic data processing equipment and systems. This has forced facilities managers to expand their activities to include technical support of these systems as well as to use them in their own management systems. The efficiency of facilities management has been greatly improved by the incorporation of automatic data processing into management decision making. However, although management decisions are dependent on the availability of accurate and timely information, the information system cannot make management decisions. The facilities manager must still make the required decisions and take the appropriate actions to maintain his hospitality enterprise in a profitable mode.

GLOSSARY OF TERMS

System indicators
A system indicator is an element of information that provides an accurate measurement of the overall health of the system.

Critical information
An item of critical information is any fact, figure, or system indicator that is essential to effective management actions or decisions.

Dashboard Approach
The Dashboard Approach is the visualization of selected items of critical information portrayed as the instrument cluster of an automobile dashboard.

Computer-specific support
This term is used to categorize automated data processing systems that apply directly to the management of operations.

Workplace-specific support
This term is used to categorize automated data processing systems that are used to control physical equipment and systems such as HVAC or electricity use that directly affect the environment of the workplace.

CAFM
Computer-Aided Facilities Management

CMMS
Computerized Maintenance Management System

CFMS
Computerized Facility Management System

CAD
Computer-Assisted Design

STUDY QUESTIONS

1. Describe the importance of current and accurate management information to a facilities manager.
2. How has the amount of management information available to the facilities manager changed? What has caused this change?
3. What is the Dashboard Approach to management information and how is it used by the facilities manager?
4. Describe the two sides of automated data processing that a facilities manager must manage.
5. How do system indicators and items of critical information affect management decisions?
6. Describe the difference between the information needed for an emergency management decision and a long-range management decision.

CHAPTER FIVE

COMMUNICATION REQUIREMENTS FOR FACILITIES OPERATIONS

CHAPTER LEARNING OBJECTIVES

After reading this chapter, the student should be able to:

1. Define the elements of effective communication.
2. Explain the need for effective staff communications.
3. Describe the adverse effect of poor communication on facility management efforts and conversely explain the benefits of effective communications on Facility Management efforts.
4. Describe common characteristics of routine communications systems.
5. Describe the importance of staff communications for efficient coordination of activities and operations.
6. Describe the detrimental effect of poor coordination and communications on the profitability of operations.
7. Explain the importance for the facility manager to "tell it like it is" for effective and efficient support of profitable operations.

The importance of accurate information to a facilities manager is clear, not only in facilities management, but also in its overall effect on operations of a hospitality enterprise. Communication is the process that distributes information to the people who need it. If the information is not shared with managers and staff who can transform it into good decisions and appropriate actions, then it is wasted. Managers and staff organizations that do not share critical information with others are defeating the organization by forcing it to operate from rumors, assumptions, and guesses. Assumptions and guesses will not support sound managerial decisions. This is especially true for facilities managers because so much of their work is invisible to the customer until some part of the facility fails or goes out of service. The only way that the facilities manager can exchange essential information with the occupants of a building is through continuous effective communication.

EFFECTIVE COMMUNICATION

Communication is a team effort, requiring the active participation of a transmitting individual and a receiving individual. If either party fails to do their part, communication does not occur. The process starts when the transmitter or sender encodes a thought into a group of words and speaks those words to the receiver, or listener. The receiver must then decode the message and translate it into thoughts. For the listener to respond the two individuals exchange roles. The listener then becomes the sender and encodes thoughts into words that are sent to the original sender who has become the listener and must decode the words into thoughts. As additional listeners and senders are added, the process becomes more complicated, but the basic process remains the same with thoughts being expressed as words and words being interpreted into thoughts. The process does not change if the medium that carries the message changes. The words can be carried by voice, written documents or messages, or physical signals, thus the encoding and decoding continues.

In any discussion of effective communications, accuracy is the main element of communication. Managers must work and practice to develop their skills in every element of the communication process. Care must be taken in encoding, to ensure that the words selected truly convey the intended meaning. There is an old adage that each person is given two ears and one mouth to ensure that they can listen twice as much as they speak. This could be interpreted that they should listen to their own words twice before they speak them. If words are carefully chosen and organized into cohesive sentences, then the probability of the successful transmission of a message is greatly increased. Conversely, the activity of decoding received messages must be practiced, so that the receiver discerns the same meaning as the transmitter intended. These two skills, coupled with good verbal enunciation, legible documents, or accurately drawn illustrations are critical elements of effective communication. They are the keys to all successful management operations, including those of the facilities manager. Communication skills are used in every managerial activity including recruiting, directing, interviewing, teaching, coaching, counseling, leading, supervising, writing, organizing, coordinating, and interacting with others. A facilities manager who does not possess the skills to deal with employees, guests, vendors, contractors, managers, and employees on a one-to-one basis or in groups, has very little chance of maintaining a profitable property. Successful communication means that the messages being sent by the facilities manager match the messages being received by the people who work with or for him and the people for whom he works.

WRITTEN COMMUNICATION

Written communication may be the most difficult form for the facilities manager to master. All managers must be able to communicate in writing because written communications assume an element of permanence. They establish a starting date for their effect and provide a valuable record for future reference. Written messages prevent confusion that can be caused by relying on the memories of the communicators. Good written documents carry information to readers in short, clear, and concise words.

To be effective, written work must be planned and organized for clear understanding. The writer should have a specific reader or audience in mind. Policies written for the staff of the engineering department will not be effective when addressed to the building occupants. The two groups of readers do not have the same background knowledge to facilitate understanding. In a similar manner, a letter from the facilities manager to the general manager will not be written in the same tone or level of formality as a directive memo addressed to maintenance staff. The facilities manager must have a purpose in mind for a written document. If the writer does not understand the reason for the message, then it will be very difficult for the reader to understand the meaning of the document. The facilities manager must focus his efforts to carry a specific meaning to the reader. Each sentence should express only one idea, and do so clearly and completely. Further, when a single sentence fulfills the entire purpose of the message then a second sentence may not be needed. Poorly written documents often seem to follow the tongue-in-cheek guideline that "one should never use a sentence when a paragraph will do." As a result the document does not carry a clear message and the result is confusion. Often the only thing accomplished is a total lack of communication.

Business writing is normally intended to convey specific information. It is important to include all of the data and guidance required to support full understanding of the meaning, but not so much that the meaning is lost. When a guest reads a policy to find out the operating hours of the hotel swimming pool, they do not need to know that it will not open until 10:00 in the morning because that allows time for maintenance on the filters and pumps. They only need to read that it will be open at 10:00 AM. Clear, concise business writing provides answers without creating more questions. It must address the reader specifically. In the example above the guest only needs to know the opening time for the swimming pool, but if the document was addressed to the hotel maintenance staff, then it would include the times and requirements for maintenance of the pumps and filters to ensure that they know what must be done to make sure the pool opens on time in a serviceable condition.

Poorly organized work is difficult to understand. Therefore, the facilities manager must learn to approach writing in the same way that other work is accomplished. Writing a topic sentence is very similar to building the foundation of a building. Once the foundation for a building is laid, the facilities manager understands that the frame of the structure must be erected. Similarly, the topic sentence leads to the construction of an outline of the document being written. When the outline is established then the sentences of the paragraphs are added in appropriate places to form the walls and floors of the document. Punctuation, connecting sentences, and qualifying points are then added to make the document flow and carry its message just as pipes, wiring, and lights are added to a building to make it functional. The facilities manager should also establish an outline or at least a list of significant points to guide the composition of an effective written message, memo, letter, policy, or procedure.

A few basic rules will also help the facilities manager to write more effective documents:

- Use specific and direct language to address the subject.
- Write in the active voice for better understanding.
- Use plain English and simple sentences, one idea per sentence.
- Follow the inverted pyramid model of writing (this will be explained).
- Use clear topic sentences to focus the reader.
- Avoid clichés and colloquial expressions.
- Avoid sexist language.
- Stress the positive effect of thoughts and ideas.
- Make a clear statement to support the topic sentence.

Using simple words and sentences is more effective than elevated and impressive words with multiple meanings. Using the inverted pyramid model is a trick to help a writer state the most important ideas first followed by supporting points and then minor points at the bottom. The facilities manager should stress the positive effect of statements by explaining to the reader what can be done, instead of telling them what they cannot do. When these elements are put together and polished with the other rules, the resulting document will be clear and effective.

The two most commonly used formats for business correspondence are the memo and the business letter. Memos usually are written to address a single subject, point, or action. Therefore, they are meant to be short and straightforward. They follow a specific format and while this varies a little in different organizations, five elements of a memo are always present:

- Name of the person to whom the memo is addressed.
- Name of the person who wrote the memo.
- The date of the memo.
- The subject of the memo.
- The body of the memo.

If any of these five elements is missing, the memo does not carry a clear message. The addressee should be a specific person or defined group of persons affected by the memo. This will prevent the reader from deciding that the message does not apply to them or incorrectly responding when they are not addressed. Identification of the writer establishes the authority or expertise of the memo and gives it a directive or official effect. The date of the memo establishes the effective date of the information included and also precludes confusion on the order of directives as to what is in effect now or what is the latest information. The subject label should be very specific to focus the contents of the memo, and the body of the memo should address only the subject listed. Good memos solve problems and establish guidance. Therefore, they should be factual and objective but not editorial in nature.

The business letter should also be clear and concise and should never exceed two pages in length. The business letter is more formal in nature and is normally used to convey information to receivers outside of the writer's organization. The facilities manager will not use this format as often as the memo, but when it is used it should be carefully composed because it displays the professional operation of the enterprise.

For an illustration of a sample memo and a sample business letter, see figures 5.1 and 5.2 on the following pages.

Figure 5.1: Sample Memo

To: Intended Reader

From: Responsible Writer

Date: Date the Memo Was Written

RE: Proper Memo Formatting Example

This is an example of a properly formatted memo. This is not an absolutely required format, but rather a common general form used in business.

Body Paragraph 1: The first sentence should be a simple, clear topic sentence establishing the reason for the memo. The second sentence should explain the required action that you want from the reader.

Notice that there are three spaces between the salutation portion at the top of the memo and the opening paragraph. Also note how the individual paragraphs are single spaced with double spacing between paragraphs. Paragraphs should not be too long. Separate paragraphs into main points. This helps your reader to follow the message that you are trying to convey as they scan through your memo. Paragraphs that are too long will discourage people from reading the contents of your memo and will seriously reduce the effectiveness of your writing.

Body Paragraph 2: This paragraph should provide important points proving or supporting your first sentence in Paragraph 1.

Body Paragraph 3: In this paragraph less-important supporting facts are provided. Some memos do not need this paragraph.

Final Body Paragraph: Provide a suitable closing sentence or sentences to confirm the required action as a result of this memo.

Finally, there is no signature at the bottom of a memo. This is different from a business letter. You may initial or sign your name at the top of the memo next to your typewritten name if you wish. Remember to keep your message clear, concise, and simple. Always proofread your work.

Figure 5.2: Sample Business Letter

Company Name
Company Address
Company Address (Second Line)

Date of Composition

(Triple space between date and address)
Name of Intended Receiver
Receiver's Title (as Appropriate)
Receiver's Company Name
Address
Address (Second Line)
(Double space between sections and paragraphs)
Dear Mr., Ms., Receiver Surname:

When writing a business letter, the most traditional method is to use the 'block' left style where all paragraphs are flush to the left with no indentations. Each paragraph is separated by TWO spaces, while the body of the paragraph itself is single spaced. The traditional font is Times New Roman, 12pt font size. Margins are 'normal' in MS Word, set at 1 inch. Try to limit the size of your paragraphs so that they contain only one main point, or are limited to a few related points. This helps your receiver to quickly scan your letter for the most important points. This also makes you look more effective as a business writer.

Paragraph 1: Explain the reason for the letter.

Paragraph 2: This paragraph provides facts or evidence supporting the reason stated in the first paragraph.

Paragraph 3: Explain any required action and the expected timeline for completion.

Final Paragraph: Thank the reader for his/her time.

Sincerely,
Triple space between salutation and name to leave room for signature.

(Signature)

Sender's Name

Never 'orphan' just your signature line on a second page. Move the last paragraph of your text to the second page to join your signature, or edit the document to fit on a single page.

In the modern business world the facilities manager must also be skilled in the use of E-mail. E-mail is a shortened term for electronic mail transmitted through Local Area Networks (LAN) and Wide Area Networks (WAN) and most managers are familiar with it. Its use has become popular for many reasons. It is less disruptive than a phone call and much faster to disseminate information than a letter or memo. Further, it does not depend on the sender and receiver actively working at their desk to receive the message. Modern computer systems will hold E-mail messages and alert the receiver to their presence on their return. Further, the use of multiple addresses allows an E-mail message to be distributed to a large number of individual receivers simultaneously.

There are a few disadvantages to the use of E-mail that the facilities manager must know. Because E-mail messages are so quick and easy to send, the sender sometimes assumes that it will be read immediately. In fact, the receiver may not read it for several hours. Therefore, for any action or response needed in less than 24 hours, the facilities manager should use telephone or direct communications. E-mail messages also do not communicate verbal inflections or body language. This means that the recipient will not be able to detect anger, urgency, disapproval, or pleasure unless it is specifically stated in the words of the message. It is especially difficult to communicate sarcasm without facial expressions or body language. Attempts at sarcasm will almost certainly be misunderstood in E-mail messages and should be avoided. A few guidelines for using E-mail include:

Don't use the "To" field when mailing more than one person.
Doing so makes the addresses of all the recipients available to all of the other recipients and some people do not want their address publicized. It is better to use the "Bcc" field for additional recipients, protecting their privacy and also preventing each receiver from knowing that anyone else received the same message.

Be sure to include an accurate "Subject" line.
The people in your organization receive many e-mail messages daily. If you include a clear, descriptive subject in the subject line, they can identify urgent or important messages quickly. It can be especially irritating to receive a message that is second or third iteration with a "ref: subject" in the subject line that is no longer correct. If the subject has been changed, the writer should make sure that the subject is changed to be accurate as a guide to the receiver.

Do not overuse the "High Priority" option.
Marking all outgoing messages as "High Priority" only serves to reduce the priority of all messages. Ensure that this designation is only used for valid urgent messages requiring immediate action.

Messages should be concise and clear.
E-mails should be short and to the point. They should not be used to carry policy statements or discuss subjects that would be more effectively handled with a memo or letter. Long E-mail messages are often not read carefully and therefore, should be avoided.

Do not write in all capital letters.
Using all capital letters in an E-mail is considered to be the same as shouting at your receiver. Most people see this as rude.

Check for writing errors.
The speed and ease of using E-mail is not an excuse to ignore the rules of spelling and grammar. It is still written correspondence and therefore should be proofread for accuracy and clarity, and reviewed carefully for correct spelling and grammar. The E-mail message is a model of the professionalism of the sender in the same way as a memo or letter.

Keep formats simple.
Fancy fonts and pretty pictures do not belong in business E-mail messages. If the receiver's computer does not share the same format then they will simply appear as computer codes interrupting the text of the message. Sometimes the message can even become large enough to crash the receiver's computer. Use Plain Text for E-mail messages.

Do not use abbreviations that are not in common use.
Facilities managers must be especially careful to not use technical acronyms or abbreviations in messages sent to non-technical recipients. The terms or expressions in common use in the engineering department often have no meaning in other departments.

Do not use "emoticons."
Emoticons are strings of punctuation marks and letters meant to approximate the appearance of a human face. They can be confusing and are viewed as unprofessional time wasters. It is best to not use them.

Include a signature at the end of the message.
The sender should never assume that the receiver will automatically identify the source of the message from the heading of an E-mail. Most E-mail programs allow for the inclusion of a signature block to be added automatically to every sent message. A signature block can provide valuable information to the receiver and establish the authority of the sender.

Proofread before you send.
Although a careful E-mail user will check grammar and spelling before the message is sent, care should also be taken to read through an E-mail message to make sure that it carries the meaning that the sender intended. This step is important because it is impossible to retrieve a message once it has been sent.

THINK before you send.
The last point that a facilities manager must consider before transmitting an E-mail message is that it is not a private means of correspondence. Employers

have the right to monitor and review any messages that are sent using company equipment, and they often do. Jokes, improper comments, or inappropriate language do not belong in E-mail messages just as they do not belong in any other written correspondence.

VERBAL COMMUNICATION

The most common form of communication is verbal communication. A great deal of information is exchanged between individuals or given to groups in direct conversation as well as in formal presentations. In either setting, the facilities manager must carefully consider the message sent and the message received. Every conversation has a starting point to establish contact and every presentation must start with an introduction to prepare listeners for the message. This is followed by the body of the message that contains the real information. The message, presentation, or statement will end with a conclusion. In a formal presentation the conclusion guides the audience to the closing statement or bottom line, and in the conversation it signals the listener that it is their turn to respond or take action as a result of the message they have received. Managers are often taught in communications classes to address presentations in three "Tell Them" steps. These steps are "tell them what you are going to tell them," "tell them," and "tell them what you told them." This is an effective model for verbal communication, but it is not complete. Listeners should hear what the sender says, but they will also note how the sender said it. The two parts of verbal communication have to be aligned with the intent of the speaker to produce effective communication. Praise delivered in perfunctory or sarcastic manner is not received as praise. Criticism spoken in an apologetic and self-demeaning voice can be misunderstood as unimportant and therefore will not be taken seriously.

Oral communication consists of several different elements that all work together to make a message that can be understood:

Verbal
The verbal part of the message is the actual wordage chosen by the sender to carry the intended meaning.

Vocal
The tone and pitch of the speaker's voice adds clarity to the message. High-pitched tones might induce excitement and urgency, while lower tones are calming or reassuring.

Volume
The actual loudness of the message also adds meaning by changing the emphasis of the words, but also is very important to ensure that the message is heard. There is an old adage that "A man will go across the street so that he doesn't have to listen to you shout, but he will lean closer to make sure that he hears you whisper the same words."

Speed

The speed of speech affects its understandability. The sender should ensure that he or she does not speak their words so fast that the listener cannot get the message. Speaking too fast can also give the impression of excitement or importance while speaking too slowly can remove the urgency. The speed of speech must match the situation while it supports clear understanding of the message.

Articulation or Enunciation

Words should be properly formed and accurately voiced. This is especially true in the English language where many words sound much alike except for the first consonant in the word. If the initial sound of the word is not clearly enunciated, the listener must attempt to interpret the meaning of the word from the context of the message and can lead to miscommunications.

Vocal Variety

A mono-tone can lead to boredom on the part of the listener. Changes in tone and pitch in coordination with significant pauses can be used to emphasize a point.

Enthusiasm

Important messages must be sent with enthusiasm to match their urgency. If the transmitter is not interested in the message, the listener will not be interested in understanding it.

The facilities manager will often find that he or she must give instructions or receive information in a very loud or hectic environment. Care should be taken to ensure that the message is received as it is intended or that the information received is accurately understood. Using the factors mentioned above effectively will greatly aid oral communication.

The facilities manager must also practice the use of body language and physical attitudes to emphasize or reduce the impact of the chosen words as appropriate. A pointing finger can give the impression of anger or directive intent, whereas poor eye contact with the listener can convey insecurity or insincerity. A smile can be apologetic or pleasant and a stern look can be professional or angry, depending on the environment. The facilities manager must always make an effort to match the physical attitude with the message to ensure effective communication. The facilities manager must also interpret information that is received from the body language of the sender and the environment of the message. It is important to identify the urgency of the message in relation to the situation at hand to guide appropriate managerial actions.

The facilities manager must orient his or her attention to listen effectively. Listening is an active function and it needs just as much effort as speaking. Every individual who speaks deserves to be heard, so the facilities manager must not only hear the words, but also accurately interpret their meaning. This is true whether the message is being spoken by the electrician's helper or the general manager.

STAFF COMMUNICATION

An effective facilities manager must communicate at all levels of the organization that occupies the property that he or she maintains. The facilities manager is an integral part of a successful staff organization. Information must be exchanged throughout the organization, in all directions. Executive management levels must receive information on the internal needs of the subordinate elements as well as the external factors with which they must contend. Department heads and middle managers must exchange data and requirements with other managers as well as their employees while they are keeping the boss informed of significant events and situations. Employees must receive the necessary guidance and direction to complete their respective tasks in an organized and supportive relationship, while providing their supervisors with the necessary information to make sound managerial decisions. The facilities manager must also communicate in three directions: upward to the executive management levels, laterally to fellow management elements, and downward to subordinate employees. To do this effectively, good communication is important, but the three directions have some important differences in coordination, execution, and timing of communications.

In the upward direction, the facilities manager must remember that the executive manager has many duties that demand attention so care must be used to make sure that the message is important and pertinent to the operation of the organization. The information provided must be accurate and complete to avoid wasted effort and ineffective managerial responses. Accurate and complete information does not mean that the message should be overly detailed, but it should contain all the necessary information to facilitate a good decision. The executive manager needs to receive bad news as rapidly and as accurately as good news. The organization is not well served by an executive level of management that does not know the problems of the operation. Information needs to be provided to the boss regularly and routinely because long periods without communication produce either uneasy anxiety, or comfortable complacency.

To produce effective communication with upper management, the facilities manager must organize communications to not only provide information, but also to use the executive manager's attention efficiently. Any problems that are presented should be accompanied by suggested solutions or options for appropriate managerial response. To ensure efficient use of interaction with the boss, the facilities manager should prepare for any meeting with an agenda of subjects or messages that need to be covered. In the case of a formal meeting or audience, this agenda might even be sent to the boss prior to the meeting so that he or she can prepare their own thoughts on current issues. Planned objectives for interactions with executive managers can also assist in keeping communications organized in a concise format and prevent diversion to less-important topics. Finally, the facilities manager must take care to pick appropriate times to talk with the boss to ensure a receptive atmosphere. Poor timing will result in ineffective communication.

Communicating with other managerial elements of the organization requires the facilities manager to become familiar with the operation or function of other departments. The effective exchange of information is much more easily accomplished between friendly and familiar co-workers than adversarial or competitive strangers. The attitude that needs to be adopted for most lateral communications is one of mutual benefit to be derived from better understanding. Each element must identify the needs and purpose of the others and the facilities manager must be attentive to the effect of his or her actions on the functions of other departments. Sharing information is more productive than directing requirements. The facilities manager must always express the purpose of supporting the operations of other departments as a service function, but simultaneously needs to ensure that the other departments understand their responsibilities to assist with that support. Close personal contact in coordination with written correspondence is much better than either is by itself.

When dealing with employees, the facilities manager must ensure that the staff feel empowered and encouraged to communicate their ideas, observations, opinions, and concerns without threat of retribution. It is important to establish an open-door policy to remove barriers to free communication from subordinates. The facilities manager must be prepared to actively listen and consider the ideas of employees without prejudice or preconceived ideas. It is unprofessional to respond emotionally or critically to employees even when they bring bad news. This is known as "shooting the messenger" and will result in employees withholding important information that is needed for efficient management. It is acceptable to correct employees if they make a mistake, but it is not acceptable to use anger as a manipulative tool in communicating urgency or displeasure to an employee.

COMMUNICATION PROBLEMS IN FACILITIES MANAGEMENT

Facilities Managers are not normally good communicators. Effort must be extended to overcome some of the communication barriers that are inherent to the position. Facilities managers usually have a background in the technical area of facilities or the logistics area of business. Therefore, they normally deal with a very physical and black-and-white sort of situation. The vocabulary that the facilities manager uses within his own department does not translate easily to the other areas of the managerial staff responsibilities. Often this leads to a compartmentalization of the facilities department in an attitude of a "not my job" reaction to many of the concerns of other departments. This is a road block to communication. The facilities manager must learn to communicate needs, requirements, and ideas to other managers and to the executive level of management in terms that they can understand. Acronyms and technical jargon should be saved for discussions within the facilities department.

Because of their background in the physical aspects of the operation, facilities managers also tend to be "doers" instead of "talkers." This can also form a barrier to effective communication with other departments and executive managers. The facilities manager sometimes may even build up resentment toward the rest of the organization because of a perception of always being left with the dirty jobs, while the others deal with the more glamorous aspects of the operation. The other departments may downgrade the activities of facilities department employees because they do not understand their contribution to operational functions. These barriers can only be defeated by more effective exchange of ideas and concerns between the facilities manager and the other department heads. The facilities manager must often make the first approach with offered assistance followed by a discussion of the shared responsibilities and requirements of the departments. Once the doors to effective communications are opened, the facilities manager must continue to communicate and keep them open. This can be done with daily status reports, distributed maintenance schedules, daily or weekly department visits, executive council discussions, or a myriad of other opportunities to communicate. But it must be pursued to keep the flow of information going for the benefit of the organization.

There are several other barriers to communication that can cause problems for facilities managers. Messages can be misinterpreted for a number of reasons. For the facilities manager the most common reason is a misperception of roles between other departments and facilities. Other departments sometimes view facilities activities as interference or disturbances rather than support or assistance. The facilities manager must be careful to schedule work and communicate requirements with the interests of the other departments in consideration. Both sides of a conversation can become defensive if they feel challenged or hindered. Communication must be used as a tool to coordinate a joint effort to meet common goals and support the greatest benefit of the operation. Many behavioral patterns or mannerisms can establish fertile ground for misinterpretation and block communication. A list of problems that form barriers to communication would include:

- Stereotypical evaluations of departments or categories of employees
- Arrogance or superiority in manner
- Inarticulate speech
- Attempted manipulation with hidden agendas
- Uncontrolled emotional reactions
- Differences in technical or social backgrounds
- Personality conflicts
- Discourteous interruptions
- Talking too much
- Talking too little
- Argumentative attitudes
- Generalizations in statements
- Shifting blame or failing to take responsibility for situations or actions
- Prejudicial opinions
- Sarcastic comments
- Discourteous behavior

SUCCESSFUL COMMUNICATION IN FACILITIES MANAGEMENT

To successfully and effectively manage a facility, the facilities manager should develop meaningful communication skills. Speaking well, actively listening, and writing effectively are essential management keys for the facilities manager. The facilities manager must have the ability to work and communicate with employees, other department managers, executive managers, suppliers, vendors, contractors, customers, and guests on a one-to-one basis. If the facilities manager masters the communications skills described in this chapter, the entire operation will benefit. Work will be completed in an appropriate manner to support the operation and the facility will receive the maintenance support that it needs to remain in a profitable condition. Strong communicators will find that they are also strong performers.

ROUTINE COMMUNICATIONS SYSTEMS

Much of the information that is exchanged between a facilities manager, facilities workers, and other departments is routine and may not be recognized as important communication. Operational schedules, event calendars, work requests, accountability reports, daily staff meetings, and other common processes and procedures are all opportunities to communicate clear messages concerning the requirements and accomplishments of the organization. If the facilities manager can read an accurate event-planning schedule, it precludes the need for a daily meeting with other departments to find out "What is going on?" It also provides the facilities managers with an opportunity to ask specific questions of the other departments to clarify needs that must be met by the facilities department to support the event schedule. Daily bulletins or staff newsletters present opportunities to inform all areas of the organization of facilities activities that may affect their operations and simultaneously inform the facilities manager of operations that may affect facilities' activities. Routine staff meetings provide a forum for the discussion of upcoming events or operational limitations for all concerned departments. These opportunities must not be wasted. The facilities manager must communicate effectively in all routine exchanges of information.

Some messages are not written or verbal. As the facilities manager walks through the building, such things as overflowing trash containers may indicate a failure on the part of staff to empty the trash or they may be a non-verbal message that the containers are not big enough to meet the needs of the operations. Or the overflowing containers may indicate that the facilities manager needs to inform the operations manager of the schedule for picking up trash so that the department managers can make sure they put the containers in the hallway at the correct time. The real indication is that better communication is needed to make sure that the trash containers are not overflowing.

THE COST OF POOR COMMUNICATION

The facilities manager must understand that there is a very high cost for poor communication. Work is harder to complete and the facility will not be maintained in an effective and efficient manner in an environment of poor communication. All managers must be aware of a few misconceptions regarding communications. These misconceptions often cause misunderstandings that could easily be avoided.

It is incorrect that communications only occur when people intend to communicate. People are sending messages at all times without speaking, writing, or intending to communicate at all. A yawn may indicate boredom, and drumming fingers on a table may indicate impatience. These actions are unintentional, but they provide an immediate signal to everyone who sees them regarding the attitude of the individual involved. Such signals are often misinterpreted. In fact, the yawner may be tired from a late night of overtime work, and the drummer may be nervous or anxious, but not impatient.

A speaker often assumes that the words that he or she uses have the same meaning to the receiver. This is not always true. As discussed previously, the perceptions of the receiver can be far different from the intention of the sender. If a manager tells a worker that their work on a particular product was "pretty good," the manager may have meant to compliment the worker. But this worker might be a person who takes a great deal of pride in their work and in fact feels slighted that the manager thought that it was only "pretty good." Care must be taken to see that the receiver gets the same message as the sender intended.

Many facilities managers think that communication is mostly done with words, but in fact a great deal of communication is non-verbal. Managers send messages with their tone of voice, facial expressions, or even the way that they walk. Sometimes they look worried or fatigued and sometimes they appear enthusiastic or agitated. Mannerisms and actions are often far more informative than words.

The assumption that non-verbal communication is silent is also not correct. A person who hums a tune while they work appears to be happy in their task. A person who grumbles under their breath is probably unhappy about something, but it may not be their work. The problem might be in their personal life. Signals are sent by laughter, weeping, tone of voice, or stamping one's foot, all of which are not silent.

When a manager is speaking to someone, communication may not actually be happening. Both the speaker and the listener must actively participate in the exchange to produce effective communication. The speaker must be sensitive to feedback from the listener. A questioning look or a scowl could indicate that the message was not received or was misunderstood. The listener should be offered the opportunity to ask questions to produce clear communications.

Messages must be articulate and precise in their meaning. To request a report "soon" may mean next week to the listener when the sender meant "today." Such terms as "occasionally, often, regularly, quickly, eventually," and "when you get time," should be replaced by more precise requirements to preclude confusion.

The facilities manager must also be aware of their listener's need for information. A worker may not need to know every detail of the reason for a directive, but they do need to know enough to allow them to complete the task efficiently. Too much information can confuse and bewilder the listener and too little information may prevent understanding of the problem. Facilities managers must be aware of the appropriate amount of information to provide for each particular audience and each particular message. Communication needs to be clear and complete, but also concise and efficient.

"TELL IT LIKE IT IS"

One of the most important things for a facilities manager to master in communications is the ability to speak to the general manager or the "Boss." The general manager must be able to trust the facilities manager to provide accurate and timely information without exaggeration or edited content. The facilities manager does not always have good news for the executive manager, but bad news must be delivered in the same professional manner. Communication needs to be clear, accurate, and delivered on time. However, the facilities manager must choose words carefully to convey messages in an acceptable manner. If the boss does not like the message, it must be because of the content and not the manner in which the message was delivered. For example, there is a great deal of difference between the phrase "that is not correct" and "that is just stupid." Both phrases can carry the same meaning, but have an entirely different impact on the listener. The facilities manager must be able to "tell it like it is," without destroying the meaning of the message.

CHAPTER SUMMARY

Effective communication is essential to professional management. Thus the facilities manager must develop his or her skills to be effective in the hospitality industry. The facilities manager must be able to interact with individuals and groups of people at all levels of the organization. Effective staff operations also require communication as a team of managers all pursuing the same goal of profitable operations. The facilities manager must be regarded as an integral element of the managerial staff of the organization. He or she must be able to coordinate their activities and requirements with the schedules and activities of the other departments within the organization. To accomplish this level of professional relations, the facilities manager must be able to not only make facilities issues understood by the other departments, but must also develop the listening skills to understand their requirements. The exchange of information that constitutes effective communication is continuous and takes many forms, including verbal, written, and non-verbal formats. Without effective and efficient communications throughout the hospitality enterprise, profitable operations cannot be sustained. The facilities manager must not only develop the skills to communicate effectively, he or she must also ensure that they are known for providing accurate and timely information in support of the overall profitable operation of the organization.

GLOSSARY OF TERMS

Active Listening
In active listening the listener must participate in the communication exchange by concentrating on the words that the speaker is saying, taking personal responsibility for understanding the message.

Body Language
Communication signals received from a person's mannerisms and posture including the hands, eyes, legs, and facial features that reveal his or her thoughts, reactions, or mood.

Feedback

Any form of communication that indicates a listener's reaction to or understanding of a message.

Hidden Agenda
A hidden agenda is an internal interest or personal goal affecting one's interaction with others that is not openly revealed.

Inverted Pyramid
A writing model that uses the image of an inverted pyramid to illustrate that important points are covered first with lesser points included in the order of their relevance or importance.

Passive Listening
In passive listening the listener does not really participate in the communication process and does not take responsibility for understanding the information that is received.

STUDY QUESTIONS

1. Describe the normal sequence of effective communication. What are the responsibilities of the speaker? Listener?
2. Explain the importance of effective communication.
3. Is there any cost to ineffective or poor communication? Explain your answer.
4. What role does the facilities manager play in routine staff communication?
5. When is E-mail communication not appropriate? Explain your answer.
6. How does a facilities manager use effective communication to support operational profitability?
7. Why is written communication important to the facilities manager?
8. When would you use a memo? Business letter?
9. Why are facilities managers not usually natural communicators?
10. Explain the importance of the term "tell it like it is." How does this term apply to a facilities manager?

CHAPTER SIX
WORKLOAD PLANNING AND STAFFING FOR FACILITIES OPERATIONS

CHAPTER LEARNING OBJECTIVES

After reading this chapter, the student should be able to:

1. Explain the need for work control in Facility Management.
2. Describe the basic tools for task identification and organization.
3. Describe the interaction between Material and Supply Management and Work Control.
4. Explain the correlation between Preventive Maintenance, Predictive Maintenance, Reactive Maintenance, and Deferred Maintenance.
5. Construct a basic Annual Work Schedule.
6. Develop a basic staff budget based on predicted labor requirements and Full Time Equivalent (FTE) calculations.
7. Describe the basic management tools used to control work and monitor productive effort.
8. Describe the basic principles of Time-Based Maintenance, Condition-Based Maintenance, Run-to-Failure Maintenance, Reliability-Centered Maintenance, and Integrated-Resource Management.

The work that is required to maintain facilities can assume its own singular identity. It can become a tyrant and master to the facilities manager. This is because facilities work must be completed or the facility decomposes and eventually becomes unusable. Therefore, there is no decision to make about the completion of facilities work. It must be done. However, the thousands of tasks involved vary greatly in immediate impact on the occupants and profitable operations in the building. Further, each task has its own required frequency, cost, and description. To manage the effort and resources, these tasks require the use of a Facilities Management System (FMS). The core of this system is called "work control" and incorporates scheduling, provisioning, and accounting for the accomplishment of tasks and projects to maintain the facility.

WORK CONTROL

Most authorities agree that there are five basic management functions: planning, organizing, staffing, controlling, and directing. The facilities manager is involved in all five, but has a special interest in controlling. In facilities management this is usually termed "Work Control."

As the business of facilities management has become more technologically complex, it has also become more expensive because of rising energy costs, increased labor costs, and more expensive materials. Therefore, the work-control responsibilities of the facilities manager must include the following objectives:

- Reduce facility degradation
- Reduce equipment and structural failure
- Reduce maintenance costs
- Establish efficient and effective staff organizations
- Provide experienced, trained, and motivated staff
- Improve planning and scheduling of work
- Manage resources to eliminate waste while providing materials, parts, tools, and equipment
- Provide a control system that regulates, accomplishes, and accommodates the measurement of maintenance production

Facilities management does not lend itself to the profit/loss analysis used in manufacturing industries. It is very difficult to allocate any individual cost involved in maintaining a facility to a specific revenue source. However, since it affects the ability to pursue all profitable operations, facility management does contribute to all profits and can be addressed as an overhead requirement for all activities. Therefore, good facility maintenance results at a lower cost or in a more efficient manner increase the potential for profit in all operations.

A conservative estimate of lost time in an average facilities maintenance organization is approximately 33% of each working day. Almost half of this lost time can be saved by the introduction of good management and work-control procedures. The proper application of planning, scheduling, and work measurement will eliminate time that is squandered by poor coordination and poor production accountability. A good rule of thumb is that every dollar ($1) expended in good planning saves five dollars ($5) in maintenance expense for labor and materials.

A good work-control program can improve productivity, reduce the number of people required to perform a given workload, and improve the quality of maintenance that is accomplished. Higher quality and quantity of maintenance activities will reduce the frequency of equipment, system, and structure failures, and the labor hours required for reactive or repair activities, as well as reduce waste in material, equipment, and tool purchases. A well-maintained facility will use less energy, require less effort to keep clean, and experience a slower rate of deterioration. The result is a greater degree of protection for the capital investment. Effective work control is good business.

A work-control system is intended to support the facilities manager in the overall maintenance management of the facilities. In his/her maintenance management role, the facilities manager has the following responsibilities:

- Planning and scheduling of the maintenance workload
- Establishing an efficient communication system for effective coordination and supervision of work
- Designing an organizational structure with clear lines of authority and grouping of related skills and equipment
- Developing controls and procedures that allow the orderly, timely, and efficient accomplishment of required facilities work
- Establishing an understandable performance measurement and quality-control function
- Developing an annual budget that identifies required operating funds as well as adequate allowances for special repair requirements and deferred maintenance work

The character and style of a facilities management organization are reflected in how it gets the job done. Success is controlled by the policies and principles of the facilities manager, but also largely influenced by the policies and principles of the owners or general managers of the enterprise. A work-approval system must be implemented that provides effective management of all work requests and requirements including identification of tasks needing immediate attention and those of a more routine nature. A well-defined list of priority categories for work, combined with a formal definition of the differing classifications of work is necessary. Sometimes the classifications must include value limits to allow for effective budget management.

A typical priority system would look like this:

Priority 1   *Hazards to Life, Health, and/or Property*
              Work required to provide or restore security to the facility, to eliminate immediate hazards to life or health, to protect valuable property, or to restore facilities or equipment to serviceable conditions.

Priority 2   *Essential Operations Support*
              Work needed to accomplish the primary business objectives, to prevent a breakdown of essential operation or housekeeping functions, or to improve the performance of a necessary system.

Priority 3   *Routine Operations and New Projects*
              Work that is not time-sensitive, but still necessary and new work to enhance operations or existing systems, that does not pose an immediate threat to operations and can be scheduled for the next appropriate opportunity.

A typical work classification system consists of the following:

Classification	Abbreviation	Examples
Maintenance	Maint.	Checking, inspecting, servicing, adjusting, minor repairs, hardware replacement, repainting, patching, sealing, random tile replacement, cleaning, pruning, trimming, fertilizing, mowing.
Repair	Rep.	Repair or replacement of obsolete, worn, broken, failed, or inoperative systems or components; restoration, rehabilitation, reglazing.
Alteration	Alt.	Modification, expansion, change in configuration or capacity, modernization.
Minor Construction	MC	New work, addition, extension, erection.
Installation	Inst.	New equipment or systems in or on an existing structure, facility, or property.
Fabrication	Fab.	Assembly or manufacture of furniture, shelving, bulletin boards, signs, picture frames; includes installation where appropriate.
Delivery/Pick up	Deliv.	Movable items such as plants, shrubs, bleachers, booths, platforms, furniture, equipment.
Loading/Unloading	Load	Material, Furniture, Equipment.
Demolition	Demo.	Disconnect, strip, cannibalize, salvage, remove, destroy, tear down; includes hauling to appropriate disposal point.
Miscellaneous	Misc.	Any work that does not fit any other category.

One of the guiding precepts for combining the priority designation with the work classification is to accomplish all work in priority order as effectively and efficiently as possible at the lowest practical cost while maintaining a consistently high level of quality.

The priority system and the work classification provide the basis for planning and scheduling the work to be accomplished. A facilities manager makes a significant change for the better when planning and scheduling activities are pulled under the authority of a central administrative element. Removing such tasks from the tradesmen and workers releases these technicians to concentrate on the quality of their work as well as providing the facilities manager with more effective work control. This central office assumes operational control for the following tasks:

- Receipt of work orders/requests following a formal procedure for work classification, priority designation, and management approval
- Compliance with a maintenance plan and/or preventive maintenance program in its scheduling function
- Operation of a service call or minor-emergency response system
- Planning all work within an established number of labor hours or authorized level of expense including all routine maintenance, preventive maintenance, or service calls
- Preparation of advance work schedules, usually on a weekly basis, and maintenance of an annual master work schedule

- Requisition of necessary materials and parts for planned and unplanned work and inventory control of established on-hand material supply stocks
- Providing pertinent shop drawings, sketches, and work authorization documents
- Maintaining progress status and cost data on all work orders
- Maintaining an accurate inventory of backlog by trade, operational area, or functional system
- Evaluating work measurement and work performance accountability
- Reporting of production levels and achievements to upper management
- Maintaining equipment and tool status and condition
- Maintaining warranty information on all equipment, material, and service work

Facilities management efforts can only be accomplished successfully by continuous and effective work-control efforts on the part of the facilities manager. To ensure that productive effort is sufficient to the requirements of the building and its occupant operations, the facilities manager must have an effective facilities management system and efficient work-control procedures.

THE BASIC ELEMENTS OF TASK ORGANIZATION

In facility management, tasks are very seldom isolated occurrences and almost never totally completed by only one person or element of the organization. Most of the things that must be done require a certain amount of technical knowledge and, for many of the major functions in facility management, expertise is required from many different disciplines. To draw a familiar analogy, consider a successful football team. The team as a whole has the collective task of winning a football game. But to be successful in its collective task, each member of the team must complete his individual task efficiently and effectively. Any individual task that is not correctly completed can cause the team to lose the game, even if all of the other individual tasks involved are completed perfectly. There is a hierarchy of tasks involved in the successful football team and also in the successful facility management team. In general, this hierarchy can be broken into two categories: collective tasks and individual tasks.

Collective tasks are produced by a combination of related individual tasks accomplished in a required sequence for successful completion. This would mean that a collective task cannot be done by a single individual, nor could it be accomplished in a single activity. Usually collective tasks have a prescribed sequence of events that must occur for their completion. For example, in the task to serve a cooked steak to a dining customer, a number of people must complete a series of tasks in a specific order: the hostess must seat the customer, the waiter must deliver a menu to the customer, the waiter must take the customer's order and transfer it to the kitchen staff, the kitchen staff must then cook the steak and transfer it back to the waiter, who then delivers it to the customer. The waiter cannot deliver the steak before it is cooked and the kitchen staff cannot cook the steak before they receive the order. Also involved in this collective task are the efforts of the butcher who cut the steak, the cook's helper who cleaned the grill, the dishwasher who provided the clean plate and cutlery to serve the steak, the truck driver who delivered the uncut meat to the restaurant, the meat-processing plant that processed the meat from the hoof to the truck, and the rancher who raised the animal. If any of these individuals did not complete their individual tasks in the correct sequence or on schedule, the customer would not have received the steak that was ordered.

Individual tasks are accomplished by a single worker and are the base level of the hierarchy of task organization. In the example of serving a cooked steak to a customer, several of the contributing tasks listed are not individual tasks but actually lower-level collective tasks. For example, the meat-processing plant had to kill the animal, drain, skin and clean the carcass, halve or quarter it for transportation, and then cure or age the meat to ensure its quality. One worker cannot do all those tasks, nor can they be done simultaneously, so again there is a governing sequence or schedule of events completed by many individuals that cannot be done in the wrong order and still be successful.

Facility management functions have a similar hierarchy of tasks often involving many different people or positions to accomplish the collective task through their individual efforts. Each one of the required individual tasks can be identified and established in the most efficient sequence for successful completion. In identifying the individual tasks, the facility manager can also identify tasks and details that can be improved or rescheduled to produce a more efficient and often more economical procedure for the collective task. To do this each individual task must be analyzed and documented into specific steps and actions. Until this analysis is completed, improvements and corrections cannot be effectively modified. Each action must be examined to determine its effect on every other action in the task. Its relationship and most effective scheduling must be determined. For example, when brushing one's teeth, one of the required actions is to take the cap off the toothpaste tube. This must be accomplished at a specific point in the sequence of events to be effective and it cannot be eliminated without degrading the rest of the process. However, the action of turning on the hot water and waiting for it to reach a high temperature is not required for effective completion of the overall task and could be eliminated without degrading the process. In addition, eliminating this step from the task would reduce energy use, water waste, and decrease the amount of time required to complete the task. Every individual task must be analyzed at this level of examination if the collective tasks of facilities management are to be streamlined into the most efficient possible operation.

Once the individual tasks have been examined and improved, two things must be done. First, the individual task must be documented in detail to ensure that it can be duplicated to the same standard of performance every time it is undertaken. Then, each of the streamlined individual tasks must be scheduled into the most effective sequence to accomplish the collective task in the most effective possible manner. Examination and analysis is then employed again to verify that each of the individual tasks is actually required to successfully complete the collective task. Further, the sequence of the individual tasks must be analyzed to ensure the greatest possible efficiency is attained. Then, in the same manner as the individual tasks, the collective task must be documented to ensure that it is accomplished in the prescribed manner every time.

On a periodic basis, the entire task analysis process must be repeated. Any changes in the system could mean that a task modification or a sequence modification may need to be implemented. Changes in personnel, equipment, structure, targeted markets, financial objectives, material resources, or managerial priorities can all require procedural or task changes to attain efficiency of operations.

THE BASIC STEPS OF WORK FLOW

In facilities management the thousands of tasks that must be accomplished are brought under control when they are identified as work orders. A work order can be issued for an individual task or a collective task. As tasks and requirements are identified, they can never be cancelled. An ignored requirement does not go away any more than a broken window is automatically repaired because it is effectively ignored. It is the job of the facilities management system and the work-control procedures to capture tasks and incorporate them into the system for efficient completion. Tasks and requirements are continuously being identified. It would be nice if the facilities manager could establish a rule that nothing can break, malfunction, or be scheduled except between the hours of 8:00 AM and 8:30 AM. It would also be wonderful if another rule could be established that enforced a limit to the number of needs or tasks that can be recognized in a specified time period. Unfortunately, buildings, occupants, operational requirements, and equipment systems do not follow such rules. Therefore, work cannot be established in a batch management model. That means that the facilities manager cannot decide to do all the carpentry work on Monday, all the electrical work on Tuesday, and all the plumbing work on Wednesday, just as he cannot enforce a rule that there will be no equipment malfunctions on weekends. The facilities manager must use the facilities management system and his work-control procedures to manage work in a continuous flow pattern.

Each task or work order in facilities management has a work process sequence that it must go through from inception to completion. This is called work flow. Some tasks go through very quickly and others go through slowly. The steps in this process include the following:

Identification of Work or Initiation of Work Order

Work is identified or a work request is received containing the required information to start the process. It must include, as a minimum, the location of the work, a description of the work to be done, the name of the person requesting the work, and the date that the request is made.

Waiting Inspection

After the work order has been initiated, the employee, technician, or project manager responsible for its completion must inspect the area where the work is to be accomplished. The scope of the work and a detailed sequence of tasks required to complete the work must be developed with a precise list of the required materials. The inspection could be nothing more complicated than an electrician identifying the type of light bulb to be replaced. In large projects, it could involve design engineers or architects and the development of a work plan by a project manager.

Waiting Materials

As the required materials are ordered, purchased, or obtained from stocks on hand, the work order passes though the process step of waiting materials. It can take several months for more complex jobs or a few seconds for the more routine actions. In either case, having actual work start before all of the required materials are available is not an effective management approach.

Waiting Schedule

After the materials are received and available, the work then moves into waiting schedule. It is now waiting for the individual(s) assigned to do the work to have the time available to complete it. This may be a matter of waiting for man-hours to be available in the work schedule or it may be that time is not available in the operations schedule for the work to be done. It is up to the facility manager to determine the appropriate time for the required work to be done. To change a light bulb the waiting schedule time period may be only moments. Replacing or repairing a major item of production equipment may mean waiting until after closing time, or a major reconstruction of a dining room might wait for several weeks for the best possible opportunity.

Waiting Work

When the appropriate schedule for the work has been established, the job is now waiting for the work to start. Until the task is physically started, it is waiting work.

In Progress

When work has physically started and is moving toward completion, the task is in progress.

Waiting Final Inspection

The physical work has been finished and is waiting for approval and acceptance by the person who requested the work or the facility manager.

Completion/Accounting

The work order is noted as completed and appropriate financial accounts are billed to pay for the work. A copy of the work order or other documentation recording the activity is filed as a part of the history of the facility condition. The final step of billing the cost of the work to an appropriate account completes the task.

THE FOUR CATEGORIES OF MAINTENANCE

Maintenance has been defined as those activities required to keep a facility or item of equipment in a serviceable condition. Many authorities have separated these activities into numerous categories but in its simplest description, maintenance can be described in four categories. They are Preventive Maintenance, Predictive Maintenance, Reactive Maintenance, and Deferred Maintenance.

1. **Preventive Maintenance** is the use of regularly scheduled maintenance activities for equipment and structures that preclude or prevent service interruption because of equipment or component failure. It includes:

   • Inspections
   • Lubrication

- Minor repair and adjustment
- Work-order initiation

2. **Predictive Maintenance** is the use of scheduled maintenance activities that identify impending equipment failures with the intent of replacing equipment and/or components at the end of their useful life, but prior to failure. Impending failures can be predicted by expected component life, performance measurements, or specific measurements and wear indicators obtained from sophisticated analytic instruments. The intent is to prevent service interruption because of equipment or component failure. It requires:

- Predictable or measured failure indicators
- Anticipated equipment life cycles
- Budgeted support funds for element replacement

3. **Reactive Maintenance** is the unscheduled repair/maintenance activities necessary because of equipment failure or service interruption. This includes all actions that are called repair. Repair requirements can actually be considered to be Preventive or Predictive Maintenance failures. Reactive Maintenance is

- The most costly form of maintenance
- A significant impact on customer satisfaction
- An operational interruption causing revenue loss
- An indication of facilities management shortcomings

4. **Deferred Maintenance** is the practice of delaying or deferring maintenance activities to a more affordable or convenient time period. Maintenance requirements from any of the other categories that do not have an immediate effect on operational objectives or requirements can be entered into this category. The reason for not completing these actions and scheduling them for a later time can be any factor that would cause a delay in completion. Deferred Maintenance cannot be delayed forever. It must be scheduled for a later, more appropriate date. If it is not scheduled and completed, it will ultimately lead to a loss of revenue because of operational failure attributable to managerial neglect. Deferred Maintenance Factors include:

- Lack of budgeted funds
- Lack of available time (man-hours)
- Lack of parts or materials
- No available break in operation schedule
- Must be a matter of written record with a scheduled completion date
- Must be managed to prevent TOTAL system failure

MAINTENANCE RECORDS

Maintenance Records are an essential element of effective Facility Management. All of the aforementioned concepts must be supported by historic records. An effective manager will manage from data. Facilities managers cannot guess at equipment or systems conditions, prior maintenance services, age of components, or any other factors affecting buildings or equipment under their care. Good management requires solid decisions based on

Figure 6.1: Annual Work Schedule

	Activity	Frequency	Weeks: 1	2	3	4	5	6	7	8	9	10	11	12	13	14	15	16	17	18	19	20	21	22	23	24	25
1																											
2																											
3																											
4																											
5																											
6																											
7																											
8																											
9																											
10																											
11																											
12																											
13																											
14																											
15																											
16																											
17																											
18																											
19																											
20																											
21																											
22																											
23																											
24																											
25																											
26																											
	Total Hours																										

verifiable information. Facilities managers must use their facilities management system, work-control procedures, and the four categories of maintenance to ensure that the correct activities are being completed at the most effective time to maintain their facilities. The objective is to keep the building and its systems in an operationally profitable condition and this cannot be done by chance. It must be managed with professional execution of solid management decisions based on good information.

26	27	28	29	30	31	32	33	34	35	36	37	38	39	40	41	42	43	44	45	46	47	48	49	50	51	52	Total Hours
																											0
																											0
																											0
																											0
																											0
																											0
																											0
																											0
																											0
																											0
																											0
																											0
																											0
																											0
																											0
																											0
																											0
																											0
																											0
																											0
																											0
																											0
																											0
																											0
																											0
																											0
																											0
																											0

SCHEDULING WORK

Many facilities' activities and tasks are cyclic and repetitive. It may be said that this work has its own schedule, in that the work does not have any concern about who accomplishes it or how much it costs. The work must be completed to maintain the physical structure and systems of the facility. Scheduling work is necessary to ensure that it is completed in proper sequence and within appropriate time frames to allow the building occupants to function in a profitable manner with minimal disruption to daily operations.

Scheduling of facility management and maintenance tasks can be very difficult if each activity is treated as a single occurrence. Therefore, it is logical to group activities into appropriate categories and establish as many tasks as possible as recurring routines. All requirements are first recorded on an overall task list. This list can never be totally complete. As new requirements are identified they are added to the list. As these new requirements are identified they are categorized and grouped as Daily, Weekly, Monthly, Quarterly, Annual, or Non-Recurring Tasks.

These categories are then entered into the Annual Work Schedule for the facility. Because most requirements are recurring and therefore cyclic in nature, a common twelve-month calendar is not a very useful tool for work scheduling. A calendar based on a working year of 52 weeks better accommodates effective work scheduling. An example of such a calendar can be found in Figure 6.1. Please note that the attached calendar allows for the scheduling of only twenty-six activities. This limitation is simply the effect of the size of the page on which it is printed. In fact, an actual Annual Work Schedule may have hundreds of activities listed and scheduled for the upcoming year. Further, a new activity may be added at any time during the year. Since it is a continuous ongoing routine, the actual start date of a particular task is not really relevant to the total schedule.

Each activity is entered into the week of the year in which it will be completed. The entry should be a number that represents the total number of work hours required to complete the task during that week. A Daily task that requires fifteen minutes per day to complete will be entered in every week of the year as 1.75 hours (.25 hrs. X 7 days) for a seven-day work week, 1.5 hours (.25hrs X 6 days) for a six-day work week, or 1.25 hours (.25hrs X 5 days) for a five-day work week. A Weekly task that requires 2 hours to complete would be entered into every week of the year as 2 hours. Monthly tasks are entered in every fourth week through the year as the number of hours required to complete the task and Quarterly tasks are entered in every thirteenth week through the year as the number of hours required to complete the task. Annual tasks are entered only once in the year with the total number of hours required for their completion.

As the Annual Work Schedule is completed, the required hours are totaled horizontally for each activity and vertically for each week. When all entries have been made, the facilities manager can easily identify the anticipated total annual cost in labor hours to complete each task and the total number of labor hours that are required in each work week to complete all tasks scheduled for that week.

These totals can be very useful indicators in the process of determining the overhead workload and associated costs to maintain the facility. The facilities manager should first compare the vertical weekly totals across the year to ensure that each week has the same approximate weekly total throughout the year. If some weeks are significantly heavier than others, then adjustments in scheduling of monthly, quarterly, or annual tasks should be made to even out the schedule and balance the weekly workload. When the weeks have been balanced as much as possible, the facilities manager should be able to identify time periods where the workload might require maximum staff attendance or minimum staff requirements. Further, periods when operational requirements preclude facility activities can be accurately identified and the requirements can be rescheduled to ensure that operations are not disturbed or interrupted. This can be very helpful when scheduling special projects, staff vacations, or other significant events. Balancing the workload also allows the facilities manager to predict required budgeting to ensure that facility maintenance activities can be accomplished with the resources on hand. The facilities manager can also anticipate when special supplies or additional labor are required and make arrangements to ensure their availability.

The horizontal activity totals for the year will tell the facilities manager the anticipated cost of doing that activity for an entire year. Analysis of these costs may reveal that some activities represent a cost that exceeds their value. This may indicate that the frequency of that activity could be reduced from daily to weekly or weekly to monthly. The facilities manager must be careful in making such changes to ensure that required activities are not reduced to insufficient levels. Further examination of the activity totals may also identify activities that could be done more efficiently and at less cost by contracted agencies or personnel other than facility staff. Other possibilities for labor savings also might be found. For example, if the cost of emptying trash receptacles in the facility seems to be too expensive, then the manager should consider reducing the frequency of that activity. Trash must be removed from the facility before the receptacles overflow, but larger receptacles might reduce the required frequency from twice per shift to once per shift. This might not appear to be a large change but it would cut the labor requirement for this activity in half. If it previously had totaled 250 hours per year it would now total only 125 hours per year. Using a minimum hourly wage rate of $7.25 per hour, the cost of this activity would be reduced from $1,813 per year to $906 per year for a cost reduction of $906 per year. This may not seem like a large amount, but if the manager can identify ten activities of equal cost reduction, a reduction of overhead costs of over $9,000 per year could be possible.

STAFFING AND BUDGETING LABOR FOR WORKLOAD

The facility manager can also use the Annual Work Schedule as a guideline for developing facility staffing requirements for the year. The total hours for each week provide a base figure for the number of personnel that will be required to complete each week's activities. It would be very simple to divide the total for each week by 40 hours to determine the number of people needed to complete the required work, but this would be completely inaccurate. A much more useful result is obtained through the use of a labor factor known as Full Time Employee (FTE).

The FTE factor is the number of annual hours that are available to the employer from a full-time staff member after hours have been extracted for legally authorized or required absences. The term Full Time is defined in the United States as a forty-hour work week for fifty-two weeks of each year. This constitutes a work year of 2,080 hours. However, an employee is not required to produce forty hours of work in a full-time position. Under current labor laws in the United States, each employee is normally authorized a specified amount of paid vacation. In most cases this is approximately 10 working days or 80 hours of work time per year. In addition each employee is authorized a specified amount of paid sick leave. Normally this is approximately one work day per month or 96 hours of work per year. Finally, an employee is paid, but cannot be required to work on a national holiday unless he or she is offered equal compensatory time or additional pay for that time. There are nine national holidays that equal an additional 72 hours of work. Thus the calculation for an FTE is

Maximum Number of work hours/year	=	2,080 hrs.
Minus Authorized Vacation	=	- 80 hrs.
Minus Authorized Sick Leave	=	- 96 hrs.
Minus National Holidays	=	- 72 hrs.
Full Time Employee work hours/year	=	1,832 hrs.
Full Time Employee productive work hours/week =		35 hrs (1,832 divided by 52)

This FTE figure of 1,832 hours per work year may differ slightly in specific firms and establishments depending on how many vacation hours or sick hours they allow for their employees, but the process of the calculation is the same. Using the FTE factor the facilities manager can then determine, from his totals on the Annual Work Schedule, how many employees will be needed to complete the required facility activities in each week and for the entire year. If the total for the year was approximately 1,832 hours, a manager might consider adding an employee to the facility staff to do these tasks. However, further consideration reveals that the answer is not quite that simple.

The facilities manager must examine the tasks further to determine the required expertise for each task. Is the task a common labor type of activity such as emptying the trash or sweeping the floor, or does it require some additional knowledge such as plumbing or carpentry tasks? If there are 1,832 hours of common labor tasks in the schedule, then an additional unskilled worker might be justified. If there are fewer than 1,832 hours of common labor tasks, then they might be distributed through existing employees as additional duties. If there are 1,832 or more hours requiring specialized skills such as plumbing, carpentry, or electrical work, then a licensed or certified technician might be needed to take care of these tasks. If the total number of hours for tasks requiring specialized skills does not meet or exceed 1,832 hours, then there are two options available. The manager can elect to train a current employee or employees to handle these jobs, or an outside entity or agency might be contracted to perform the tasks.

If tasks are distributed through existing employees, there are several factors to consider. The facilities manager must first consider the current workload of the employees. If they are already fully committed then the addition of more tasks might mean that not only might those tasks not be completed, but also the employee's primary duties might also be disrupted. This is an important factor because overworked employees often do none of their duties completely, resulting in degradation of the facilities in the long run. Further, the wage rate of the current employees must be considered. If a highly skilled chef is being paid $55 per work hour, for two reasons, it would not be sensible to assign him or her the additional duty of washing the windows in the dining room. The facilities manager would not pay any other employee $55 per hour to wash windows. The task does not justify that wage rate. Further, while the chef is washing the windows, no one is managing the kitchen and supervising the cooking.

Current employees may not have the required level of expertise for some tasks. If the task must be completed by a licensed plumber or a certified electrician, it could not be assigned as an additional duty to the cook's helper or the bell captain. Some tasks might need some special skills short of an actual licensed technician and these might assigned to existing employees who have time available, but additional training may be required. For example, changing the air filters on the HVAC system does not usually require a certified refrigeration specialist, but if this task were assigned to the cook's helper, that individual would need to be trained to complete the task correctly. Many preventive maintenance activities do not require a great deal of technical expertise, but needed repairs that are identified during cleaning or inspection of equipment might need the attention of a certified technician. When training common labor employees to do such preventive maintenance work, they must be carefully instructed on the limits of their capabilities and responsibilities. Such employees must know that they are to call for assistance when they discover problems beyond their ability.

CONTRACTING TO COMPLETE A TASK

Training of existing employees will incur costs to pay for the training and in time lost from their other duties. For example, the chef might be trained to repair his own gas burners, but during training his services would not be available for kitchen supervision. Further, after he is trained, any time he is required to do repairs he is not cooking or supervising his staff. In fact, the result is that he would be drawing chef's wages to do plumber's work. This might be the option that the manager chooses, but he should think through all of the costs and factors carefully.

Contracting to have work done by an outside entity is another option. This is a common practice and should be considered when the facility staff does not have the expertise, tools, equipment, or the available time to complete the required tasks and the volume of the tasks do not justify expansion of the facility staff or investment in the required equipment and tools. It is very unlikely that a single privately owned restaurant would have a qualified refrigeration specialist on its staff to service its refrigeration equipment. However, a hotel with 640 window air conditioners might have enough work requirements to have its own refrigeration specialist with his own equipment. Therefore, the restaurant manager could establish a contractual agreement with a refrigeration or plumbing and heating company to provide preventive maintenance and repair services to his restaurant, but the hotel facilities manager might be able to justify the funds and resources necessary to establish an internal capability to maintain his HVAC equipment.

All facility maintenance activities can be contracted out and there are multiple companies and agencies that can perform such required services. The only thing that cannot be placed under contract is the management responsibility to ensure that the service is completed and managed to the benefit of the establishment. Contractors can be employed very easily, but they are not ultimately responsible for the results of their efforts. The facilities manager must monitor and supervise all contractors to verify the timely and effective performance as well as the quality of their work. A contract to complete a service for the firm will provide the expertise and the tools to do that work, but the manager is still responsible to ensure that the service is completed correctly and on time.

WORKLOAD PRODUCTION MANAGEMENT

The base document for the management of a facility is the Work Order (also sometimes referred to as a Work Request). This document starts and ends the process of any action to maintain and manage a facility. It allows for the accumulation of financial cost and manpower requirements, which drives the facility-management budget. It provides a demand-history base for the ordering of equipment, parts, and services for all elements of the facility, and serves as the main source of information for the facility condition history. It is the most important document in any system of facility management.

A work order acts as a trigger to initiate management action for the work-control center/ authority of the facility. It must contain the following information as a minimum:

- Location of the work to be done
- Description of the work to be done
- Name of person requesting/authorizing the work
- Date the work was requested

More sophisticated or larger operations/facilities may require additional information on a work order such as:

- Work order sequence number
- Building/area name/number
- Required completion date/time
- Urgency of request
- Exact location of work
- Expense approval by appropriate authority
- Budget/financial account number/information
- Detailed description of the work required
- Estimated cost of work
- Special scheduling instructions
- Completion inspection date
- Assigned coordinator/inspector

For a small operation the work order and work order register may consist of a pad of paper on the manager's or secretary's desk or a notebook in the custodian's pocket. It might even be made up of no more than a dated checklist of periodic duties for the facility operators. In larger operations it may be a computer-generated document printed on the facilities manager's printer. For organizations the size of a large hotel or a resort or college campus, it may be a multi-copy, multi-color preprinted form with a register index number already embossed onto the paper and a complete report data base could be associated to it by index or sequence number.

Whatever form it takes, the work order must be a managed document that provides a chronological history of the facility management actions that are used to support the operations of a functional physical facility. It is essential first to identify the work or tasks that can and should be captured by a documented work order. This is part of the scheduling process that has already been discussed, but the work order is the instrument that executes the scheduled work and accounts for its completion.

Required tasks or maintenance actions can be addressed in the following categories: Daily, Weekly, Monthly, Quarterly, Annual, Long Range, and Non-Recurring. The Daily category includes the myriad of tasks required to keep a facility clean and functional. It may include Preventive Maintenance tasks as well as those actions required to maintain operations on a daily basis. Weekly tasks are usually slightly less repetitive than Daily Tasks, but they also are the normal requirements to keep a facility functional and operating within the minimal prescribed standards of performance. Monthly tasks are usually more technically involved than the Daily or Weekly and often consist of preventive maintenance actions and inspections on major items or systems in the facility. The Annual category normally is a scheduled visit or task for a technical inspection or service of equipment or systems in the facility that is beyond the capability of the operating staff. Many annual inspections are requirements established by local ordinances or regulations. Non-Recurring tasks are usually Reactive Maintenance activities such as repairs or adjustment requirements that occur unpredictably. They may actually occur more than once, but by their nature they cannot be brought into a routine or scheduled recurring task list.

In developing a task list, the facilities manager creates a list of the actions to be completed. The first list will be a continuous document noting all required activities from the daily to the long range. Non-Recurring tasks may be listed but they will not lend themselves to planned tasking or scheduling because of their unpredictable nature. It is probably more productive to simply remember that Non-Recurring tasks will require some amount of time, energy, money, and materials and therefore must be acknowledged in the budgeting processes for those resources. If a Non-Recurring task does seem to be popping up more regularly than expected, then it should be "Routinized." It must be analyzed and either added to one of the other categories or added to a Preventive Maintenance inspection sequence to preclude the disruptive operational effect of its uncontrolled recurrence.

All activities will be recorded on the task list in the order in which they are identified. This list is never complete and cannot be compiled in a single sitting. This is because new tasks will be identified continuously throughout the life of the establishment. Every time a new piece of equipment is installed, a wall is repainted, or a facility system is inspected, something new will be noted and added to the list.

Each activity on the list must be sorted into its appropriate category from Daily to Long Range. This will establish a separate list for each category and allows them to be scheduled more effectively. Starting with the Daily requirements, the facilities manager must determine if each or any of the listed activities are critical, expensive, or difficult enough to warrant a separate work order to record their completion. For example, if the activity was of such a nature that its omission or mismanagement would affect the survival of the facility, then it might warrant a separate and distinct work order to verify that it was accomplished and properly recorded. But it is more likely that most Daily activities are minor enough that they could be listed in a daily task list on one overall daily work order or simply listed on a daily activity checklist or task sheet. However, this document should be dated and signed either by the employee who completes the task(s) or the supervisor who is responsible to ensure the task(s) are accomplished. A new daily work order, daily task list, or daily check sheet should be issued for every working day. Completed orders, lists, or sheets should be filed as a historical record of activities.

Weekly activities are by their nature more labor intensive, of longer duration, or of a more critical status and might warrant a separate work order to maintain a record of their completion, or they may be routine enough that they might be recorded on a weekly work order, task list, or check sheet. These documents must also be signed and dated in the same manner as the daily check sheets by the employee completing each task or the supervisor responsible for its completion. A new weekly work order, check sheet, or task list should be issued at the start of each work week and completed sheets should be filed as a historical record of activities.

As Monthly, Quarterly, and Annual tasks are analyzed, it usually becomes apparent that the expense and complexity of these operations, coupled with the required expertise, will normally dictate that they be handled as a separate work order or element of work and not be listed as a task on a list. This will not only allow them to be accounted for and completed in an effective and efficient manner but also permits more effective scheduling for future planning and staffing decisions. Some of these actions or tasks will require detailed planning to ensure that the proper technicians are supported by an adequate budget and sufficient material resources, permits, and time to complete the requirement.

As was mentioned earlier, small and simple operations may not require an actual "Work Control System." In fact, daily or weekly checklists coordinated with a series of notes on the secretary's or manager's calendar might be sufficient to meet the needs of the facility. But, in larger and more complex operations such as resorts, hotels, or large office buildings, a more formal and elaborate system is often necessary to control the required facility work. In such cases, a formal work order system with sequenced work order numbers indexed to a "Work Order Register" is more effective. The work order register is the general ledger of a work-control system. All transactions and activities are recorded on the work order register to enable the facility manager to manage and maneuver his work force. The register is the document that records the progress of a work order through the work process.

The Work Order Register must, as a minimum, record the date of request of each work order, the location of the work, the person requesting the work, and the date of completion. In small organizations these data could be recorded in a notebook on the secretary's or manager's desk but in larger and more complex facilities, the register will record the status of every work order in every step of the work process. An example of a simple work order register is presented in Figure 6.2.

A work order for a simple procedure such as the replacement of a light fixture could be captured on a single sheet. Further, its entry in the work order register or the manager's notebook might be a single line that records that the work was requested and completed on the same day. This single transaction has little meaning by itself in the history of facility condition. However, because it was documented and recorded in the facility condition history, it could lead to the discovery of vital cost-consuming conditions. For example, if the same light fixture was replaced on a frequent basis such as once or twice a year, it might not be noticed each time it is replaced, but discovery of the recurrence may indicate that there is a larger problem involved. When the facilities manager is reviewing his notebook or the work order register, the frequency of this light fixture failing might lead him to examine the wiring supporting the fixture or to discover a water leak on upper floors or in the roof that is shorting out the fixture. Without the records, the recurring nature of this problem might not be noticed in the bustle of normal operations.

WORK ORDER REGISTER

Figure 6.2: Example Work Order Register

Sequence Number	Date of Request	Location of Work	Person Requesting Work	Description of Work	Date Completed

Further, a large number of open, uncompleted work orders on the register might lead to the discovery that maintenance personnel or technicians are not operating in a productive manner. A large number of the same kind of work orders such as slow drains in the kitchen or clogged toilets could lead to the discovery of a major sewer problem. A large back log of uncompleted work might suggest that a facility is understaffed and in like manner, the absence of work waiting for attention over a long period of time may indicate that a facility is overstaffed. All of these indicators are the result of documented work orders being recorded, either in an informal or a formal manner, as actions in the facility history or on the work order register.

When a work request must be delayed because of estimated, costs, operational schedules, non-available materials, or other considerations, then the work request should be added to the management category of Deferred Maintenance. This does not mean that the requirement is forgotten, but rather it is postponed until a better or more affordable time in the future. Planning should be initiated for the completion of the required work. The work request should be entered in the work order register with a remark indicating that it is in a deferred status. The target date for completion might also be noted in the work order register. Because the deferred work order is captured in the work order register, it cannot be forgotten. It will always appear as unfinished work when the facilities manager reviews the work order register.

CONCEPTS, MODELS, AND PRINCIPLES FOR MAINTENANCE MANAGEMENT

There are several approaches to maintenance planning available to the facilities manager. These concepts are not cookbook instructions, but instead they provide management strategies to guide scheduling and tasking for effective anticipation of equipment and system problems. None of them can be used exclusively. They must be combined for efficient maintenance management.

Time-based management is an approach to preventive maintenance that establishes maintenance activities scheduled solely by the passage of time. Using this approach maintenance activities are scheduled in a recurring cycle based on elapsed time since the last service of the equipment or systems. Maintenance work is done on a daily, weekly, monthly, or annual basis with no regard for the condition of the system or amount of use of equipment since its last service. This can either cause an unacceptable operational condition because needed maintenance is delayed until the time scheduled for its completion or it can lead to wasted labor and resources working on systems or equipment that have not been used. The best example of this would be changing the oil in an automobile every ninety days regardless of its mileage during the maintenance period. If the car has not been used, then perfectly good oil is being removed and discarded, causing an unjustified cost. On the other hand, the car may have been used for extensive travel under dusty and adverse conditions causing the oil to deteriorate long before the end of the maintenance period. This would mean the car would be running for part of the period with oil that is not protecting it from wear and metal fatigue. Some items respond very well to time-based management such as interior paint or window washing, but other items might be damaged or incur increased cost with this approach.

Almost opposite to time-based management is condition-based management. Under condition-based management, systems and equipment receive maintenance service because of their condition regardless of the time elapsed since their last service. This will require continued inspection or monitoring of the equipment or systems. In general, this approach will maintain operational conditions very well, but because time is ignored it becomes difficult to schedule maintenance activities so that they do not interfere with operations. Work cannot be scheduled until specific levels of condition are met regardless of pending use. Further, if this approach is used exclusively, equipment or systems cannot continue to be used when those specific levels of condition occur. Without consideration of operations, the equipment or systems must be serviced immediately to prevent damage or reduced serviceable life. This strategy requires the use of test equipment or measuring instrumentation to provide accurate measurements of condition. Using the automobile as an example again, condition-based scheduling would change the oil in the engine only when viscosity or filter tests indicated that the oil was dirty or ineffective. This prevents wasting serviceable oil simply because of its age. It also extends engine life by replacing unserviceable oil before the engine shows adverse effects.

Some systems or equipment might fall into categories either by dependability or low replacement costs that justify a strategy of run-to-failure management. In this approach, equipment or components are allowed to operate until they fail and are then replaced. This is a very cost-effective method to care for inexpensive components that do not control critical operations. For example, a small secondary motor in an HVAC system might have a replacement value in materials and labor of $150 and an expected life of five years. If this motor were serviced as a time-based preventive maintenance system, it might receive an hour of labor at an average cost of $25/hour on a quarterly basis. This would amount to $100 worth of labor per year for five years with no appreciable extension of the expected life. Over five years this would increase the maintenance costs of the $150 motor to $650 over the five years instead of simply allowing it to fail and replacing it for $150. In a similar manner, the same motor might receive $500 worth of labor in monitoring and testing in a condition-based strategy and still not have received any extension to its serviceable life, which would also increase maintenance cost with no appreciable benefit. It is much cheaper to manage such items as run-to-failure components.

Time-based, condition-based, and run-to-failure strategies can be combined into a reliability-centered maintenance (RCM) approach. Reliability-centered maintenance is used by the facilities manager to manage systems and equipment according to the most sensible method for each component or element within the system. Some items are best managed by a time-based approach such as interior or exterior paint, or landscaping elements. Others, such as HVAC filters or kitchen equipment, is better managed in a condition-based approach. Still others such as light bulbs or inexpensive subcomponents are more appropriate to the run-to-failure approach. Under reliability-centered maintenance, the facilities manager analyzes his property in detail and attempts to apply a combination of the three strategies to keep the structure operating in a profitable mode at the lowest required expense. It is designed to maintain the reliability of the entire facility in an integrated maintenance management system.

When the facilities manager uses a strategy of reliability-centered maintenance and adds the consideration of optimizing the resources available to accomplish it, such as labor and materials, through an organized scheduling and control system, the result is referred to as integrated-resource management (IRM). Under integrated-resource management, the facilities manager not only uses the most appropriate maintenance strategy for the different systems of the structure, but also uses every possible resource, tool, or technician to the best advantage. The objective is to obtain the most effective results by using the best resource, in the right quantities, at the best time. The facilities manager can only achieve this objective through a methodically organized, actively managed, and professionally executed maintenance management system.

CHAPTER SUMMARY

Task identification and work-control activities are essential for effective facility management. A systematic and well-managed work-control procedure will ensure that a facility stays in an operable condition and provides quality response to facility needs in a cost-saving and efficient manner. The work order is the basic document used to establish a work-control system. Using a task-classification system in combination with effective priority-assignment criteria makes it possible for the facilities manager to successfully control and manage thousands of tasks as they move through a predictable work flow. The maintenance management system and its inherent work-control function are the primary management tools of the facilities manager.

GLOSSARY OF TERMS

Facilities Management System (FMS)
The organized procedures and policies in place to control and manage facilities operations and maintenance activities.

Preventive Maintenance (PM)
Maintenance activities designed to keep a system or item of equipment in service-able condition and prevent service failures or interruptions.

Predictive Maintenance (PM)
Maintenance activities designed to replace components and items of equipment prior to predicted failure and prevent service failures or interruptions.

Reactive Maintenance (RM)
Maintenance activities designed to return equipment or systems to a serviceable condition following a service failure or interruption, also known as repair activities.

Deferred Maintenance (DM)
Maintenance activities that have been delayed for any reason and rescheduled for future completion.

Full Time Equivalent (FTE)
The amount of production received from a full-time employee during a year after subtracting paid vacation, paid sick leave, and paid national holidays.

Time-Based Maintenance (TB)

A maintenance strategy that schedules maintenance activities in response only to elapsed time from previously completed activities.

Condition-Based Maintenance (CB)

A maintenance strategy that schedules maintenance activities in response to system or equipment conditions.

Run-to-Failure (RTF)

A maintenance strategy based on servicing or replacing components or systems only after they have failed or become unserviceable.

Reliability-Centered Management (RCM)

A maintenance management strategy that uses Time-Based, Condition-Based, and Run-to-Failure maintenance concepts in combination to ensure that all systems and items of equipment are scheduled for maintenance in the most efficient manner.

Integrated-Resource Management (IRM)

A facility management strategy that combines resource management with Reliability-Centered Management to optimize resource utility and maintenance management for maximum efficiency.

STUDY QUESTIONS

1. What characteristic of facilities-related work requires that it be controlled and managed?
2. What management tools are used by the facilities managers to ensure that properties stay in serviceable, operational, and profitable condition?
3. How are tasks indentified? Categorized? Organized?
4. Define:

   a. Preventive Maintenance
   b. Predictive Maintenance
   c. Reactive Maintenance
   d. Deferred maintenance

5. Explain the difference between individual tasks and collective tasks.
6. Explain why maintenance scheduling is based on a fifty-two-week annual schedule.
7. How does the annual schedule support budgeting requirements? Staffing requirements?

8. How does the concept of Full Time Equivalent (FTE) affect staffing requirements?
9. Define and explain the interactions between:

   a. Time-Based Maintenance
   b. Condition-Based Maintenance
   c. Reliability-Centered Maintenance
   d. Integrated-Resource Management

10. What is the basic objective of all work-control and maintenance management efforts?

CHAPTER SEVEN
MECHANICAL, ELECTRICAL, AND PLUMBING (MEP) MAINTENANCE MANAGEMENT

CHAPTER LEARNING OBJECTIVES

After reading this chapter, the student should be able to:

1. Describe the requirements for the coordination of mechanical, electrical, and plumbing (MEP) systems into an integrated facility system.
2. Explain the application of management tools and principles to specific MEP equipment concerns.
3. Explain the differences between facility management of MEP equipment in a lodging operation versus a food service operation.
4. Describe the characteristics of an effectively balanced MEP system and the effect on profitable operational activities.

The three primary utility systems in any facility are the electrical, water and wastewater, and HVAC systems. There are other utilities available and used in many buildings, but these three are always present. Quite often these systems are studied and taught as separate entities. In fact, they work together in a relationship of interdependence, and none normally operates in the absence of the other two. Therefore, only the basic characteristics of the three can be studied as stand-alone subjects. The management of these systems must be addressed as an integrated management system that focuses on their interaction and shared operational concerns.

MECHANICAL, ELECTRICAL, AND PLUMBING SYSTEMS

To understand the relationships between mechanical, electrical, and plumbing (MEP) systems, the facilities manager needs to understand the history of their development and growth. The mechanical system in a building includes the HVAC system and all of its required hardware. This includes the ductwork and the items of required equipment such as fans, filters, dampers, air handlers, etc. The electrical system includes all of the wiring and electrical distribution equipment, the supported electrically powered appliances and components, and their related management and control elements. The plumbing system is comprised of all of the piping and items of equipment that distribute, contain, and carry water and wastewater into and out of the building.

Of the three systems, development of the mechanical system began first as early men began to pursue a comfortable environment in their dwelling place. Their first approach was to find a cave that had an entrance small enough to reduce the influence of external wind, and some sort of natural outlet in the cave roof to allow smoke and fumes from their fires to escape. As they began to move to man-made shelters such as huts and tents, they still had to develop ways to reduce the invasion of uncomfortable external air while allowing the induction of enough ventilation to preclude suffocation, and provide a vent for smoke and gases to exit the shelter. They discovered that the temperature within the shelter could be controlled by damping the speed of air movement from the outside to the inside, while they simultaneously reduced the speed of smoke exhaust. By controlling the intake and escape of air within the structure, they were able to gain control of the temperature levels within the shelter to improve their own comfort. As dwellings became more permanent in construction, the hearth, chimney, door, flue damper, and window were invented as man developed more expertise in controlling his own personal comfort. The role of the facility manager at this point included the provision of heating fuel and control of airflow, as well as maintenance of the structure of the dwelling.

With temperature under control and the development of HVAC and mechanicals well underway, early man turned some of his attention to the development of plumbing for water supply, because he had to leave the comfort of his warm dwelling to get a drink of water. The invention of the bucket enabled water to be carried from its source to the interior of the dwelling, and for hundreds of years such implements were used not only to bring water in, but also to carry wastewater out for disposal. The development of mechanical systems began as man pursued comfort, but plumbing began its development in the pursuit of convenience. The next important invention was piping as a conduit for water. Pipes made possible the introduction of running water into the dwelling and the expulsion of wastewater without the labor of carrying it in a bucket. Running water was not only convenient, but bringing water into the house either with the bucket or through pipes meant that water could be stored or supplied inside the heated comfort of the dwelling. This meant that the heated air would not just provide comfort, but it also prevented the water from freezing during the winter, making its availability much more convenient even under adverse conditions. Simultaneously, the water stored inside the dwelling also supplied a way to extinguish the fire that provided the heat if it got out of control. So the water system was integrated as an additional control tool on the mechanical system, which helped to make it available during cold weather. The role of the facilities manager expanded to include the maintenance of the water supply and wastewater disposal systems.

The last element of the MEP trilogy of systems to begin development was the electrical system. As the potential of electric power began to be identified during the nineteenth century, it was realized that this new source of energy not only could provide clean heat and light, but also provide a much more efficient means to force and control the flow of air to support comfort, as well as the power to move water to provide more convenience. These three systems, when integrated into a structure, allow for comfort, convenience, and efficiency. Because they have developed into modern facilities structures as integrated systems, these three systems must be managed as integrated systems. The role of the facilities manager in supporting the operations of his occupants and the facility structure itself now incorporates, comfort, convenience, and efficiency as primary issues through the MEP systems.

MANAGEMENT TOOLS IN AN INTEGRATED APPROACH

Facilities managers cannot address one of the primary systems without considering the effect on each of the other two. The tools of maintenance management must be applied to the building structure in an integrated approach. Time-based management issues cannot establish separate schedules for the primary systems. The standards and requirements of each item of mechanical equipment, every part of the electrical system, as well as water systems components must not only be included in the schedule, they must also be entered in a coordinated sequence. Servicing an electrical distribution panel may even have an adverse effect on an electric pump supplying water to some element of the HVAC system if it is not done as a coordinated maintenance operation. Condition-based maintenance approaches must be modified to support the needs of mutually supporting components in different systems. A water pump may be operating within its required performance specifications, but the condition of the electric motor that turns it may be marginal and subject to failure. Further, the pending failure might be the result of marginal performance by the HVAC equipment that is cooling the mechanical space where the equipment is installed. All elements must be considered as a single system for maintenance scheduling.

Run-to-failure principles also cannot be practiced in separate systems. A single electric motor may not justify regular maintenance cost based on its own low replacement cost, but the system that it supports might suffer devastating effects for the facility if it is allowed to fail. It might be the tiny motor that controls the position of the HVAC variable speed fans that provide cooling to the central processing unit of the automated operational management system. The motor itself could be allowed to fail with no direct adverse effect on the operation of the establishment, but failure of its controlled system might disrupt all profitable operation. Reliability-centered maintenance management must ensure the functional support of the profitable operations as an integrated system, and not just the function of each component. The facilities manager has to use his or her management tools to provide a profitable environment for the occupants of the building, and cannot center that management on the individual systems.

LODGING UTILITIES VERSUS FOOD SERVICE UTILITIES

Although the same management tools are used, in most cases the facilities manager of a lodging operation must deal with a much more complex integrated MEP system than does the facilities manager of a food service operation. Where the food service operation is normally a single structural unit engaged in only one revenue-producing operation, the lodging operation can have several different operations ongoing in the same structure and each with diverse requirements and schedules. Further, the primary function of providing lodging requires the maintenance of many duplicate units that all must have identical MEP-support capabilities. Because of this increased complexity, lodging facilities usually have a single individual identified as the facilities manager. And, depending on the scale of the operation, he or she will be responsible for the management of several supporting technicians or staff members. In food service operations, the general manager usually assumes the role of facilities manager as an included duty in his or her job description.

Lodging facilities are much more likely to have in-house staff members who are proficient in the maintenance and care of the building. Therefore, the maintenance management system will be more organized, and with a much greater capacity for in-house response to work requests and requirements. The facilities lodging manager must be more aware of the interdependence of his or her three primary systems, because they are supporting revenue-producing operations continuously with no closed time during the operational day or week. The interoperability and integration of maintenance efforts is constant because the functional requirements are constant, and all systems must be maintained in a profitable mode at all times.

Most food service operations do not maintain maintenance technicians on staff. Most do not have a sufficient quantity of work to justify the full time employment of technicians, but most are not in operational mode twenty-four hours a day. This allows the facilities manager to maintain his or her systems with contractors, and to schedule work periods and requirements for times when the revenue-producing areas are not in operation. Thus, the facilities manager is able to more easily integrate maintenance operations for particular items without disrupting the functions of related or connected components of other systems. This advantage, however, does not allow the facilities manager to concentrate on only his or her plumbing while ignoring the HVAC and electricity. It only means that there are periods in the operational day when revenue-producing functions are not disrupted if one system is shut down to allow work on another. During operating hours all systems must be active, and protection of the interdependency of MEP systems must be remembered when work is being done so one system does not keep all systems from being available during revenue-producing time periods.

PROFITABILITY OF A BALANCED APPROACH TO UTILITIES

If the facilities manager can effectively balance the management of MEP systems into an integrated program, service interruptions and unexpected problems can be greatly reduced. Further, the reduction in service interruptions will result in much higher levels of satisfaction for the occupants of the facilities. Guests and other department staff members will enjoy a much more efficient and supportive environment. This level of satisfaction will be reflected in increased profitability for several reasons. Probably foremost of these is that satisfied guests and patrons will return for additional visits. They will also spread the good reputation of the hospitality enterprise, which results in new customers. The revenue-producing operations in the building will operate more efficiently and provide better service or products because of the reliability of the profitable environment within the facility. A final reason for increased profitability will be realized through the more efficient operation of the facility itself. The profitable environment will be supported with lower energy and maintenance costs because the three primary systems are operating as an integrated and balanced system. Customer and department complaints will be reduced. Therefore, nonrecurring service requests would also be reduced, allowing the facilities manager to plan, schedule, and complete maintenance requirements in an organized and efficient manner. Material and labor costs would be less, with funds becoming available to spend on systems to improve their effective performance at lower expense.

CHAPTER SUMMARY

The mechanical, electrical, and plumbing systems within a facility cannot be efficiently maintained or operated as stand-alone systems. They are dependent on each other, with the condition of each affecting the conditions of the other two. The facilities manager must approach the care and maintenance of these systems as an integrated MEP system. All activities have to be planned with consideration of the interoperability of the three systems. If the facilities manager can do this successfully, the resulting reduction in service interruptions, and reduced cost of maintenance activities, will ensure that the revenue-producing departments and occupants of the building enjoy a profitable environment. The resulting levels of customer satisfaction will ensure the continuing profitable life of the hospitality operations in the building.

GLOSSARY OF TERMS

MEP
Acronym that represents mechanical, electrical, and plumbing systems as a single integrated system.

STUDY QUESTIONS

1. Why must utilities system maintenance activities be coordinated on a single schedule? Explain.
2. Explain the use of time-based and condition-based maintenance management in an integrated MEP system.
3. Which is more difficult to manage, the MEP systems in a lodging facility, or the MEP systems in a food service facility? Explain your answer in detail.
4. Why is a well balanced MEP maintenance management system considered to be a benefit to the profitability of an operation? Justify your answer in detail.

CHAPTER EIGHT
FACILITIES MANAGEMENT TO OPERATIONS MANAGEMENT

CHAPTER LEARNING OBJECTIVES

After reading this chapter, the student should be able to:

1. Explain the correlation between operational activities and facility management activities.
2. Describe the conflict between the fixed schedule of facility management requirements and the variable schedule of operations management.
3. Describe priority management systems that coordinate operations with facility management.
4. Explain methods and procedures used to manage repetitive requirements.
5. Describe different creative schedule adjustments that would relieve conflicts between operations and facility activities.
6. Explain the requirement for facility management to always be in support of operations management.

The operational functions of a building's occupants are supported by the activities of the facilities manager and his or her staff. Many of the occupants consider those activities to be secondary to their operations. In fact, the two elements must be coordinated and managed to ensure that the structure remains in a healthy, profitable condition. Occasionally, facilities functions will take precedence over operational functions, especially when the facilities manager must complete essential tasks to prevent the interruption of revenue-producing operations. Conversely, facilities requirements should be scheduled and managed as much as possible to prevent interference with ongoing operations. There is a perpetual need for the facilities manager to coordinate facilities activities with operational functions.

THE CORRELATION OF FACILITIES AND OPERATION ACTIVITIES

The facilities manager must ensure that the structure and systems under his or her control provide a profitable environment for the revenue-producing operations of the occupants. He or she must also maintain the condition of the building to the highest possible level. Usually these responsibilities go together very well. Occasionally, however, the required maintenance activities interfere with operational activities, and at times scheduled work must be adjusted or delayed to support revenue production. At other times, revenue-producing activities must be reduced or shut down so that necessary maintenance tasks can be completed to extend the revenue-producing life, or to prevent more serious future service interruptions for the occupants. The two sides are correlated because one does not exist without the other. Revenue-producing operations are not possible unless the facility is maintained, and there is no need to maintain the facility if revenue-producing activities cannot occur.

The question is not "Which came first? The chicken? Or the egg?" It is more an exercise of feeding the chicken to produce the eggs for sale to obtain money needed to buy grain to feed the chicken. It doesn't really matter where in the process you start, because all parts must be completed for continued success. You must maintain the building to support the revenue-producing operation to justify the effort to maintain the building.

MAINTENANCE SCHEDULES VERSUS OPERATIONAL SCHEDULES

To properly maintain the property, the facilities manager must establish a maintenance management system (See Chapter 6). One of the elements of that system is the facilities work schedule. The tasks on the schedule are usually repetitive in nature and are most effective if they are completed within a consistent time frame. For example, daily tasks must be completed every day, weekly tasks must be completed every week, and monthly tasks should be completed every month. But weekly tasks that are completed on the last day of a week, and then immediately completed again on the first day of the next week, are not being completed as a weekly task. Nor can a monthly task be completed on the last day of one month, and then immediately done again on the first day of the following month. Such work scheduling would mean that weekly tasks would be done twice in a two-day period, and then not done again for twelve days, and the monthly task would be done twice in two days, and then neglected for eight weeks before it is repeated. Since such scheduling would not adequately maintain the building, revenue-producing operations would probably suffer as well. To be effective, repetitive maintenance activities should be scheduled at regular intervals. The elapsed time between iterations should be cyclic and relatively uniform to ensure consistent levels of property condition and systems performance.

The operations schedule is not usually as easily controlled. Occupancy rates, the number of meals served, or even peak periods are not as easily predictable. Further, special events and requirements resulting from outside influences such as holidays or customer requests must be taken care of when they occur. Although some things are predictable and can be anticipated, such as Christmas Day, the Christmas party catering schedule cannot be established with any accuracy until the reservations are received. In fact, every scheduling factor that is influenced by factors outside the establishment, such as customer requests or unexpected business surges, cannot be reliably predicted with pinpoint accuracy. Because of this unpredictability, conflict between the semi-fixed maintenance schedule and the more fluid operations schedule are going to happen.

Because the facilities manager's schedule is cyclic, and therefore predictable, it can be planned and managed more easily than the operations schedule. In most cases, it will be the facilities manager who adjusts schedules to accommodate operational requirements.

But the facilities manager cannot just change his or her schedule to meet operational requirements without careful consideration. He or she must think about the long-term effect of such changes. If the change creates a tangible threat to the condition or physical health of the building, then alternatives must be sought. Adjustments can be made to complete the scheduled work either before the operational event or after the event. Some work might be scheduled to after-hours periods to prevent interference, while other activities might be moved to off-season schedules for some enterprises. Tasks can be added to the deferred maintenance list and scheduled for a later date. Some services may be unavailable for events on the operational schedule while maintenance is deferred. If it does not interfere with the revenue-producing activity, this may be the best solution. In unusual cases, the maintenance activity cannot be rescheduled and the operational activity must be rescheduled or possibly cancelled. This should only occur when delay of the work would result in an unhealthy or unsafe condition, or incur significant costs or difficulties in the future. For example, the repair of a roof leak or the rescheduling of a preventive maintenance service to a later date does not necessarily threaten future revenue-producing activities, but the inspection of an elevator is a legally mandated requirement that must be accomplished within a prescribed timeframe or the building can be closed by government authorities until it is completed. In the case of a mandated action, the operational activities must be curtailed or modified to allow the action to be completed.

PRIORITY MANAGEMENT IN OPERATIONAL SCHEDULES

All facilities management work can be incorporated into a priority assignment system such as is described in Chapter 6, but the facilities manager must educate the other managers of the occupant operations on the use of this system. The primary staff members must not only understand the priority assignments made by the facilities manager, they must also use the same priority system when requesting work or support from the facilities manager. If the requesting departments establish their work request priorities effectively, it will assist the facilities manager in scheduling work in the most appropriate sequence to support profitable operations. If the entire operation uses the same system, scheduling conflicts are reduced because all managers understand the relative importance of each task.

The facilities manager must encourage other department heads to go a step further in priority assignment. While all departments understand that the highest priority is assigned to work that restores interruptions in service to profitable levels, they also need to provide the facilities manager with guidance on the available time periods for priority work. High priority work must be accomplished immediately to restore service, but each part of the operation must identify the most appropriate time in their operation's schedule for normal and low priority work. For example, the rooms division may tell the facilities manager that the best time to take care of normal operations work to prevent interference with guests is between the checkout and check-in times. The food service manager may prefer that normal and low priority work be done during late night to early morning hours while no food preparation or serving is in progress. The recreation department might request that all swimming pool maintenance be completed in the morning hours and that no major swimming pool work be scheduled during the hot summer months. Using such time-priority guidance in coordination with work priorities, the facilities manager has a much greater chance of minimizing interference with revenue- producing operations, and of completing required maintenance activities within prescribed time periods.

The facilities manager should publish his or her maintenance schedule as management information for other department managers. This would give them the information to adjust their more flexible schedules to reduce interference. No reservations manager will ever enjoy telling a customer that his or her reserved room is not available because of maintenance. They would much rather have told the customer that the reservation they wanted was not available and offer them alternate accommodations, than to tell them that a mistake was made and no rooms are available at this late date. If the facilities manager makes sure that the maintenance schedule is published, such errors and customer dissatisfaction can be prevented.

MANAGING REPETITIVE REQUIREMENTS

Beyond the repetitive preventive maintenance procedures called for in the operating manuals for equipment and primary systems, the facilities manager must use the maintenance management system to respond to repetitive requirements that are not covered in maintenance instructions. As requirements occur for the second or third time, the facilities manager must establish effective procedures to handle them in a normal routine. If this is not done, then every recurrence is a new crisis demanding managerial attention. It is much more sensible to identify such tasks and address them with proper managerial planning. First, thought must be expended to identify the cause of the repetitive action. Usually the problem symptoms are not the root cause. The initial planning should include the identification of preventive maintenance work to reduce the conditions causing the repetitive requirement. The preventive maintenance task can then be scheduled into the standing work schedule to complete in work priority sequence, and a time frame that supports and does not interfere with revenue-producing activities. The second step is to develop standard procedures to respond to the repetitive requirement if the preventive maintenance task is not completely effective. If the problem cannot be prevented entirely, it must be anticipated and dealt with to minimize its effect. It might be incorporated into a predictive maintenance program, so that work could be completed within the most appropriate time identified for normal priority work by the affected operational departments, instead of reactive work to correct interruptions during inconvenient operational periods.

WORK SCHEDULE ADJUSTMENTS

Communication with the other departments and an active management effort on the part of the facilities manager will reduce the occurrence of schedule conflict between the operational schedule and the facilities work schedule. Nonetheless, conflicts will always be present. The facilities manager must adjust the work schedule to accommodate key operational requirements, but cancelling activities is not appropriate. Schedule manipulation is the key. An item of conflict can be avoided by rescheduling a maintenance activity to a more appropriate time or date. The development of a staggered work schedule for facilities staff could make technicians available to complete work after-hours or over weekends when the operations schedule is open. Activities can also be scheduled in managed parts. For example, not all elevators need to be maintained simultaneously. Scheduling individual units at different times can reduce the effect of out-of-service conditions. All the air handlers in the building should not be serviced at the same time, and painting guestrooms a few at a time leaves rooms available for guests and preserves revenue flow during a renovation.

One of the main problems for the facilities manager when resolving a conflict is the reaction of the operational department manager to the requirement. The immediate response is usually a heated phone call or message to the facilities manager from the department manager, with words to the effect of "You can't do this!" At this point, it would be a mistake for the facilities manager to try to force the issue. What should have been done to prevent this confrontation was coordination prior to the event, through a published maintenance schedule so that the complaint could be received without a disruption of ongoing work in progress. By notifying the supported departments that work is scheduled, they have time to voice their complaint early or adjust their own schedules to accommodate the work. If their response were as described above, then the rejoinder from the facilities manager should be to quietly ask, "When would be a more appropriate or convenient time for this work to be completed?" The departments must understand that the work will not be cancelled, but that some amount of schedule adjustment is possible. If the operational department managers feel that they have some latitude and room to influence the maintenance schedule, they will normally cooperate much more readily.

FACILITIES MANAGEMENT IS ALWAYS IN SUPPORT

The facilities manager cannot forget that his or her actions must always support the operational departments. The facilities manager may be responsible for the building and all of its systems and equipment, but the mission is to maintain the building as a profitable environment for the operational occupants. Facilities management planning must be detailed and complete. The facilities manager cannot simply react to the requests from the departments and guests for repairs. Maintenance activities must be scheduled and coordinated well in advance to ensure effective care for the structure. Emergency responses to broken or failed systems often indicate inaccurate planning and scheduling rather than unforeseen problems. A well-maintained building provides a profitable environment for the operational departments. To be well maintained, the facility manager of the building must have an effective maintenance management system and a well-planned maintenance schedule. That schedule must reflect a conscious effort to make sure that the operational departments never suffer a service interruption that would reduce their profitability.

CHAPTER SUMMARY

Facilities management and operations management must work together to optimize the profitability of an establishment. They are dependent on each other—and because of this, conflicts in schedules will occur. This is caused by the relatively static nature of the maintenance schedule in contrast with the volatile nature of the operations schedule. To be effective, the schedule for maintenance activities must ensure that tasks are done in appropriate intervals to protect the property and the systems in the building. Simultaneously, the much less predictable operations schedule must be protected from disruption or service interruption. The facilities manager must expend the management effort to resolve conflicts between these two schedules so that the establishment can stay in a profitable mode. Conflicts must be resolved and the property must be maintained. The use of a maintenance management system that includes a priority assignment procedure is vital to the effective resolution of scheduling conflicts. But the facilities manager must educate the supported operational managers on the use of priorities assigned to work, and the use of priorities assigned to time frames, to create a system of cooperation and coordination. The job of the facilities manager is to provide the operational managers with a profitable environment.

GLOSSARY OF TERMS

Rooms division
The managerial department responsible for controlling the occupancy of guest rooms in a hotel.

Maintenance schedule
Developed by the facilities manager to control the completion of required maintenance activities within prescribed time frames and constraints.

Operations schedule
The event-planning tool for all operating sections of a hospitality establishment.

Repetitive requirements
The facility care or maintenance tasks that are not called for by published preventive maintenance guidance. They occur in response to unexpected factors. They are repetitive if they occur more than once.

STUDY QUESTIONS

1. How are maintenance schedules and operations schedules correlated?
2. What causes conflicts between maintenance schedules and operations schedules?
3. What does "priority time management" mean?
4. List and explain the actions that a facilities manager can take to resolve scheduling problems and conflicts.

CHAPTER NINE
FINANCIAL MANAGEMENT FOR FACILITIES OPERATIONS

CHAPTER LEARNING OBJECTIVES

After reading this chapter, the student should be able to:

1. Describe the financial management responsibilities for facility management.
2. Construct a basic budget using zero-based budgeting principles.
3. Explain the cost-control tools available to the facilities manager.
4. Explain the false economies of shortcuts, quick fixes, and cheap substitutes.
5. Describe the basic principles of production accounting.
6. Describe the benefits and problems associated with effective warranty management.

To be effective, a facilities manager must manage all of the resources required to maintain a property in a profitable condition. One of the most important of those resources is the funding required to support facilities activities. The facilities manager must be an effective money manager to meet the requirements of his or her tasks. This means that the facilities manager must be proficient in the use of provided funding to obtain maximum value for resources expended. The allocation of those funds in the form of a sufficient budget must be developed and justified by the facilities manager to support the maintenance of the property. The operations managers of most hospitality establishments do not fully comprehend the costs associated with facilities activities, and must be convinced of the funding requirements to sustain a profitable environment.

FINANCIAL RESPONSIBILITIES OF A FACILITIES MANAGER

The financial requirements for facilities management are separated into two major headings: Property Operation and Maintenance (POM), and Utilities expenditures. Both usually amount to 10 to 15 percent of revenue for a U.S. hospitality operation. The *Uniform System of Accounts for the Lodging Industry* (USALI) has published standard formats for POM and Utilities accounts, which are illustrated in *Figures 9.1* and *9.2*, respectively. These lists do not include all of the expense headings that occur at every hospitality establishment, and in some cases additional items will be needed. But they offer a very good example of the myriad of financial requirements that the facilities manager must budget and control.

POM activities are labor-intensive, and for most properties wages and employee benefits will approach 50 percent of POM expenses. This is especially true for organizations that complete most work with in-house staff. Some of this expense can be transferred to contract expenses in areas of non-labor costs for those organizations that reduce their in-house work with contract maintenance. To budget for POM expenditures, the labor needs for the task lists, described in Chapter 6, are used to determine the required number of labor hours for employees and technicians, and establish expected staffing levels. Using that information and the wage rates for different employees, provide the basis for the amount of funds to be budgeted for labor. It is important to remember that outsourcing labor by using contractors does not reduce the labor required, but moves those labor costs to contract costs. The value of anticipated parts and materials costs are then entered into the list of expenditures, along with administrative costs to complete the estimated POM budget.

The Utilities budget does not have as many components as the POM budget, but careful planning is still required to establish an accurate estimate. The facilities manager must use historic utility consumption rates and totals from previous years to establish the base figure for a Utilities budget. Anticipated increases and reductions in consumption for each utility must then be added to the base figure. The consumption totals are multiplied by the anticipated utility rates to provide the total Utilities budget. Electricity cost will normally be the highest single element of the Utilities budget.

Fig. 9.1. Source: *Uniform System of Accounts for the Lodging Industry,* 10th Rev. Ed. Lansing, MI: Educational Institute of the American Hotel and Lodging Association, 2006.

Property Operation and Maintenance

Current Period:(date)

Expenses:

    Payroll and Related Expenses:

        Salaries, Wages, and Bonuses:

            Salaries and Wages...$

            Bonuses and Incentives..

            Total Salaries, Wages, and Bonuses..

        Payroll Related Expenses:

            Payroll Taxes..

            Supplemental Pay..

            Employee Benefits..

            Total Payroll-Related Expenses..

        Total Payroll and Related Expenses..

Other Expenses:

Building..

Complimentary Services and Gifts...

Contract Services...

Corporate Office Reimbursables..

Decorations...

Dues and Subscriptions..

Electrical and Mechanical Equipment...

Elevators and Escalators..

Engineering Supplies...

Equipment Rental..

Floor Covering...

Furniture and Equipment...

Grounds and Landscaping..

Heating, Ventilation, and Air Conditioning...

Kitchen Equipment...

Laundry and Dry Cleaning...

Laundry Equipment..

Licenses and Permits..

Life Safety..

Light Bulbs..

Miscellaneous..

Operating Supplies..

Painting and Decorating..

Plumbing...

Swimming Pool..

Telecommunications...

Training...

Travel—Meals and Entertainment..

Travel—Other..

Uniforms...

Uniform Laundry...

Waste Removal...

Total Other Expenses..

Total Expenses..$

Fig. 9.2. Source: *Uniform System of Accounts for the Lodging Industry,* 10th Rev. Ed. Lansing, MI: Educational Institute of the American Hotel and Lodging Association, 2006.

Utility Costs

Current Period: (date)

Utility Costs

    Electricity...$

    Gas...

    Oil...

    Steam...

    Water..

    Sewer...

    Other Fuels..

    Utility Taxes...

Total Utility Costs...$

============

When the facilities manager has developed the POM and Utilities budgets, he or she then becomes responsible to manage the use of the approved funds to complete the planned maintenance tasks. Unfortunately, not all requirements can be planned. In every element of the POM and Utilities budget the facilities manager must consider unexpected or non-recurring requirements and emergency needs. A good maintenance management system greatly reduces such occurrences, but they cannot be totally eliminated. Several factors such as the age of the building, weather, location, and structural condition can all induce unexpected costs and must be considered. The facilities manager must make allowances for such problems in the anticipated requirements that are included in the budget. The resulting budgets must be sufficient to maintain the property in a profitable condition.

The facilities manager must serve as the contract manager for the property, as well as the landlord for the building occupants and revenue-producing departments. If renovations or restorations are required within the building, an additional role of project manager must be added, and in some cases the facilities manager and his staff will act as contractors to other departments. In all of his or her dealings with revenue-producing elements of the organization, the facilities manager must manage financial requirements uniformly. Each labor hour and item of material must be priced identically for every activity or requirement for effective financial management to occur. In the case of POM expenses, this is relatively easy. But it becomes difficult to separate the cost of the electrical lighting used by the accounting department from the cost of electricity used by the recreational swimming pool, unless a system of submeters is installed.

The consumption of utilities is measured by meters provided by the supplier, such as the water meter and the electric meter used to determine the overall consumption charges for a property. To identify utility consumption of a particular revenue-producing department, a submeter that captures consumption data for that department as an isolated entity must be installed. When a facilities manager does this, it not only allows the allocation of consumption to a particular operation, it also provides a factor for the operations manager to use in assessing the profitable contribution being made by that department. Therefore, submetering encourages departments to be more careful in their use of facilities, because their expenditures are no longer hidden in the overall utility costs of the property.

Some requirements affect the entire property and cannot be allocated or submetered to a single department. When such requirements exceed the POM and Utilities budgets established to support the operation of the establishment, they are considered to be capital expenditures. The replacement of a roof or rewiring of the building would be capital investments, as would the replacement of furniture, fixtures, and equipment (FF&E). Such expenditures must be planned-budgeted, and completed under the supervision of the facilities manager. In most cases, these activities are caused by wear and tear over the expected life of the system or equipment involved, but occasionally they are brought on by a weather disaster such as flood or wind damage, or a man-made emergency such as fire, theft, or vandalism. In any case, the facilities manager is responsible for the financial management and execution of such activities.

ZERO-BASED BUDGETING

In many organizations, the general manager or the facilities manager establishes the annual facilities budgets based entirely on the costs incurred in previous years. This is a very simple process that uses the accounting records to identify previous expenditures. And under the assumption that the same property is being maintained, this process infers that costs and requirements will remain constant or static. Other companies use a formula approach that bases cost estimates on a percentage of overall costs per square foot of maintained property, or total costs incurred per number of customers served, or some other arbitrary relationship to estimate requirements for the coming year. Neither of these approaches is accurate because they do not allow for changing conditions.

A budget based on a previous year's expenditures or an arbitrary formula infers that every year will be the same for the facilities management effort. In fact, everything has changed. The property is a year older and so is equipment, structure, wiring, and piping. Every part of the property has incurred the wear and tear of another year of service. The operational environment has also changed. Utility consumption charges, labor costs, and material costs are all going to be different from the past. Therefore, the facilities manager must develop the annual budgets with a method that allows adjustments to be made for every predictable or planned expenditure. Zero-based budgeting provides a more accurate method for budgeting, and a more easily defended justification for individual requirements.

The facilities manager who uses zero-based budgeting starts his budgets for the coming year at zero. He or she then adds the value of anticipated or planned requirements in every category of the budget as they are identified and defined. Labor costs can be found by analyzing the annual maintenance schedule for each task as described in Chapter 6. When the annual schedule of tasks is completed, it provides the labor cost for every recurring activity and task. The frequency of the recurring tasks also provides the information to develop the materials requirements for those tasks. The current material costs can then be identified and added to the budget. Estimated non-recurring costs for reactive maintenance requirements are then added into each budget category. These estimates are based on experience or property history, but also include considerations for equipment and system age, condition, current materials, and labor costs.

The facility manager must also add anticipated special projects and capital requirements to the budget. Restoration, renovation, or replacement needs are added to the zero-based budget for the coming year to prevent such expenditures from depleting maintenance funds. Capital improvements and projects usually represent large amounts of money that cannot be supported by operating funds. By making them a budget item using zero-based budgeting, the facilities manager isolates those costs for more effective management and protects other elements of the property from neglect. Shortfalls in funding are easily identified and cannot endanger normal operations.

Zero-based budgeting also provides the facilities manager with the ability to negotiate with upper management for funding. Using this method of budgeting, the facilities manager can very easily explain the effect of budget reductions by pointing out the tasks or projects that cannot be completed if funding is reduced. This is very valuable because it illustrates to higher management the effect of under-financing facilities activities. This method also allows the facilities manager to very quickly identify how funds are being used because the expenditures are isolated and clearly assigned to specific requirements and activities. Finally, because the cost of each task or activity is isolated, funding shortfalls and overages are very visible for reference in developing budgets for subsequent years.

COST-CONTROL TOOLS

Once the annual budgeting process has been completed and operating funds are allocated, the facilities manager must establish systems and routines to not only control the productive efforts of his or her staff, but also to control the use of budgeted funds. To the external observer this would seem to be very similar to the management of a checking account, but it is complicated by the variety of tasks and personnel involved. Some items, such as projects and capital expenditures, must be managed separately from other funds to prevent overspending or underspending. Overspending will take funds away from other activities, and underspending may affect the delivery of the finished project in the prescribed time frame or at the required level of quality. Other parts of the budget must be controlled at a steady rate of expenditure throughout the budget period to ensure that the task concerned is completed at a given rate of delivery. Utility accounts and preventive maintenance tasks fall into this approach to financial management. Still other tasks are seasonal and should be controlled to ensure that funds are not expended prior to their intended use. The facilities manager monitors and manages all of these items through the use of cost-control tools.

The cost-control tools used by the facilities manager are not the same as those used in the accounting department. For example, a facilities manager cannot simply stop expending funds for a particular task when it runs out of funds. Trash must be collected and disposed of even if the trash-collection category of the budget has been expended. Instead, the facilities manager must find ways to ensure that those allocated funds cover the entire year. In the case of trash and garbage, equipment changes or the establishment of policies precluding the collection of half-empty dumpsters might reduce the rate of fund use to prolong the funded period of service. Policies limiting the uncontrolled spending authority of subordinate employees can also help the facilities manager to control spending. If an electrician is limited to the cost of repair on a single non-recurring work order without prior approval, it prevents him or her from completing unnecessary work or unexpected work that might damage funding. For example, if a plumber knew that a single work order cannot exceed a value of $50 without approval, then that plumber would ask the facilities manager for permission prior to completing the work. The facilities manager could then make a decision to expend or save the funds.

Management policies such as those listed above can be incorporated into the Maintenance Management System (MMS) described in Chapter 6. In doing so, the facilities manager institutes a system of cost control to ensure that funds are used effectively and efficiently to maintain the property. Further, the use of the MMS to control funding use can be easily converted into similar controls in a Computerized Maintenance Management System (CMMS) or a Computerized Facilities Management System (CFMS). By using these systems, cost-control efforts can be automatically inserted into routine operations. In fact, the CFMS not only will routinely control costs for maintenance and project activities, it can also be programmed to control utility costs by controlling operating hours, or levels of service provided by energy using systems such as lighting and HVAC equipment.

SHORTCUTS, QUICK FIXES, AND SUBSTITUTES

Under the heading of cost control, the facilities manager is often tempted to use less expensive quick fixes or temporary shortcuts to keep systems, equipment, or structures in operation. Sometimes the shorter results of such tactics can seem to be beneficial, but the long-term consequences are often disastrous to the overall operation and its profitability. Many household items appear in buildings from mysterious sources and are used in attempts to keep things running. Such items as duct tape, chewing gum, toothpaste, paper clips, and rubber bands have been used to repair circuit breakers, fuses, holes in walls, sagging hinges, smoke alarms, door locks, extension cords, and hundreds of other symptomatic faults. Invariably, over time, the results have not been profitable. Usually the fault is amplified, expanding the cost of a simple repair to a major service interruption. Replacing fuses with tinfoil plugs, paper clips, pieces of wire, or taping circuit breakers closed have resulted in fires that have destroyed entire establishments. The facilities manager must train staff members and himself or herself to avoid the enormous expense of unprofessional work and short-term fixes.

Building systems are expensive and sometimes complicated. Many systems require the use of very expensive specific components and materials. A cheap substitute or alternate will sometimes fit, but the life or efficiency of the equipment is often affected. Remanufactured electrical parts and motors are often substandard in performance. Reconditioned filters and bearing systems are often just cleaned for appearance and will not provide sufficient levels of protection for the system. The facilities manager must evaluate the quality of rebuilt or reconditioned components very carefully. Sometimes savings may be realized, but the early demise of a building or a major operating system because of substandard components would greatly increase the actual cost. Even newly manufactured parts and components must be inspected for quality. After-market manufacturers sometimes use lower-quality materials to create "knockoff" items. A knockoff is a copy made to resemble or fit in the place of an original manufacturer's component—but not to the same quality specifications. The resulting low-cost and low-quality item can also reduce the efficient life of a major building system. The savings produced by using shortcuts, quick fixes, and cheap substitutes is a false economy and should be avoided by the facilities manager.

PRODUCTION ACCOUNTING

The fastest way for the facilities manager to reduce costs to the lowest possible level is to accomplish no work. This is not a viable option. The recurring tasks identified on the annual work schedule (see Chapter 6) are required to maintain a property in profitable condition. Therefore, they must be accomplished. Further, counting completed work orders or completed tasks does not account for production labor costs. Several completed small tasks would seem to indicate a very productive workday, but they might not add up to the amount of effort needed to complete a single large task. The facilities manager cannot effectively account for production or justify the amount of labor costs incurred until he or she begins compiling the number of man-hours expended on each completed task. A man-hour equals the work of one worker for one occupied hour. By totaling the number of man-hours expended on a single task or work order, and then comparing that to the number of hours required to complete the task, the facilities manager can derive a value for the amount of production achieved in comparison with the cost of the labor expended.

If a task is listed on the annual work schedule as requiring 3.5 man-hours per week to complete, but seven man-hours were expended to accomplish it, only 50 percent of the expended cost is accounted for as productive work. The facilities manager should investigate to identify the problem. It might be the efficiency of the assigned worker, which would indicate a need for managerial disciplinary action. Unforeseen difficulties might have occurred that required more effort, or the original man-hour requirement for the task may have been wrong. It does not matter what caused the discrepancy. The facilities manager has to investigate and take action to ensure that labor costs are not being wasted with nonproductive man-hours.

What if the facilities manager learns that the task on the annual work schedule that required 3.5 man-hours per week to complete is actually being accomplished with only two man-hours of work each week? This would mean that the work was being done with only 60 percent of the anticipated labor cost. This would indicate an unexpected high level of production, and therefore a reduction in expected labor cost. The facilities manager must investigate this situation just as he or she would look into a low level of production. It might be learned that the assigned worker is not completing the entire task or not doing the task correctly, something has changed in the task that makes it easier to accomplish, or the original man-hour requirement for the task was wrong. Again, no matter what the discrepancy, it must be investigated. If the work is not being done correctly, the damage costs incurred may greatly exceed the savings from the reduced labor costs. If the work is being done correctly with a lower amount of expended effort, then the annual work schedule should be adjusted to allow the application of those unneeded man-hours to other tasks.

When a facilities manager takes the necessary steps to properly account for production, he or she is ensuring that acceptable quality levels of work are being provided at the appropriate level of cost. In doing so, the property is maintained in a profitable condition and allocated funds are being used in an efficient manner. The facilities staff is also being trained to work productively and effectively.

WARRANTY MANAGEMENT

Most reputable manufacturers, suppliers, and service contractors will warrant their products or services for the quality of materials and workmanship for an established amount of time or period of service. The management of warranties on services, materials, supplies, or equipment can be a very important element of financial management for the facilities manager. Many organizations and establishments spend large amounts of money replacing or repairing equipment and materials because they do not take advantage of warranty guarantees. The facilities manager should establish a warranty file or record that captures and tracks warranty factors for supplies and appliances as they are purchased and installed.

Warranties will vary on the conditions and components that are covered, and on the period of time or service that is covered for each item. The facilities manager can begin warranty management for his property with a policy that establishes preferred manufacturers, contractors, and a vendor roster for the property. Only those who routinely offer guarantees or service warranties would be listed on this roster. When equipment, supplies, or materials are needed, the vendors on the preferred list would be approached first to fill the requirement. Even if no vendor on the preferred list can provide the needed item or service, the purchasing process should include an inquiry to prospective suppliers on their warranty policies for their products or services. The facilities manager must then record warranty information so that claims are made effectively if faults in service or quality are discovered.

The facilities manager must ensure that each warranty is carefully examined so that mishandling or improper operation of equipment, or improper application or storage of an item of material, does not void or reduce the warranty coverage. Often, improper application or installation can render a warranty worthless. Some warranties require technical support or service by manufacturer-certified or licensed technicians, or the use of specified lubricants, detergents, or consumable supplies. These factors must be noted and complied with to ensure that funds are not wasted on repairing faults and failures that would have been covered by properly managed warranties. The period of coverage and the start date of the warranty period must also be noted and carefully monitored. Warranty periods can be very short for some materials or services, and care should be taken that they do not expire before faults are noted and reported to the vendor. Others might cover several years for major items of equipment or some materials, such as roofing surfaces or paint products, and these items must be monitored to prevent warranty coverage from being forgotten over time. Some mechanical equipment or their associated items of supply, such as vehicles or tires, are covered by warranty for periods of service measured in hours of operation, number of cycled functions, or miles of use. Such terms will require that instruments or record systems be installed and used to provide a history of use on such equipment. The start date of each warranty must also be noted as an item of record. Manufacturer's or vendor's warranties on some items that have a limited storage life may start on the date of manufacture, while other warranties may start on the day that the item is applied or installed. Equipment warranties often start on the first day of service or operation. This information must be captured so that the facilities manager can ensure that funds are not wasted by lapsed warranty coverage.

By actively managing warranty coverage, the facilities manager can often benefit the property greatly by avoiding unnecessary repair and maintenance costs. Warranties of hundreds of items of equipment, materials, or services cannot be monitored and managed from the memory of the facilities manager. A written record of warranty information and activity must be established to avoid unnecessary and often unanticipated costs.

CHAPTER SUMMARY

The facilities manager must be an effective financial manger to successfully maintain a building in a profitable condition. He or she must establish an accurate maintenance budget for the property and expend that budget efficiently throughout the fiscal year. The facilities manager cannot depend on chance or unsupported estimates to establish an accurate budget. Actual costs and specific objectives must be established to complete planned production requirements. The most accurate method to use is zero-based budgeting. This tool not only develops appropriate funding levels, it provides supporting justification for the required funds. When an accurate budget is provided it must be incorporated into the facilities management and maintenance management systems, allowing the facilities manager to control costs and ensure that funds are used properly to maintain the property. The proper management of funds ensures that work is completed correctly and good decisions are made in the purchase of materials, equipment, and services. The avoidance of cheap materials and low-quality work combined with effective production management allows the facilities manager to meet the requirements of the property effectively. The facilities manager must use materials, equipment, and services purchased from reputable manufacturers, and manage all warranty provisions to protect the best interests of the property, as well as its occupants, employees, and owners. The facilities manager is responsible for the efficient and effective use of financial resources to maintain the building in a profitable condition.

GLOSSARY OF TERMS

Property Operations and Maintenance (POM)
Referring to all activities to maintain a property except those costs involved in the purchase or consumption of utilities resources. Because facilities operations are

labor-intensive, the largest single element of POM is labor costs in the form of wages and benefits. Labor costs approach 50 percent of all POM costs.

Zero-based budgeting
Establishes budget values by justifying each anticipated cost for the coming year to add them to the projected budget. By starting at zero, this method ensures accurate and sufficient cost projections while preventing excess funding and wasted resources.

Man-hour
A measurement of labor equal to the productive effort of one worker for one hour.

Warranty
A written guarantee of the quality of a product or service that establishes a responsibility for repair or replacement for the manufacturer or vendor if the specified level of workmanship or quality is not met.

STUDY QUESTIONS

1. Describe the two major categories of facilities-related financial requirements.
2. How do the financial management responsibilities of the facilities manager relate to the profitable operation of a building? Explain.
3. Describe the use of zero-based budgeting. Why is this method of budgeting more effective for a facilities manager?
4. How does the facilities work schedule relate to budgeting for annual facilities costs?
5. Describe the cost-control activities used by the facilities manager.
6. How does a facilities manager control production levels?
7. Describe the financial effect of shortcuts and quick fixes.
8. What must a facilities manager do to effectively manage warranty issues?

CHAPTER TEN

ENERGY MANAGEMENT

CHAPTER LEARNING OBJECTIVES

After reading this chapter, the student should be able to:

1. Explain the concepts of effective and efficient energy management and the conflict between them.
2. Describe the application of energy conservation concepts in facility management activities.
3. Describe the process of developing a managed approach for the application of energy- conserving concepts.
4. Explain the use of an energy use index to effectively monitor energy conservation efforts.

Many business failures and bankruptcy proceedings are the result of mismanagement on the part of facilities managers. Over the last 30 years, this mismanagement has often occurred in energy use. Obtaining the energy needed to operate a hospitality enterprise represents a significant portion of operating expenses. Energy costs have consistently risen over the last three decades, and the forecast is that that they will continue to increase for a number of reasons. Facilities managers have no control over the rising cost of energy, but they must develop methods and means for managing those costs effectively and efficiently to maintain a profitable environment for the revenue-producing occupants of their property. If a good energy management program can be devised for his building, a facilities manager can greatly assist his or her hospitality operations in producing generous profits.

EFFECTIVE AND EFFICIENT ENERGY MANAGEMENT

A good energy management system is an optimum balance between effective and efficient energy management. The facilities manager must pursue this balance. It is not enough to simply improve the efficiency of energy-using appliances and systems. If the HVAC system in a building is set to its most efficient level of operation for lighting, cooling, heating or ventilation functions, then energy usage is minimized. But this may not represent the most effective management levels for the operational side of the facility. While the most effective settings are those that ensure customer or occupant comfort, these levels do not always obtain maximum efficiency in energy consumption. The facilities manager must manage energy use to improve efficiency without sacrificing effective comfort control for the building. If efficiency is produced but effectiveness is reduced, the opportunity for profitable operations is threatened. For example, the best way to reduce energy consumption during the summer would be to suspend air conditioning. This would violate the comfort expectations of the customers, who in turn would take their business elsewhere. In the winter, energy consumption could be reduced by not using the heating system, but this would also have a detrimental effect on customer expectations. In addition, these extreme energy reduction measures might produce physical damage to the structure—through humidity during the summer months and frozen utilities during the winter. Both of these conditions would threaten the future profitable status of the property.

Achieving effective levels of performance for all energy-using systems is essential to maintaining the profitability of the operation. Pursuing increased efficiency while maintaining that profitability is the objective of energy management. Many methods and measures are available to the facilities manager to improve efficiency without losing effectiveness. The facilities manager can select more energy-efficient appliances and equipment, or adjust energy-using activities to more effective time periods. Systems can be equipped with more accurate controls and instrumentation to ensure precise operation, and staff members must be trained in the proper use and control of equipment, appliances, and systems.

ENERGY CONSERVATION CONCEPTS

It is important for the facilities manager to understand that the objective of energy conservation measures is not only the reduction of energy use. It is also the efficient use of energy to achieve effective operations. The facilities manager must identify and master the exploitation of energy management opportunities (EMOs). An EMO is an opportunity to conserve energy while achieving optimum system performance. The factors involved with the development of an energy management program include many elements that are not within the control of the facilities manager. For instance, climate, location, topography, building configuration, materials used for construction, and methods of facility construction are not elements that the facilities manager can adjust. EMOs must be found within the maintenance of operational standards and systems confronting those factors. Building systems can be managed to produce energy conservation.

Many actions and adjustments are available to conserve energy. The reduction of infiltration and exfiltration of conditioned air from a building can produce a significant improvement in efficiency of energy use. Infiltration is the uncontrolled leakage of unconditioned air into the building, exfiltration is the uncontrolled leakage of conditioned air out of the building. Both increase energy costs to maintain appropriate comfort levels for occupants. Leakage is affected by the amount of insulation provided in the building envelope and all of the openings in that envelope. Some openings are intentional, such as doors and windows, while others might be the result of poor maintenance of wall integrity, producing cracks and holes. The application of caulking material, paint, and wall coverings can help reduce the maintenance problems.

Double- and triple-glazed fixed windows will reduce the radiant movement of heat through the building envelope, while automatic door closures, revolving doors, and double-barrier doors can reduce the passage of air in and out of the building. Blinds, shades, and tinted or reflective glass can also reduce radiant heat loss during the heating season, and heat gain in the cooling season. Increasing air pressure inside the building can prevent the movement of air and energy loss from infiltration, while decreasing pressure can reduce exfiltration. Even the effective use of landscaping to shade parts of the building can reduce energy use without loss of comfort. All of these items are only a small portion of the EMOs available to the facilities manager. EMOs must be incorporated into a management plan to achieve an appropriate balance between effectiveness and efficiency.

DEVELOPING AN ENERGY MANAGEMENT PLAN

The facilities manager is the primary manager of the physical property and therefore must address all energy management activities. But without the involvement of operational elements and occupants of the property, effective and efficient energy management is very difficult. The facilities manager must gain support and cooperation from all departments to reduce energy usage. An energy management team or committee must be formed for the property. The facilities manager is a member of this team, but it must also include an operational manager with the authority to implement operating policies throughout the organization. Representatives and key personnel from all departments along with revenue-producing occupants must also be active on the energy management team. This team is responsible for the development and implementation of the energy management plan.

The first step in the development of the energy plan is to conduct an energy survey of the property. The survey establishes both the existing condition of the building itself and the current levels of energy use. All departments must be involved in contributing information for this survey, because they dictate the operational energy needs for the property. All installed equipment, appliances, and systems must be examined to provide current operating efficiency and energy use. Information must be gathered for consideration of the energy management team.

In analyzing the information gathered in step one, the energy team identifies possible EMOs and compiles them into a prioritized list of energy-saving activities. When this list is established, the second step has been completed. As such, the current situation has been analyzed and corrective actions have been identified.

To move to the third step of energy plan development, the prioritized list is developed into a schedule for the completion of adjustments and corrective actions to reduce energy use and improve the efficiency of the operation. The energy team must discuss and consider this schedule very carefully. This is the opportunity for the representatives of the revenue-producing departments to ensure that their operational needs are met. In this discussion the facilities manager must identify the physical requirements for each action or adjustment. Conflicts between the needs of the departments and the proposed actions are resolved by the operations manager.

The fourth step is the establishment of energy use goals to be met within a prescribed time frame. These goals are usually based on an operational year. Short-range goals of less than a year are not usually used because most adjustments and corrective action will not produce consistent results in shorter periods of time. A full operational year will normally produce measurable results that can guide energy management efforts in subsequent years.

The fifth step is to implement the plan and evaluate the results for future adjustments. The facilities manager is the primary action officer for the plan because he or she has direct control of the physical property. In this role, the facilities manager is also responsible for the measurement of the results of the corrective actions. The primary tool used for the measurement of an energy management plan is the energy use index.

ENERGY USE INDEX

An energy use index (EUI) measures in British thermal units (Btu) how much energy a building consumes per total air-conditioned square foot over a given time period of either a month or a year. The primary function of an EUI is to facilitate comparison of total energy consumption from one time period to another. It does not take weather or increasing energy costs into consideration, nor does it facilitate the comparison of one building to another. An EUI allows the facilities manager to compare the energy use of his building to itself in previous time periods. This provides a means to measure the effectiveness of energy-saving efforts.

The calculation of an EUI is a simple, but extensive process. It must include all energy consumption in the building. A sample EUI calculation form is provided in *Figures 10-1a* through *10-1c*. This form can be modified to include any energy use factors that were not included, or to remove those that are not present in a particular building.

The area of the building must be established to make the EUI effective. First, the facilities manager must determine the amount of gross conditioned square feet in the property. Unconditioned spaces such as equipment rooms or elevator shafts must be subtracted to prevent overestimation of the efficiency of energy use in the building. Access to complete plans for the structure are not required, but the actual measurements of each individual conditioned room must be included in the total. When this total has been determined, it should be entered into the form in the blank provided for "Gross Conditioned Square Feet."

Heating degree days are determined by calculating the difference between the mean outdoor temperature in a 24-hour period and a base temperature of 65 degrees Fahrenheit. Cooling degree days are determined by calculating the difference between outside mean temperatures in a 24-hour period and a base temperature of 75 degrees Fahrenheit. Degree day data is essential in comparing EUIs from different years. If energy consumption was higher in January of one year when compared with January of another, it might be because of a higher number of heating degree days. The number of heating degree days or cooling degree days for each month should be recorded in columns 2 and 3 on the EUI calculation form.

The facilities manager should record electrical energy data in columns 4 through 12 of the EUI calculation form. This data is available from records and utility bills. The quantity of kilowatt hours (kWh) should be recorded in column 4, and the demand charge should be entered in column 6. The billed utility fuel-adjustment charge is entered in column 7, and the total billed amount is entered in column 8. The billed demand is entered in column 9, with the actual demand listed in column 10 as kilowatts (kW). The number of kWh used for the month is entered in column 11. The number of thousands of British thermal units (M Btu) is calculated by multiplying the number of kWh entered in column 11 by the conversion factor listed at the bottom of the EUI calculation form (*Figure 10-1c*) and entered in column 12.

If the property uses purchased steam, that data is recorded in columns 13 through 19 of the EUI calculation form. In column 13, the facilities manager lists the cost rate of the steam, and any demand charge rate that is imposed is entered in column 14. The total cost of steam for the month is entered in column 15, and actual and billed demand should be entered in columns 16 and 17, respectively. The facilities manager should enter the actual monthly steam consumption in thousands of pounds of steam (M lb) in column 18. Total M Btu can be calculated by multiplying the number in column 18 by the conversion factor listed at the bottom of the EUI calculation form (*Figure 10-1c*) and entered in column 19.

The facilities manager should list any fuel oil use by the property in columns 20 through 25 of the EUI calculation form. Heavy oil (usually grade No. 6) data is entered in columns 20 through 22, and light oil (usually grade No. 2) data is entered in columns 23 through 25. To calculate the number of gallons used per month, the facilities manager must determine the amount of oil required to fill the property storage tanks since the previous fill. If the tanks are not filled on a monthly basis, the facilities manager must make approximations based on historical consumption patterns to determine the gallons used in a specific month. In columns 20 and 23, the total cost of the two categories of oil consumed should be entered. The total quantity of two categories of oil consumed during the month should be recorded in columns 21 and 24. The total M Btu used can be calculated by multiplying the numbers in columns 21 and 24 by the conversion factors listed at the bottom of the EUI calculation form (*Figure 10-1c*) and entered in columns 22 and 25.

Natural gas data includes the cost of gas consumed (including any taxes and fuel-adjustment charges) plus demand charges. Natural gas consumption is usually measured in therms. One therm is equal to approximately 100 cubic feet of gas. The facilities manager should record the cost rate for gas in column 26 and the demand charge in column 27. The total natural gas bill for billed cost for the month should be entered in column 28, and the quantity of gas consumed should be entered in column 29 as thousands of cubic feet (Mcf). The total M Btu used can be calculated by multiplying the number in column 29 by the conversion factor listed at the bottom of the EUI calculation form (*Figure 10-1c*) and entered in column 30.

If the property uses coal, the facilities manager should record the total cost and tons consumed in columns 31 and 32 of the EUI calculation form. The method of counting tonnage is the same as that used for estimating oil consumption. The total M Btu used can be calculated by multiplying the number in column 32 by the conversion factor listed at the bottom of the EUI calculation form (*Figure 10-1c*) and entered in column 33.

Figure 10-1a. Sample Energy Use Index (EUI) Form (Page 1)

Energy Use Index (Page 1)

Year: _____

Building: _____

Gross Conditioned Square Feet _____

Electricity

Month	Heating Degree-Days	Cooling Degree-Days	kWh Cost	Demand Charge	Power Factor Adj.	Fuel Adj.	Total Cost	Billed Demand (kW)	Actual Demand (kW)	kWh Used	M Btu
1	2	3	4	5	6	7	8	9	10	11	12
January											
February											
March											
April											
May											
June											
July											
August											
September											
October											
November											
December											
Year Total											

Figure 10-1b. Sample Energy Use Index (EUI) Form (Page 2)

Energy Use Index (Page 2)

Year: _____

Building: _____

Gross Conditioned Square Feet _____

Month	Steam							Oil, Heavy			Oil, Light		
	Steam	Steam Demand Charge	Total Steam Cost	Demand Actual (lb/hr)	Demand Billed (lb/hr)	Steam Used M ib	M Btu	Total Cost	Gallons Used	M Btu	Total Cost	Gallons Used	M Btu
1	13	14	15	16	17	18	19	20	21	22	23	24	25
January													
February													
March													
April													
May													
June													
July													
August													
September													
October													
November													
December													
Year Total													

Figure 10-1c Sample Energy Use Index Form (Page 3)

Energy Use Index (Page 3)

Year: _____

Building: _____

Gross Conditioned Square Feet _____

| Month | Natural Gas | | | | | Coal | | | Totals | | | |
	Com-modity Cost	Demand Charge	Total Cost	Mcf Used	M Btu	Total Cost	Tons Used	M Btu	Total Cost	Cost per Sq.Ft.	Total M Btu Used	EUI
1	26	27	28	29	30	31	32	33	34	35	36	37
January												
February												
March												
April												
May												
June												
July												
August												
September												
October												
November												
December												
Year Total												

Conversion Factors

Energy		Conv. Factor (SI)		M Btu (kJ)
Electricity	_____ X	3,413	(3,600)	= _____
Purchase Steam	_____ X	1,000	(kg x 2,326.4)	= _____
Natural Gas	_____ X	1,030 *	(L x 38.6)	= _____
Propane	_____ X	2,500*	(L x 95)	= _____
Oil	_____ X	138	(#2 Oil)* (L x 5.2)	= _____
		148	(#6 Oil))* (L x 5.6)	_____
Coal	_____ X	26,000*	(kg x 30,238)	= _____
Other Fuel	_____ X	_____		= _____

* Use Actual Values If Known

At this point, the facilities manager has entered all of the data required to produce good management information regarding energy use on his property and to develop an EUI. Adding the costs recorded in columns 8, 15, 20, 23, 28 and 31 provided the total cost of energy consumed for that specific month. This number should be entered in column 34. To determine the total cost of energy used per square foot, the facilities manager would divide the number in column 34 by the gross conditioned square feet on the property, and record that number in column 35. The total M Btu of energy consumed is calculated by adding columns 12, 19, 22, 25, 30, and 33 and entering the result in column 36. Finally, to determine the EUI for the specific month, the facilities manager would divide the number in column 36 by the gross conditioned square feet of the property. Annual totals or year-to-date totals and EUIs can be determined by adding the columns vertically.

These totals and the use of the overall EUI for the property enable the facilities manager to determine the effect of energy-saving adjustments, new equipment, new services, and other factors affecting energy consumption by comparison between similar time periods. Once data has been captured for a full year, comparisons can be made from any given month to the same month in the previous year. It would not make sense to compare July with January because the number of heating and cooling degree days are not comparable, but a July to July, or October to October comparison can be very useful in determining changes in the efficiency of energy use.

CHAPTER SUMMARY

The facilities manager is the key player in the energy management program for any property, but he or she must be cognizant of the effect of energy use on operational interests. The most efficient use of energy does not produce the lowest costs in energy use. Instead, it must be justified by producing the lowest possible costs in energy use while maintaining operational conditions to produce a profitable environment. Further, all forms of energy must be considered in developing the program, because energy sources often supplement each other, a savings in cost for one might result in an increase in cost for another. Tools such as the energy use index can be used by the facilities manager to balance efficiency and effectiveness at optimum levels for the property.

GLOSSARY OF TERMS

British thermal unit (Btu)
One Btu is equal to the amount of heat required to raise the temperature of one pound of water one degree Fahrenheit.

Building envelope
The exterior surfaces of a building that enclose the building's interior space. The building envelope includes walls, windows, doors, roof, and exposed floors.

Degree day
The difference between the outdoor mean temperature over a 24-hour period and the given base temperature of the interior of a building.

Demand charge
An additional charge assessed by a utility company for the maximum rate at which electricity is used over a set time period. It is designed to cover the fixed costs of generating, transmitting, and distributing a large amount of electricity at one time.

Energy management opportunity (EMO)
An opportunity to conserve energy while achieving optimum system performance for the energy expended.

Energy use index
A measurement of the quantity of energy consumed by a building, expressed as the number of Btu(s) per gross conditioned square foot per period of time, usually established as an annual measurement.

Exfiltration
The uncontrolled leakage of conditioned indoor air out of a building.

Infiltration
The uncontrolled leakage of unconditioned air into a building.

Kilowatt (kw)
The unit of electrical energy used to measure the power that is available for work. One kilowatt equals 1,000 watts.

Kilowatt hour (kWh)
The unit of electrical energy used as the base for consumption charges billed by a utility company. One kilowatt hour equals 1,000 watts in one hour of time.

Natural gas data
Includes the cost of gas consumed (including any taxes or fuel-adjustment charges) plus demand charges. Natural gas consumption is usually measured in therms.

Therm
A measurement of natural gas consumption equal to a cubic meter of volume.

STUDY QUESTIONS

1. Explain the concept of an energy management system balanced between efficiency and effectiveness.

2. Can energy use be limited to minimum levels and still meet the needs of a profitable operation? Explain your answer.
3. Define the objective of energy conservation efforts.
4. What is the difference between infiltration and exfiltration? Why are these concepts important to energy management programs?
5. Who would you select as members of an energy management team? Explain the reason for each member you select.
6. Describe the five steps required to develop an energy management plan.
7. What is the real purpose of an energy use index (EUI)?
8. What data is included in the calculation of an energy use index (EUI)?
9. Define "heating degree days".
10. Define "cooling degree days".

CHAPTER ELEVEN

INTEGRATING TECHNOLOGY INTO FACILITIES MANAGEMENT

CHAPTER LEARNING OBJECTIVES

After reading this chapter, the student should be able to:

1. Describe the increasing complexity of technology as it affects facility management.
2. Describe the beneficial and detrimental effects of technology on facility management operations.
3. Explain the necessity to expand facility management operations to accommodate the progress of technology.
4. Describe the integration of modern technology into "system" controls.
5. Describe the necessary actions to integrate different elements of equipment at multiple levels of technology into effective facility management operations.
6. Explain the structural considerations for the integration of technology into facility management operations.
7. Describe the predictable future of technology in facility management, the pending benefits, and the problems involved.

The word "technology" is generally associated with computers or automatic data processing equipment in current business environments. Facilities managers must educate their staff and occupants about the effect of modern technology on facilities issues, and also how the building itself affects their use of technology. For most occupants and operational managers, attitudes toward physical structures and building operating systems are largely unchanged in regard to technology. They are well versed in the expanding uses for technology within their areas of operation, but often unaware of the technology being used by facilities managers to support their operational environment. Most workers think of technology as solely the computer on their desk or the cell phone in their pocket but don't understand, or even think about, the fact that technology is redefining the tools and methods used by the facilities manager.

THE INCREASING COMPLEXITY OF TECHNOLOGY

Technology use in facilities management not only concerns the building and its systems. It also includes technology applications that integrate profit-producing operations with facilities management activities. Simultaneously, the technology that can be used in a building is determined partly by the existing systems within the structure. For example, modern technology may be applied to the management of electrical power within a building, while the available electrical system can limit the amount or type of technological hardware that can be used in the existing structure.

Computers have created new methods and means for doing work at levels of speed and efficiency that were previously impossible. Not only have computers changed the way we do work, they have also created new jobs and functions that did not previously exist. Building controls and systems can now be operated or adjusted from the facilities manager's cell phone from remote locations. E-mail is the most widely used application of modern technology in the world, and computers are so pervasive that modern workers have no choice but to learn to use them. Technology has invaded every aspect of the business world. Several elements or applications that started as separate efforts have become integrated and overlap. Just in normal management operations these overlapping areas include:

- Microfilm, microfiche, compact disks, flash drives
- Wirebound local area networks (LAN) and telecommunications
- Computer-generated presentations and graphic support
- Fax, photocopying, remote or centralized printing
- Voice and data transmission
- Graphics, word processing, spreadsheets
- Data bases
- Cordless phones and wireless LAN
- Cell phones and smart phones
- Wireless computer communication
- iPads and electronic books
- More to come

As these systems and tools have developed, the application of technology has become more complex. Traditional organizations depended on paper to record information, statistics, and management data. Today, paper records are known as hard data and information being handled by electronic storage devices and systems known as soft data. The differences between the two become blurred as management uses the stored materials to make decisions and manipulate resources. Electronic storage is becoming more reliable as the technology is developed, with paper records moved to being used primarily to record or store legally accountable records. Such documents as contracts, tax records, deeds, legally binding notes, permits, and certifications are still maintained on paper as the primary record for business, but even these are often printed copies of electronic records.

All managers, including the facilities manager, must understand the relationship between data and knowledge to use technology effectively. Facts and figures stored in any system are called data. Data is only useful when the manager uses it to interpret results, conditions, situations, and make decisions. The data then becomes management information. As this information is used and developed to produce operational procedures, policies, and directions, it becomes knowledge. The facilities manager has more data available than ever before, and as the enormous amounts of facts and figures have expanded, the computer has provided the technological tool to sort, catalog, and classify them into information that adds to the body of management knowledge.

TECHNOLOGY—BENEFICIAL OR DETRIMENTAL?

Nearly all building operating systems now depend to some degree on modern technology to control, monitor, or automatically maintain them. These systems, such as lighting, plumbing, HVAC, security, fire detection, and energy management all operate as coordinated elements so the technology applications that control them also overlap. This has required that older workers not only tolerate changes in the systems, but also learn to use new tools. New and younger workers have used computers all their lives and have no trouble with the new tools, but they have no knowledge of the old tools that the older workers depended upon. As an example, a computer-literate worker may quickly produce superb management documents and reports, complete with integrated multicolored charts that are excellent aids to the development of excellent management decisions. But that same worker is just as likely to plug his or her computer, coffee pot, printer, electric space heater, paper shredder, photocopier, and iPod charger into the same electrical outlet and become totally bewildered when the circuit overloads and all of his equipment goes down. Every worker who uses automatic data processing equipment to complete their job must be supported by other workers who maintain the older levels of technology on which the modern equipment depends.

The increased efficiency of a computer-managed system might be hidden behind enormous initial installation costs, and confronted with workers who do not understand why a new way was needed to do an already existing task. The older worker hides his or her fear of technology behind the question that "everything was working fine, why should it change?" The facilities manager also learns very quickly that modernization must be done in all areas because of the integration of the building systems. One system cannot be changed without changing the supporting and supported activities around it. He or she will also note very quickly that the workload to support a building increases as more information becomes available to the building occupants. This is not just added tasks to support the new technology, but work generated because the occupants can see much more of the previously obscure activities that support their operations.

The facilities manager must also realize that electronic control and information systems are very vulnerable to attack. This is especially true of those systems that can be accessed by building occupants. The world of modern technology has even developed personality related names to these invasions and assaults—names such as viruses, worms, moles, Trojan horses, and many others, all of which allude to an almost alien life form that has invaded the building. In the effort to improve efficiency, modern technology also brings an increased threat to the security of the property and its revenue-producing occupants.

TECHNOLOGY EXPANDS FACILITIES MANAGEMENT

The facilities manager must address the application of technology in two categories: systems and equipment that are used by building occupants to support the management of revenue-producing activities, and those that are used to support the maintenance of the workplace or building itself.

Computer-specific support must be provided to computers and equipment systems that are used directly by the occupants in business operations. The facilities manager also becomes his or her own customer in this area because these systems provide management activities in the administrative activities of the facilities manager. Office automation that supports revenue-producing operations such as accounting, inventory, payroll, marketing, sales, etc., fall into this area. It also includes telecommunications systems for voice and electronic transmission of data and information. The facilities manager could also add CMMS, CFMS, CAAD, asset tracking, repair parts/materials inventory, work scheduling, and budget control to computer-specific support requirements

Workplace-specific support must be provided to computers and equipment systems that control or define the physical structure or work environment of the building itself. This includes building systems such as HVAC, fire safety, security, or energy management systems that are monitored and/or controlled by computers. It also provides technical support for elements that are driven by the technological requirements of the equipment itself, including wiring, cabling, and environmental specifications for the use of such automated equipment as heating or cooling.

The facilities manager must develop and maintain the ability to support the equipment for both the administrative and the physical systems of modern technology. There is no option available to the facilities manager. He or she must integrate modern technology into the management and operation of the property. Once new systems have been adopted, and the workers in the revenue-producing activities and the facilities management operations learn to use and begin to depend on modern technology, they will not go back to the old systems. The facilities manager must have technicians available either on staff or by contract to support automated equipment. Technicians for the older systems, however, must still be available as well. The occupant must have someone to call on when the computer buttons don't work, but the facilities manager still has to be able to respond when the commode doesn't flush or the roof leaks.

BUILDING SYSTEM CONTROLS

The use of modern electronic technology is developing much more rapidly than the technology of the physical systems managed by the facilities manager. Although the physical laws involved in the assurance of human comfort have not changed, the methods and materials used to provide that comfort have gradually evolved to become more efficient, more easily installed, less expensive to maintain, and more dependable. Modern technology is revolutionizing the management of those materials and methods to improve efficiency and reduce the cost of operations even more in the future. The technology applications for business, administration, and building systems overlap and new combinations of management strategy must be developed. One of these strategies is the automation of building controls. Automated control systems are now available to provide life safety support and efficient fire suppression with no intervention by human operators. Energy management and environmental management of a property are now accomplished with measured data and supporting information provided from automatic sensors and monitors. Often these devices send their information to a central processing unit (CPU) that responds to the reported conditions with automatic adjustment to heating, cooling, or lighting equipment. Security of properties has been greatly enhanced with remote surveillance cameras, enabling a single operator to observe and manage entire structural complexes from a single security office. Several of these control systems have now been linked through telecommunications systems, so that a single manager can monitor and adjust the environmental parameters of an entire property from a remote location from his or her cell phone. All of these control systems have enabled the facilities manager to multiply his or her management presence for more effective and efficient operation.

Modern control systems have become essential tools, but they do come with a few problems. The facilities manager must maintain the flexibility in his or her staff to physically respond to malfunctions in the control system. This often requires the availability of specifically trained technicians, either by contract or on permanent staff. Further, the controls must maintain building systems at levels of operation that support the revenue-producing activities. The electronic equipment must not dictate operational levels within the facility. Instead, the facilities manager must remember to program them to maintain levels required for profitable operation. The successful implementation of automatic controls in building systems requires the facilities manager to consider and resolve several factors as the system develops. These include issues concerning the role of maintenance and the retrofitting of the structure to incorporate the new control systems. Management must decide how the building should operate to support a profitable environment, and the control system must be designed to meet those needs.

TECHNOLOGY AND EFFECTIVE FACILITIES MANAGEMENT

The successful integration of modern technology into facilities management requires careful selection of the CFMS to support the property, effective planning and scheduling of the installation/implementation of the system, and effective training of the system operators. A key concept is to remember that permitting change to occur as gracefully as possible might cost more financial assets in the short run but will produce greater gains over the life of the property. There are many CFMS and CMMS approaches available, and all have strengths and weaknesses. The facilities manager must take the time to study several possible systems until one is found that meets the needs of the building and its occupants.

The three basic types of a CFMS are those that manage energy systems, those controlling building operations, and those that link to corporate information systems. Any of the three can provide improved:

- Long term operational planning
- Space planning/management

- Furniture/equipment management
- Real property/lease management
- Maintenance/facilities operations management
- Work-control management
- Strategic facilities planning
- Budget planning and control

CFMS are much more efficient if they are interfaced with other operational systems in the property. If the operational systems and the CFMS are compatible, the overall management effectiveness of the facilities manager and the operational manager are greatly enhanced. To make this selection the facilities manager must:

- Assess the impact of a proposed CFMS on existing technology in the building
- Orchestrate required construction and installation of equipment in the structure
- Document all decisions for future reference
- Inform and train occupants and staff on the use and control of the CFMS

The planning tasks for the installation and implementation of the CFMS falls to the facilities manager, not only because of his or her direct interest in the system, but also because the facilities manager has the best combination of managerial skills and technical awareness to recognize the effect of each proposed change on the profitability of the property. The facilities manager should remember that the greatest cost in moving from any manual management system to a CMMS or CFMS is the training of the workforce to use the new system, and the transfer of required historical and structural data into the new system. Data entry is labor-intensive and therefore very expensive.

STRUCTURAL CONSIDERATIONS

When installing modern technology, the facilities manager must consider the effect of the new equipment and procedures on the existing structure and, conversely, the effect of the existing structure on the new system. The electrical system of the old building may have to be expanded to accommodate the increased power demand, and it may be found that the existing wiring does not meet the specifications for the new equipment. The facilities manager must decide whether to address this issue with a wiring-intensive solution or an equipment-intensive solution. The wiring-intensive solution requires the entire building to be rewired and upgraded to meet the needs of the new system. This is a very expensive and intrusive approach. The equipment-intensive solution calls for the purchase and installation of auxiliary equipment such as surge protectors or local transformers to protect the new equipment. The existing HVAC system may also present problems. Since automatic data processing equipment produces heat, it adds to the heat load in the building and also may have its own requirements for environmental conditions that the existing HVAC system cannot meet. The most expensive way to address this problem would be to redesign and rebuild the entire HVAC system. An alternative would be to install the equipment in isolated areas with supporting local HVAC appliances specifically to protect the new data processing equipment.

The facilities manager must address many other issues when installing modern technology in an existing structure. As new systems are developed or installed, and systems replaced or improved, these issues will need to be dealt with repeatedly. They include:

- Advancing obsolescence of existing structure and equipment
- Required utility upgrades
- Constant retraining of staff and occupants
- Incompatibility of different generations of equipment
- Additional support skills/equipment for specific systems

Flexibility is the key for the facilities manager to deal with the continued introduction of new methods and equipment. The overlap of business and facilities systems will require the development of new strategies and plans for investment in hardware, software, and training—as well as the disposal of outdated equipment and obsolete systems. The facilities manager is the only person in an organization who sees the full and true cost of the application of new technology.

IMPACT OF FUTURE TECHNOLOGY

As the development of technology accelerates, the facilities manager must continue to make strategic decisions, balancing short-term costs of development with the long-term potential for improved efficiency and profitability. The facilities manager must support the use of new technology while planning for the predictable obsolescence of existing and new systems. This applies to the operational systems used by the revenue-producing occupants, as well as the facilities systems that provide them with a profitable environment. The projected role of the facilities manager in modern technology is to plan for the technological obsolescence of all the management tools in a property, while orchestrating the installation and implementation of the technological advancements that replace them.

GLOSSARY OF TERMS

Central processing unit (CPU)
A computer that coordinates and links the activities of other units or sources of input.

CFMS
Computerized facilities management systems

CMMS
Computerized maintenance management systems

STUDY QUESTIONS

1. Has modern technology increased the complexity of facilities management? Explain your answer.
2. Why do older workers resist the use of modern technology?
3. Why must new workers understand old technology?
4. Can a facilities manager concentrate only on the modernization of facilities operations? Explain your answer.
5. Does the integration of modern technology improve facilities management operations or only complicate them? Explain you answer.
6. Is the integration of modern technology necessary? Why?
7. What factors must the facilities manager consider when selecting new control systems?
8. What structural changes might need to be addressed for the integration of new levels of technology into existing buildings?
9. How will the facilities manager cope with or use new technologies in the future? Explain your answer.

CHAPTER TWELVE
THE ENVIRONMENTAL IMPACT OF FACILITIES OPERATIONS

CHAPTER LEARNING OBJECTIVES

After reading this chapter, the student should be able to:

1. Explain the concept of "sustainability" in facility management.
2. Describe the management and conservation of environmental resources.
3. Explain the correlation between economic, environmental, and equity factors in "sustainability."
4. Describe the importance and practical application of re-use and recycling in facility management.
5. Describe the concept of "environmentally friendly facilities."
6. Describe the ethical conflict between protection of the environment and support of the owner's business objectives.

A hospitality establishment must operate profitably within its environment. When environment is mentioned, most people immediately visualize mountains, rivers, forests, and other such natural resources, but the hospitality firm must consider all of the factors of its environment, man-made as well as natural. The attitude of modern travelers is shifting toward an interest in doing business with "green" organizations. Therefore, organizations that make a visible management effort to establish an environmental management program are attractive to customers and more beneficial to the entire business community. Sustainability, in reference to the environment, has become an extremely important concept with international interest in the hospitality industry. The international Organization for Standardization (ISO) has established guidelines for the management of environmental issues with its ISO 14000 series of international agreements. The American Hotel and Lodging Association also formed a standing Committee for Quality Environment in the 1970s to assist its members in the development of policies and procedures to reduce environmental damage. The facilities manager has a primary responsibility in maintaining the long-term profitability or sustainability of the organization.

THE CONCEPT OF SUSTAINABILITY

The World Commission on the Environment and Development (WCED) defined the concept of sustainability in its 1987 activity report as "meeting the needs of the present without compromising the ability of the future to meet their own needs." The original emphasis was on the conservation of natural resources, but the concept has grown over the past two decades to include all elements of the business environment. Many hospitality corporations and establishments have put forth enormous efforts to achieve a balanced level of sustainability, but none has been totally successful. Because of the physical requirements of any program for sustainability, the facilities manager is a prominent manager in the effort.

In the hospitality industry, sustainability refers to the continued profitable existence of the organization with minimal damage to the surrounding environment. In fact, the effort in recent years has turned from minimal damage to an emphasis on contributing to the overall condition of the environment. Sustainability addresses three integrated areas of importance, often referred to as the three E's of sustainability: economics, equity, and environment. All must be addressed with an approach of balanced management to produce the desired longevity of profitability. Economics addresses the financial health and revenue flow of the operation, equity is concerned with the effect of the establishment on the surrounding business community, and environment refers to the use of natural resources and materials.

MANAGEMENT AND CONSERVATION

Resources are wasted if they are only preserved. Preservation means that those resources are not used at all and therefore do not produce any benefit for an organization or a business community. Resources must be used to produce products and services. Uncontrolled use, however, usually becomes abuse, leading to waste of those resources and eventual depletion of available supplies. The only tool that can be used to prevent either extreme is effective management that uses resources wisely while conserving them for future use as well. Conservation is the use of resources to produce benefit over time without depleting the resource. A good example of conservation can be seen in the United States forest industry. In the early history of the country, forests were cut without any active management to conserve them. The attitude was that the resource was unlimited and self-sustaining. In fact, a great deal of damage was done to American forests and the land surrounding them. This damage began to be recognized in the early twentieth century and controls were introduced to manage the forests. Over the past century, lumber companies have been forced to abandon clear-cutting methods of production. They must now replant trees and leave a prescribed number of trees per acre to reseed the forests. These requirements and other related controls have saved the American forests. Forest products are still available to be used, but lumber is now referred to as a renewable resource because it is protected from depletion by managed conservation.

The facilities manager must use this same approach for the resources and environment that support the operation of his property. By conserving and managing resources with a controlled system, he or she ensures that revenue-producing operations have the materials, facilities, and utilities to allow effective operations without damaging the future availability of those resources. On a broader note, the facilities manager who uses effective conservation techniques further ensures the survival of the surrounding business community by not depleting shared resources.

THE CORRELATION OF ECONOMICS, EQUITY, AND ENVIRONMENT

When discussing sustainability, the term "economics" refers to the management of operations to produce revenue. The facilities manager must manage the physical resources of the establishment to allow for revenue production. These resources include not only the property itself, but the natural environment that surrounds it, and the business community in which it operates. To operate profitably without endangering the future of the business requires that the facilities manager establish procedures and policies that control the use of those resources. Many factors have been introduced in recent years concerning this element of sustainability. Energy management has a direct economic effect on the organization by reducing operating costs. Effective energy management also protects the natural environment by the reduction of wasted resources, and the community benefits because reduced demands keep energy costs from rising. Effective waste management can also affect the profit levels of the establishment by reducing the loss of valuable resources and cutting the cost of disposal. It might even produce revenue through the recycling of waste materials. Further, because customers prefer to frequent businesses that protect the environment, the reduction of waste can encourage higher levels of revenue for the organization.

In a sustainability program, equity addresses the distribution of commerce within the business community. The facilities manager must recognize the business community in the policies and procedures of maintaining the property. A healthy environment depends on the availability of a mixture of services and products to attract and accommodate customers. One business cannot dominate the community in all areas. For example, a large hotel might select a location adjacent to a major highway and establish a robust operation. Because of this hotel, the gas station across the street might enjoy an increase in business selling fuel to the customers of the hotel, and a restaurant down the street might also experience an increase in sales. The introduction of the hotel was a stimulant to the business community. But if the hotel includes a gas station in its venue that undercuts the one across the street, and installs a restaurant with a similar menu to its competitor at a reduced price, the surrounding business community does not experience growth from the hotel's presence. If the hotel can force the two competitors out of business, then it removes any customer choice from the local market, possibly resulting in fewer customers who would be interested in doing business with the hotel. The hotel would have introduced an inequitable situation in the local business community while damaging the market for all three competitors.

In a similar manner, if a restaurant were to establish an operation in a small community known for its beautiful trees, and installed a large parking lot that removed a good number of those trees, it would damage the tourism for the entire community. A large manufacturer could contaminate the water table for a community and destroy the inhabitability of the land. A golf course could kill the fish in a fishing lake by not controlling its fertilizer runoff and in the process destroy the business of the entire area. Such actions would all violate the principle of equity under the concept of sustainability.

Both economic and equity factors can damage the natural environment. The pollution of streams, destruction of woodlands, exploitation of mineral deposits, etc., can destroy the economic health of a community. The uncontrolled exploitation of profitable resources leading to overuse or unfair competition can also destroy a market. When economic and equitable abuses have a detrimental effect on business, they produce a corresponding amount of damage to the natural environment. The environmental damage in turn will prevent the expansion or growth of economic opportunities in the area. The facilities manager must balance the activities and requirements of the property to produce a profitable situation without damaging any of the three elements of economic, equity, or environmental factors.

REUSE AND RECYCLING

Recycling has become a very popular concept over the past twenty-five years. But it is not new. Materials have been recycled for centuries. It has been incorporated into heavy manufacturing, with metal recovery or scrap reclamation in a number of different products. The thing that is new is that the consumer has become aware of the economic and environmental benefits of recycling. Reuse has also been around for many years. In the days of home-delivered milk, the bottles were returned for reuse. Beer kegs, wooden cargo pallets, bread trays, cardboard boxes, and wine barrels are usually used several times before they are discarded. Even then they may be recovered and used for an alternative application before they are actually thrown away. Many people confuse reuse and recycling. If an item is reused it is simply cleaned and put back into service. A recycled item is used as raw material to produce new products. For example, a beer keg remains a beer keg until it is discarded, but an aluminum beverage can is not refilled. The beverage can is used as raw material to be melted down and recast into a new product, possibly a new can. A milk jug that is cleaned and refilled is reused, but a plastic milk jug that is shredded and woven into patio carpet has been recycled.

To effectively manage his or her resources, the facilities manager must incorporate both reuse and recycling into the sustainment program of his or her facility. This will require that the facilities manager study the materials that are being used and identify opportunities for their recovery. Aluminum cans can be gathered by housekeepers and receptacles can be provided for customers to deposit empty cans for collection. Gas bottles and bread racks can be returned to suppliers to be refilled. Even heat can be captured in the kitchen exhaust hood and used to supplement water heating. The only limit is that the facilities manager must verify that the recycled or reused materials are actually being used. It is a waste of resources to gather wooden pallets so that the vendor can remove them and carry them to the sanitary landfill, and many hours can be invested in the gathering of aluminum cans that are stockpiled and later buried because they cannot be transported to a point where they can be reused. The facilities manager must carefully study the property to identify opportunities for reuse and recycling, but it must be done as an organized and managed procedure. There are eight steps in this process:

1. Designate a responsible leader (this can be the facilities manager). This person is in charge of and held responsible for the process. If the organization is large enough, this could also be a committee of several people from different departments.
2. Analyze or audit the potential materials for recycling or reuse.
3. Identify markets for the materials that have been identified. A destination for the recycled materials must be found before an effort is committed to collecting them.
4. Establish working agreements with the companies, individuals, or industries identified in step three.
5. Purchase the equipment needed to handle the materials to be recycled such as receptacles, shipping containers, shredders, dumpsters, etc.
6. Train the staff to recycle or reuse the identified materials.
7. Coordinate with suppliers to purchase recycled or reclaimed materials for use in the operation. If the organization uses recycled products, then the incentive to recycle materials is created.
8. Monitor, measure, and evaluate the program to verify that materials are being handled correctly and benefits are being realized.

ENVIRONMENTALLY FRIENDLY FACILITIES

The goal of a facilities manager pursuing a sustainability program is to operate the property as an environmentally friendly facility. An establishment that recognizes the need to balance economic, equity, and environmental issues to ensure the longevity of its own profitable operation, and also the health and life of the market, is an environmentally friendly facility. The facilities manager of such a property incorporates resource conservation into the facilities management policies and procedures of the organization. By doing this, the entire organization becomes known as a socially responsible operation interested not only in its own success, but also in supporting the survival and success of the community. The customer can see this in the areas of energy management, recycling, reuse, and fair completion exhibited by the establishment. Social responsibility or contribution to the community can also be seen in the practice of good citizenship and contribution to the life of the community. Such actions as sponsoring little league baseball teams, adopting highway sections for litter control, hosting church group bake sales, or putting up advertising posters for high school cheerleading squads are also evidence of contribution to the community. They show an awareness of social responsibility that the local community respects and will respond to. The facilities manager starts this process by maintaining a property that houses a profitable operation without damaging the economic, equity, or environmental factors of the business community.

ETHICAL CONFLICT OF SUSTAINABILITY

The facilities manager will sometimes discover an ethical conflict in a sustainability program. It is the responsibility of the facilities manager to maintain the property in a profitable condition that achieves the business goals of the owner of the property. Sometimes those goals are to maximize profits over a short period without regard for the factors of sustainability. In this situation, the facilities manager must decide if he or she can support those business goals at the expense of the environment. The alternative is to not damage the environment, but to fail to meet the owner's goals. The facilities manager may have to confront the owners and inform them of the dilemma. The facilities manager may decide to support the owner or may even decide to leave the organization if the dilemma cannot be resolved, but clearly he or she has an ethical obligation to both the owners and the environment to make sure that the issue is understood and considered.

CHAPTER SUMMARY

Sustainability is a concept of long term business operation without damage to the business and natural environment of an organization. The facilities manager is a key player in this concept. Because the physical structure must be maintained and operated in a profitable mode, mismanagement of resources to produce profits constitutes a threat to the environment. The facilities manager must manage his or her property to balance the requirements of the business with the economic, equity, and environmental concerns of the business community. If this is done effectively, the organization becomes known as a socially responsible and environmentally friendly facility. Today's customers are very interested in doing business with such establishments.

GLOSSARY OF TERMS

Sustainability
A concept of business operations defined as "meeting the needs of the present without compromising the ability of the future to meet their own needs."

Economics
The first factor of sustainability. In this context it refers to the management of operations to produce revenue: The financial health and revenue flow of the enterprise.

Equity
The second factor of sustainability. It refers to the effect of an establishment on its surrounding business community. Equity addresses the distribution of commerce in the business community.

Environment
The third factor of sustainability. In the sustainability concept, environment addresses the effect of an establishment on the natural environment.

Recycling
The process of collecting products and materials to be returned to manufacturers to be used in the production of new products.

Reuse
The process of collecting products and materials to be reused in their designed role.

STUDY QUESTIONS

1. List the three E's of sustainability. Explain each.
2. Explain the difference between preservation and conservation of resources.
3. Why does the facilities manager have primary responsibility for the sustainability program?
4. Explain the difference between recycling and reuse of products.
5. Define an environmentally friendly facility.
6. Explain the ethical responsibilities of the facilities manager within the sustainability concept.

CHAPTER THIRTEEN
OUTSOURCING/CONTRACTING FOR FACILITIES OPERATIONS

CHAPTER LEARNING OBJECTIVES

After reading this chapter, the student should be able to:

1. Describe the reasons and justification for outsourcing or contracting facility management activities.
2. Explain the benefits and advantages of outsourcing and contracting facility management activities.
3. Explain the disadvantages and costs of outsourcing and contracting facility management activities.
4. List the minimum requirements of an effective contract.
5. List and describe the use of the tools associated with effective contract management.

Nearly all restaurants and hotels contract with external companies to complete some or all of their facilities maintenance requirements. If a task or requirement for work is identified, either by the failure of a system or component, or by routine maintenance needs, only two options are available to the facilities manager. The work can be done by either in-house staff, or a contractor must be engaged to complete the work. Facilities requirements are met for most hospitality properties by a mix of internal staff efforts and external or outsourced contract work.

WHY OUTSOURCE OR CONTRACT?

The facilities manager must consider using contracted or outsourced efforts to complete required maintenance tasks when the capability to complete the tasks effectively or efficiently does not exist within the internal facilities staff. Some of the factors to consider:

- The internal staff does not have the expertise, licensing, or required certification to complete the task.
- The property does not have specialized tools or equipment required for the task.
- The internal staff does not have time available to complete the task.
- The task is too small to justify the use of internal staff.
- The task is too large for the capacity of the internal staff.
- There is a temporary shortage of internal staff.

- The tasks represents an emergency that cannot be addressed by the internal staff.
- The required task presents a liability risk if completed by internal staff.

Many requirements do not justify or allow the use of internal employees. For example, it is very unlikely that a single privately owned restaurant would have its own qualified refrigeration specialist because it would not have enough work to justify the full-time employment of such a technician. But a hotel with 700 package air-conditioning units (PAC) might have enough work to justify employing its own refrigeration specialist with his or her own equipment and tools. Therefore, the restaurant facilities manager could establish a contractual agreement with a plumbing and heating company to provide preventive maintenance and repair services to the restaurant, but the hotel facilities manager can justify the funds and resources necessary to establish an internal capability to maintain the hotel's HVAC equipment. Many tasks such as elevator maintenance, trash hauling, window cleaning, kitchen duct cleaning, landscaping and yard work, pest control, water treatment, and HVAC controls calibration are contracted out to specialized service firms. Each facilities manager must survey his or her property to identify those required activities that would be handled more efficiently with outsourcing versus internal staffing.

There is a growing trend in the commercial real estate industry to outsource entire facilities operations to external firms. This is an extension of the practice of outsourcing those items that exceed in-house capabilities by replacing internal facilities staff completely. Hospitality firms such as ARAMARK, Sodexho, and Servicemaster are active in this type of outsourcing. In the United States, this has not become a very strong influence in the hospitality industry, but there are indications that it may grow in the future. The facilities manager of a property sometimes extends such complete service to occupants of the property that are not actually part of the hospitality establishment. For example, hotels that occupy only a portion of their property with retail enterprises, such as retail shops attached to the lobby or firms renting office space in the building, could contract with these occupants to provide complete facilities services. This could provide a means of turning these areas of the building into actual revenue centers for the facilities manager to support other activities.

The facilities manager must remember that the task can be outsourced or contracted, but the responsibility to ensure that work is performed cannot. It is possible to outsource all facilities maintenance tasks, and there are many companies and agencies that can provide the required services. The only thing that cannot be contracted is the management responsibility for the property. The obligation to maintain the establishment in a profitable condition remains with the facilities manager. Contractors can be employed very easily but they are not ultimately responsible for the results of their efforts. The facilities manager must monitor and supervise all contractors to verify the timely and effective performance as well as the quality of their work. A contract to complete a service for the facility can provide the expertise and the tools to meet property requirements, but the facilities manager is still responsible to ensure that the service is completed correctly and on time.

THE BENEFITS OF OUTSOURCING

There are thousands of tasks required to maintain any hospitality facility in a profitable condition. The facilities manager realizes several advantages from the effective use of contractors. The first is that specialized maintenance activities are expensive, both for labor and for the materials and tools required. Workers with specialized skills are often highly compensated. To retain this level of expertise without sufficient requirements to employ them completely is a waste of labor costs. Thus, contracting specialized tasks out to external sources produces significant cost avoidance for potentially idle internal technicians. Reducing the internal staff by using contracted work also removes the administrative cost of employing a standing staff. Requirements for time keeping and personnel administration, including tax and insurance management costs, are transferred to the contractor.

Many specialized requirements are seasonal or scheduled over long periods of time, such as the winterization of swimming pools, roof inspections and repair, boiler cleaning and duct cleaning. These activities require expensive specialized equipment that represents an enormous capital investment. This cost is transferred to the contractor when such activities are outsourced.

Certain activities such as elevator repair, the maintenance of fire safety equipment, security equipment, installation of electrical wiring, and the maintenance of steam-related equipment—all of which must be performed to prescribed or mandated standards—impose a high level of liability on the facilities manager. When such actions are performed by qualified contractors, those contracting firms assume some element of that liability, and therefore share the responsibility or risk involving failure that's connected to improper work. This greatly reduces the financial risk to the property owners and the facilities manager.

A contractor who completes a large amount of a particular type of work recognizes an economy of volume. This means that a firm that specializes in one specific area of expertise can often perform work within that area at a much lower level of cost than a facilities staff that only does the task occasionally. This can most easily be seen in the simple landscaping task of mowing a lawn. If a restaurant has a small grassed area in front of its building, the lawn-mowing equipment needed to mow this small area will cost the same as the equipment to mow a larger area of grass. Further, someone on the staff would have to be scheduled periodically to operate this expensive equipment to complete the job, and that individual might actually be employed at a higher wage rate than would normally be paid for someone to run a lawn mower. In addition, whatever that staff member is actually employed to do—e.g., cooking or maintaining building systems—is not being accomplished while he or she is out mowing the lawn. While all of these factors make mowing the lawn very expensive if done by an internal staff member, a contracted landscaper uses the lawn-mowing equipment, but distributes the cost of that equipment over many customers. The workers in the landscape company are paid a wage commensurate to the task, and the primary function of the internal employee is not abandoned to complete the task. The cost of mowing the lawn in front of the restaurant is greatly reduced.

THE COST OF OUTSOURCING

The facilities manager loses detailed control of the workers' actions when a task or operation is outsourced. To ensure that quality of work is maintained, the facilities manager must implement quality control policies to monitor contractor's performance. The workers that the contractor uses will not have the same loyalty or sense of ownership as internal staff members, so the facilities manager must maintain a strict system of accountability and inspections to protect the property. This is partly done in the initial selection of the contractor before agreements are established. The facilities manager must carefully screen contractor candidates to verify their ability to do the work, capacity to meet the needs of the property, and ethical business practices. As a guarantee of quality work, a carefully constructed legal agreement that includes the right to cancel should be completed for every contractual relationship.

When entering into a contract with an outside firm to work on the property, the facilities manager must be aware that the outside workers constitute a security risk to the establishment and its guests. The facilities manager has not personally interviewed or screened these workers and must require the contracted firm to do so. Even then, he or she should take steps to limit the access of contracted workers to only those areas necessary to do the contracted work. In no case should an outside contractor or outside workers be given keys, or in any way allowed unlimited access to the property. The contractor should provide the facilities manager with a list of those workers who will be assigned to the contract, and the facilities manager must insist that any substitutions be formally communicated prior to the worker's arrival on site.

There is also a cost dealing with reaction time requirements involving the use of outside contractors. This does not normally affect routine work such as landscaping, painting, cleaning, or preventive maintenance, but in key areas such as plumbing, HVAC, or electricity, the facilities manager needs to consider possible emergencies. On large properties, the internal staff might need to retain emergency capability to reduce reaction time to leaks, power outages, or failed refrigeration units, even if the major amount of work has been outsourced to a contractor. Other properties should include reaction time requirements in the contractual agreement, which the contractor must meet in responding to emergencies.

EFFECTIVE CONTRACTS

The key to outsourcing is the written agreement or contract. The facilities manager must exercise great care in issuing a contract to ensure that the property is protected against substandard work, and that the contractor responds to the needs of the establishment effectively and efficiently. There are several specific elements that should be present in an outsourcing contract:

- *Insurance* The contractor must carry sufficient insurance to cover injuries to workers and liability for problems caused by the work. The insurance policy should cover both the contractor and the property. The certificate of insurance should state, "Owner Also

Covered" in the remarks section of the standard certificate. A copy of this certificate must be provided to the facilities manager and retained on file.

- *Term of contract* An effective contract has a specific start date and a specific end date.
- *No automatic renewal* There is no incentive for a contractor to improve performance if the contract is automatically renewed. The contract should stipulate that there is no automatic renewal, and require the contractor to rebid the contract in competition with other firms.
- *Cancellation* To protect the property from abuse of the contractual agreement or poor performance of the contractor, the facilities manager must have the right to cancel the agreement on short notice for lack of performance. To provide complete protection to both the property and the contractor, both parties should have the right to cancel the contract with thirty days' notice without cause. In addition, the contract may stipulate penalties for nonperformance by the contractor.
- *No conflict of interest* The contract should clearly state that the contractor is not an employee, relative, or agent of the property owner or facilities manager.
- *Non-assignable contract* A contract requiring the contractor to use his or her own employees to complete all work. The contractor must be prohibited from assigning the contracted worker to a subcontractor.
- *Clear specifications* A very detailed description of the contracted work should be included in the contract. This description should list the specific details for each task to be performed and the frequency for each task. If the facilities manager wishes to require any particular materials or manufacturer's products to be used, this should be clearly stated in the specifications.
- *Payment and fees* The contract should list specific rates to be paid for each task or each hour of work performed. This list should be very carefully written to identify the fee for every task included in the contract and include a clause covering any possible additional service. It does not matter if this schedule of fees and payments is established as a basic hourly rate or as a task fee list, but it must be constructed with controls and stipulations to prevent overcharging for services rendered. It also should withhold all payments until the work completed is inspected by the facilities manager and approved for payment.
- *Reaction requirements* For standing maintenance contracts, the facilities manager should insist that the contract stipulate the reaction requirement for response to work requests. This reaction requirement should clearly list maximum reaction times for routine work, after-hours work, and emergency work, to ensure the property is supported for nonrecurring needs and unanticipated service interruptions.

All contracts should be reviewed by legal counsel for the property prior to completion. Nontechnical contracts, such as landscaping, window cleaning, and janitorial services, can be negotiated as a standard contract form designed by the facilities manager with review by legal counsel. Technical contracts with code or other regulatory requirements, such as elevator maintenance, electrical maintenance, or HVAC maintenance, require a specific agreement designed for that service.

The American Institute of Architects (AIA) has developed sample contract formats that are effective in protecting the general interests of both the property and the contract. The

AIA Document A101, Standard Form of Agreement Between Owner and Contractor, is used for complex requirements with large scopes or complex agreements. AIA Document A107, Abbreviated Form of Agreement Between Owner and Contractor, is a shorter version of A101 and is designed for more simple applications. These formats can provide a good start for the facilities manager in developing a good standard contract format for his or her property. They should be modified as required for the particular work to be completed and reviewed by legal counsel for the property before being completed.

CONTRACT MANAGEMENT

The facilities manager must manage contractors and contracts with the same amount of attention he or she would exercise in the supervision of in-house staff members. Contractors are engaged to complete work for the property, but they do not assume ownership of that work. The facilities manager retains responsibility for the timely and proper completion of that work. To do this well, the facilities manager must ensure that contracts are clearly written to include all of the elements listed in previous paragraphs. Contracts must include detailed descriptions of the tasks to be completed, the time frame for their completion, and the quality of materials to be used. The facilities manager must screen and qualify all prospective contractors to verify their capability and capacity to complete the requirements of the contract. To do this, he or she must interview the contractor, demand evidence of licensing and certification as needed, and request reference information including the names and contact information for previous clients. These clients should be contacted before the contract is completed to learn the professional reputation of the prospective contractor. The validity of provided licensing and certification documents should be verified by inquiry with the appropriate issuing agencies. Finally, the facilities manager must consider the interview results with his or her own judgment to select the best contractor to provide the required service.

When contracts have been signed and the work has started, the facilities manager should inspect the work just as if it were done by an internal employee. Any discrepancies should be brought to the immediate attention of the contractor for appropriate correction. The facilities manager should maintain a record of all work completed and maintain a log of interaction with each contractor supporting the property. Such logs should be kept in chronological order with requirements, tasks, corrective actions, and complaint resolutions clearly noted as a formal record of business with each particular contractor. These logs provide a legal body of evidence if the facilities manager should decide to terminate the contract, but more frequently they provide the basis for consideration of the continuation of the relationship with a particular contractor when the contract expires and renewal is needed.

CHAPTER SUMMARY

Most hospitality establishments do not maintain the expertise or the capacity on their staff to complete all of the required tasks to maintain a profitable operation. The facilities manager must review the requirements of his facility and identify those tasks and requirements that can be more efficiently completed by an outside contractor. Tasks that require a specialized skill or equipment that is not available, or exceed the capacity of internal staff to complete, should be identified for outsourcing. The facilities manager retains the responsibility to make sure that these tasks are done properly and efficiently. To ensure that outsourced activities are completed effectively, the facilities manager must understand the elements of an effective contract and the tools to manage contractual agreements. The effective and efficient use of contractors enables a facilities manager to maintain his or her property in a profitable mode without expanding staffing or equipment costs.

GLOSSARY OF TERMS

PAC
Package air-conditioning unit. This is a self-contained unit that provides comfort heating and cooling to a specific area or space. Often referred to as window air conditioners.

Contract
A binding legal agreement between two parties.

Outsourcing
The concept or process of contracting a requirement to an external firm or agency.

STUDY QUESTIONS

1. List the conditions that might require a facilities manager to consider use of an outside contractor to complete a task.
2. What are the advantages of outsourcing? Explain.
3. What are the disadvantages of outsourcing? Explain.
4. List the essential elements of an effective contract. Explain each item listed.
5. What responsibilities are retained by the facilities manager when outsourcing a function or task?
6. How can a facilities manager ensure that outsourced tasks are being done properly?
7. What can a facilities manager do if a contractor is not completing tasks as specified in the contract?

CHAPTER FOURTEEN
FACILITIES PLANNING AND DESIGN

CHAPTER LEARNING OBJECTIVES

After reading this chapter, the student should be able to:

1. List and describe the design process and its phases.
2. Explain the difference in design emphasis between a food service operation and a lodging operation.
3. Explain why facility management concerns should be addressed in all phases of design.
4. List and describe outside influences on design such as codes, regulations, zoning requirements, and the Americans With Disabilities Act.
5. Explain the integration of growth considerations into design activities.
6. Describe the process of renovation design and management.

Facilities managers usually work in structures and properties that were designed and built long before they were hired. In some cases this means that the facilities manager must maintain systems and equipment that was not designed with any consideration for maintenance or operational repair. Access to valves and controls is sometimes difficult. The systems installed may have met the immediate needs of the establishment, but do not have the capacity to support growth or technological progress. In some cases, especially in food service operations, the facility was never designed to house a restaurant so the structure and utilities of the building present difficulties in maintaining a profitable environment. When a hospitality establishment is designed and built, it is of great benefit to the future of the business if the facilities manager is hired during the first stages of concept development and then participates all the way through to operating the building. The influence and assistance of an experienced facilities manager in the design process can help ensure a long and profitable life for a hospitality enterprise.

THE DESIGN PROCESS

The design process for a hospitality establishment is a long and intricate process involving a great number of people. In the case of lodging establishments, the process can take from two to four years to complete. Food service operations are not usually as complex so they don't normally require that length of time, but they still require careful planning. The construction of a hospitality establishment is an enormous exercise in organization and coordination. The exact sequence of activities varies in detail for each design, but follows a general pattern for most. The three main phases are the development phase, the design phase, and the construction phase. Within these phases a number of processes or steps must be completed, including development of the operating concept, establishing the feasibility of the concept, identifying and coordinating the efforts of the design team, establishing physical space requirements, refining the operational standards, developing construction and engineering criteria, preparing the project budget, and establishing the overall project schedule.

In the development phase, the first step is to visualize the concept for the project. This comes from the owner(s)/developer(s) of the proposed establishment. Several issues must be identified and organized in this step, with the intent of solidifying an identifiable and clear idea of the proposed structure including a good description of the services and operations that the final product will provide. The owner(s)/developer must:

- Identify the project business objectives
  - Financial
  - Operational
  - Longevity of operations
  - Future expansion plans
- Establish the feasibility of the project
- Select and form the project design team
  - Design team
  - Construction team
  - Management team
- Identify development issues
  - Regulatory
  - Environmental
  - Legal
- Estimate the overall budget for the project
- Estimate the overall schedule for the project
- Secure financial backing for the project
- Complete all required business or contractual agreements for the project
  - Design
  - Construction
  - Management

Identifying the business objectives can also be called the conceptual stage of a project. It is in this stage that the vision of the future structure is developed. The idea of building a hotel or restaurant must be clarified so that all those involved are envisioning the same picture of the completed project. The owners must be able to describe this vision in enough detail that the design team knows what it is attempting to build. Whether the owners are proposing a large resort hotel or a roadside overnight motel, the idea has to be well enough developed as a concept that it can be communicated to the project team to ensure that the project achieves the owner's desired results

When the owner or owners have developed the concept, the feasibility of the project must be established. This is normally done by hiring a consulting firm to prepare a feasibility study for the proposed project in relation to the proposed location. The selected firm should have experience and credibility in the hospitality industry. Further, the consulting firm should have no direct interest—in any form—in the proposed project to ensure that the report received is totally neutral. The feasibility study has three objectives: assesses current and future demand for the proposed establishment and its services in the proposed location; makes recommendations for adjustments to the proposed services in reference to the location; and it estimates operating expenses and anticipated revenues for the proposed project in the location. Usually this report will address the following headings or subjects:

- *Area analysis of the proposed location* This is an analysis of the economic environment of the selected area and the suitability of the proposed establishment for this area.
- *Market analysis of the proposed location* This is an assessment of the current demand for the services or products of the proposed establishment and future growth opportunities in the location. It also identifies existing competitive properties and their projected growth.
- *Proposed facilities* This is a suggested description of adjustments to the services of the proposed establishments to provide a more effective match to the selected location.
- *Financial analysis* The consulting firm provides an estimate of the projected revenue and expenses for the proposed establishment over a five- to ten-year period.

If the owners find that the feasibility study indicates that the proposed establishment is not economically feasible for the projected location, the feasibility consultant may be requested to extend the study to identify better locations, cities, or regions for the project. The report should include explanations of any assumptions and documentation to support the findings of the consulting firm.

The desired result of the feasibility study is to ensure that the proposed project has the potential to meet the established business objectives of the owner(s). Once that has been confirmed, the owner(s) must select and form the design team. This team will normally be headed by an architect or architectural firm that advises the owner(s) on required members and who controls the efforts of the team. The team will consist of engineers (civil, mechanical, electrical, acoustical, illumination, etc.), interior designers, food service consultants, landscape architects, and others as required for the proposed establishment. This team expands as the project proceeds, to incorporate construction contractors who make up the construction team and the management team hired by the owners to operate the establishment.

These three teams must complement each other and, to some extent, overlap in their functions. The owners are members of the design team because they must approve the design as it develops. The construction team must be consulted by the design team to ensure that the design can be constructed to the requirements of the owners. Finally, the design team and the construction team must coordinate and consult with the management team to verify that the final design will support the business objectives of the owners.

As the pre-design stage of the project continues, the three teams work together to identify all the requirements to build and operate the establishment envisioned by the owners. The initial element of design is the development of the overall estimated budget for the concept. This is not a detailed estimate, but more of a ballpark figure to assist the owners in obtaining financial backing for the project. It will often be quoted as large round figures in the thousands, hundreds of thousands, or millions to establish the scope of the project for potential investors. Normally these estimates will be supported by conceptual drawings, site elevation drawings, or preliminary schematic floor plans. These plans are graphic depictions of the owner's vision as modified by the feasibility study. These estimates also include requirements for issues identified in local building codes, zoning ordinances, Americans With Disabilities Act (ADA) requirements, and environmental factors for the selected location.

All hospitality establishments must be designed and constructed to meet a variety of regulatory standards. Such standards as municipal zoning requirements, building and fire codes, and local building permit ordinances are all intended to protect the public from faulty designs and unsafe structures. These standards can govern such issues as street setbacks, building height, building materials, and construction criteria. They can also affect the sale of alcohol, noise limits, and occupancy limits. The design team must ensure that its design meets the requirements of all such standards. Meeting these standards will often increase the construction costs for hospitality projects.

Although the construction estimates will grow to meet the requirements of the owner and regulatory requirements, they may still only represent 60 to 65 percent of the total cost of opening the restaurant or hotel. Construction costs do not include furnishings, professional fees, pre-opening expenses, and initial stocking and staffing costs. The owners, with the assistance of the management team, must include their own estimates for those expenses when seeking financial support.

Quite often potential investors will also require a five- or ten-year business plan for the establishment and a preliminary schedule for the construction. These are projections developed through coordination between the owners, the design team, the construction team, and the management team. The preliminary schedule is an estimate of the projected opening date for the completed project. Financial backers need this information to tell them when they can expect to receive some return on their investment. The input of the projected facilities manager would be very helpful to develop design requirements, construction costs, and operating costs for these plans.

When financial backing has been obtained, more specific design information is then developed. In concert with the design team, the owners must complete a space allocation for the proposed facility. This space allocation is a general outline of the various amounts of space that will be devoted to each of the proposed services. For example, a hotel without any food service facility might devote 95 percent of its space to guest rooms, or with a food service element it might only have 65 percent of its structure devoted to guest rooms with 35 percent assigned to food service. This space allocation provides guidance to the design team in developing the detailed design of the facility.

The owner provides additional guidance as operational criteria is developed to detail the anticipated services. For example, the owners must decide the interior HVAC performance criteria for the building. A standard of 72 degrees Fahrenheit with an allowed deviation of plus or minus 5 degrees would require different equipment than a standard of 74 degrees with allowed deviation of plus or minus 10 degrees. In a restaurant, the operational criteria for lighting in a 24-hour coffee shop would differ greatly from the lighting requirements for a fine dining menu.

The owner's concept also drives the construction and engineering criteria for the design. For example, does the owner have a multistory building constructed of marble and brick in mind or is it a group of single-story wooden cabins surrounding a central dining facility? As the vision is further explained to the design team, it allows the architect to guide the design to match the owner's concept of operation. Engineering criteria must be established for heating, air conditioning, ventilation, water supply, electrical power, lighting, fire and safety protection systems, and communication systems. The design team must ask for clarification of the owner's concept to ensure that the resulting structure is suitable to the business plan. The owner and the management team must remain deeply involved in the design process to provide guidance and approval for the design.

As the design team develops drawings of the owner's vision, the first step of the design phase is the production of the schematic drawings. Schematic drawings are most often called floor plans, and they are the initial drawings depicting a graphic representation of the completed structure. The schematic drawings provide the tool for the design team to move into the design development stage of the design process. As the schematics are polished and tailored to meet the owner's approval, the concept becomes clear to the design team. During design development the design team is in constant communication with the owner and the architect, making suggestions and modifying the drawings until the team and the owner agree on the structure's design. At this point, the design team begins to produce actual construction documents.

As the construction documents are finalized, the design team will coordinate with the construction contractor to ensure a clear understanding of the specifications and final plans for construction of the project. Material specifications are developed and utilities systems are designed and drawn. When the construction documents are completed, they will provide the actual instructions needed to build the establishment. The construction contractor will then review the documents to verify the constructability of the designed structure. After this review, construction cost estimates are finalized for the owner's approval. The design team, the owner, and the contractor will usually go through a process called "value engineering" as these estimates are developed. In value engineering, the materials and specifications are adjusted to ensure that the owner's concept and operational criteria are produced at the lowest possible construction cost. Once final approval is received, the project can move into actual construction.

FOOD SERVICE VERSUS LODGING DESIGN

Although lodging and food service operations go through a similar process, the basis of the concept is different. While the main goal of the lodging enterprise is to sell guest room nights to people from out of town, the restaurant design is driven by the sale of its menu items to people within five to ten miles of its location. More simply, the central drive of a lodging design is the guest room and the central theme of a restaurant design is the menu.

In the design of a hotel, the functions and features of the guest room are reflected in all parts of the design. A motel next to the highway specializing in overnight rest for drivers will differ in appearance and functionality from a five-star destination resort. This outward appearance also helps the customer to identify what to expect in the guest room. An overnight guest would be looking for a clean room, a comfortable bed, a clean bathroom, with a color television for entertainment. In contrast, a business executive might expect computer connections, a wet bar, and a desk with a telephone. The functionality and amenities of the guest room designed for a particular level of customer will drive the entire design of the facility. Most overnight motels will not have a food service element or a lounge, whereas the higher level of lodging, selling a more elaborate guest room, may also require a swimming pool, exercise room, lounge, restaurant, a recreation area, gift shop, business support center, and several other amenities.

Food service establishments are designed to match the menu to be served. Even from the street, a restaurant serving Chinese food will not resemble a café specializing in western barbecue. Although a fine dining restaurant may still be able to prepare pizza in its kitchen, the pizza parlor probably will not have the proper oven to cook anything other than pizza and related dishes. The back-of-house for a fast-food restaurant will not have the preparation area of the large-scale steak house, and the soup and salad restaurant will not have the frozen storage equipment of a frozen yogurt stand. Not only does the scope change in reaction to the size of the establishment, the equipment and décor will be structured to support the menu. Fast food hamburger-based restaurants will have vinyl paneling because of the grease fumes in the air, where a casual family dining facility may have paint or wallpaper. The entire physical design of a restaurant is driven by the menu it serves.

THE ROLE OF THE FACILITIES MANAGER IN DESIGN AND DEVELOPMENT

When the design team is developing the design of a building to match the vision of the owner, it often does not consider the life of the structure beyond the opening day. If the facilities manager for the establishment is hired and added to the design or the management team during development, then interest in the maintainability of the building and its systems is injected into the design process. The facilities manager is the technical manager who will be forced to make the results of the design team effort into a profitable atmosphere for the management team. This places the facilities manager in the position of asking questions during the design process, such as, "How much power does this equipment use?" "What is the expected life of this paint?" "Are there any special tools or equipment needed to support this system?" and "What are the warranties on these products and materials?" The facilities manager ensures that the design of the building is operable, maintainable, and durable.

The facilities manager also has the role of planning for future growth. He or she ensures that the equipment selected, systems installed, and décor applied meets the initial operational requirements of the owners while simultaneously influencing the incorporation of future expansion and growth into the design. Extra capacity must be incorporated into every system to ensure redundant capability. When a primary system incurs a service interruption, the facilities manager must maintain the profitability of the building with secondary or supporting systems. Design teams often do not even consider redundancy of primary systems. The facilities manager will have this factor in mind throughout the design process because when systems break down, he or she will be the one the owners will hold responsible for maintaining the establishment.

DESIGN FOR THE LOCATION AND ENVIRONMENT

To be a viable and profitable hospitality enterprise, the building and its system must be designed to exist in the selected location. A hotel with a Hawaii-based theme may be profitable in northern Minnesota, but it will not be able to do it with palm trees and pineapples growing in the front yard. A roadside overnight motel will not work well in the middle of Manhattan, New York City, and a fifty-story, five-star hotel will be very much out of place in Manhattan, Kansas. The structure must be designed for the location, the business, and the natural environment. This may seem obvious when external appearances are considered, but it extends to areas and subjects that do not show on the surface. The energy used in the structure needs to be selected to match economically available sources in the location where the structure is built. Wall treatments must tolerate the environmental factors of the particular location. Wallpaper and fabric coverings do not do well in high humidity, and a heavy grease atmosphere and impermeable vinyl surfaces become brittle in cold climates. Tall buildings can be unsafe in areas with high winds, and single-story structures are very expensive to build in areas where land values are high. The design team must make an effort to meet the owner's vision with structures that are appropriate to the environment in which they must operate.

DESIGN FOR FUTURE GROWTH

Buildings are built to meet the owner's requirements and needs on opening day. Unfortunately, as they age and customer expectations change, buildings become outdated and obsolete. Successful hospitality establishments grow in popularity and expand their services and operations to meet the demands and expectations of their customers. Because of these factors, buildings must be designed and constructed to allow for changes and additions. In other words, the original design team for a structure must include space or capability for growth. HVAC and other utility systems must be designed with more capability than the original building needed. Kitchens must be equipped for expanding volumes of sales, and dining rooms must be placed in areas that allow for expansion of seating capacity. If such allowances are not included in the original design, the hospitality establishment will reach a maximum level of operations and stagnate at that level. Predictably, such limits will eventually reduce the life-span of the enterprise.

REDESIGN FOR RENOVATION

In the same way that buildings must be designed to allow for expansion, all structures must go through an almost constant state of renovation to maintain a profitable life. The facilities manager must continually upgrade, modernize, and renew the facility with a renovation plan or program. Hospitality operations have a predictable life cycle. If they are well designed, they will enjoy a period of immediate market domination on opening day. But this begins to decline very quickly. After a phase of great profitability, hospitality operations will move into a longer period of strong performance. But as they continue to age, profitability also declines and will eventually slip below acceptable levels. To prolong the phase of strong performance, the facilities manager must engage in continuing efforts to renovate the property.

Renovation plans or programs include four levels of projects:

- Special projects are related to upgrading specific systems or elements of the facility. Such projects do not change the design of the building in any significant way. Special projects include installation of computer access systems, security system upgrades, or modifications to meet changing regulatory standards, such as ADA requirements.
- Minor renovations replace or renew furnishings or finishes within the facility, but do not change the basic design of the building. Replacement of wallpaper or wall finishes, carpet, furnishings and linens, or curtains would represent activities included in a minor renovation. Also, the use or layout of areas within the facility do not change and new services are not added. Minor renovations are intended to renew existing facilities. Normally, such activities occur after about six years of use.
- Major renovations renew all furnishings and finishes within a space in the structure. This may include actual changes in the layout, size of spaces, or supporting systems. In a major renovation, plumbing, electrical wiring, and all other utilities are upgraded to meet improved specifications. The renovated space is reopened as an entirely new area of the facility that meets the most modern standards in operation and decoration. Usually, a space must be completely renovated after twelve to fifteen years of operation.
- Restoration is the complete rebuild of an entire building. All utilities and non-load-bearing walls are completely removed and the building is gutted. The floor plans are reconfigured and all new systems are replaced with modern equipment and materials. When a renovated building is reopened, it is a completely new facility that meets the latest standards and regulatory requirements. For a building to stay in profitable operation, restoration will occur every twenty-five to fifty years.

The renovation program for a hospitality operation is sometimes called the capital projects program. To establish a renovation program, the facilities manager must survey the property to identify systems and areas that are beginning to show signs of deterioration. This survey cannot be done once—it must be repeated periodically. An annual survey is usually appropriate for most properties. When the requirements have been identified, the facilities manager must prioritize them into projects that need immediate attention to maintain profitability, projects that will begin to affect profitability if they are not corrected in the next twelve months, and projects that must be completed within the next five years to maintain profitable operations.

The design of a renovation project can vary from a simple decision by the facilities manager to upgrade a single item of equipment or paint a single room, to the appointment of an entire design team to plan a restoration. In some cases, the design for special systems, such as a computer access systems or new kitchen equipment, is completed by the contractor who will install the system. This is often the case in smaller properties with a limited in-house facilities staff. In larger properties, the internal staff may complete the entire project. In the case of a restoration or a major rebuild, a design team will usually complete the design and pass the construction requirements to a general contractor. In all renovation projects, the facilities manager is the primary representative of the owner(s), with responsibility to complete the project and return the facility to operations as quickly as possible. It is the facilities manager who maintains the facility in a profitable condition.

CHAPTER SUMMARY

Buildings must be designed and constructed correctly to support the hospitality enterprises that they house. The facilities manager is a key factor in providing the guidance to the design team to ensure that this is done effectively. Although the design team designs a structure that will be fully operational on its opening day, the facilities manager is responsible for maintaining that facility in a profitable mode throughout the life of the enterprise. The design process is difficult and complex, but the facilities manager should be involved in every step of the procedure.

GLOSSARY OF TERMS:

Design team
The group of design experts (engineers, consultants, décor specialists) under the supervision of the architect who actually produce the design documents, including construction documents for a building.

Construction team
The group of contractors, usually under the supervision of a general contractor, that actually builds a structure to match the construction documents.

Management team
The management personnel and agencies hired by a building's owner(s) to operate the building and its revenue-producing functions. The facilities manager is a member of this team.

Street setback
The distance that a building must be moved back from the edge of the public roadway or street.

Value engineering
The process of comparing products and construction methods to ensure that the needs of the building owners are met at the lowest possible cost.

Capital projects
Projects that go beyond normal operating maintenance activities. The cost of such projects cannot be allocated to a single customer, but must be addressed as overhead costs supported by all sources of revenue.

Schematic drawings
Architectural drawings that depict the floor plan as seen from directly above the building. These drawings are used to establish the spatial relations of different functional areas of a building.

STUDY QUESTIONS:

1. What are the functions of a feasibility study? Explain the importance of each.
2. Who supervises the activities of the design team?
3. Describe the role of the facilities manager in the design of a building?
4. Define value engineering.
5. Why is planning for growth important to consider during the design of a building? Explain.
6. How does design of a lodging facility differ from design of a food service facility? Explain.
7. What is meant by the terms operational, engineering, and construction criteria? Explain.

CHAPTER FIFTEEN
HEALTH, SAFETY, AND SECURITY CONCERNS FOR FACILITIES OPERATIONS

CHAPTER LEARNING OBJECTIVES

After reading this chapter, the student should be able to:

1. Describe the ethical and legal requirements for safe management practices.
2. Describe the health, safety, and security responsibilities of the facility manager.
3. Describe the liability risks involved in facility management in the hospitality industry.
4. List the legal requirements for facility management in the hospitality industry.
5. Discuss the factors and procedures for effective fire safety programs.
6. Discuss the factors that affect guest room safety.
7. Discuss the increasing security threats in hospitality operations and some of the tools available to the facility manager to protect the facility.

Safety records in the hospitality industry have improved in recent years, owing to a number of reasons. Increased management awareness of safety risks combined with increased demands and expectations of customers for safe accommodations have made safety a key issue in facilities management. The facilities manager must understand safety and security issues and needs, not only in relation to the well-being of customers and staff, but also because of the significant financial effect of safety risks and accidents.

THE ETHICS OF SAFETY

The guests and customers in a hospitality establishment have a right to expect safety and security. Traditionally, inns and roadhouses of the past were considered to be safe havens from the dangers of travel, and once a guest entered they were to be protected from bandits, brigands, and other threats to their safety. In the modern hospitality industry, this expectation of protection from harm has expanded to include safety from fire, sickness, injury, and other losses from accidents or incidents. The employees of the establishment also have a right to expect a safe working environment where they can earn their wages without injury or risk. The facilities manager is ethically obligated to maintain a safe physical environment for the customers and employees of the property, and also to protect the owner of the property from loss due to accidents or unsafe conditions.

In pursuing a safe environment, the facilities manager is acting as an agent for the owner or the general manager to ensure the physical safety of the building and its occupants. But he or she cannot effectively manage safety without the interest and support of top management. Senior management must be sincerely and actively interested in a safety program for it to be successful. If the "Boss" is concerned, then all subordinate employees will also be concerned with safe operations, and safety becomes everybody's responsibility. When all employees at every level understand this ethical obligation to provide safe operations for customers and employees, and to protect the owner from loss, an effective safety program can be achieved.

SAFETY RESPONSIBILITIES OF FACILITIES MANAGEMENT

The facilities manager has a key role in any safety program because of his or her direct responsibility for the physical structure of the building. The facilities manager installs or supervises the installation and maintenance of all safety and security equipment or systems on the property. He or she also has direct responsibility for the safe installation, construction, maintenance, and operation of all equipment and systems throughout the structure.

The training of staff members and occupants on the use of building systems and equipment safely is also within the facilities manager's responsibilities. Operating procedures must be written, implemented, and supervised for the entire property. By training building occupants to follow those procedures, the facilities manager not only fulfills his or her responsibility for safety on the property, he or she also shares the responsibility for safe operation with the trained staff members. Before being trained in proper procedures, employees cannot be held responsible for accidents, but once they have been taught, it becomes their responsibility to follow those procedures. This makes all employees responsible for safety. The facilities manager does not reduce his or her own responsibility, but actually shares it by training staff members and occupants on safe operational practices. Training must be repeated to retain its effectiveness, because employees become relaxed and careless if they are not periodically retrained.

MANAGING SAFETY PROGRAMS

In many properties a visitor may see posters and publications openly displayed that proclaim an interest in safety. Such slogans as "We put safety first!" or "Safety goes in before the name goes on!" have a nice ring to them. But they are ineffectual if not supported by a well managed safety program. Such programs involve all employees as well as management personnel in a risk management effort, and are often implemented in coordination with insurance agencies providing coverage to the property. It is very important that a single individual or a specifically assigned safety committee be placed in charge of the safety program. The role of this person or team is to provide leadership to implement the program, and they must have the authority to enforce policy and procedures for safe operation. For this reason, the facilities manager is always a member of the committee and often the designated chairman or safety officer for the property.

Basic elements of a good safety program include:

- Composing and distributing to all employees a written safety policy that states the commitment of management to safety and the expected actions from employees.
- Obtaining employee thoughts on safety matters related to their duties.
- Conducting regular safety inspections of the property, both formal and informal in nature.
- Establishing realistic and attainable accident reduction goals with monitoring procedures and appropriate reward plans for improved performance.
- Requiring employee accountability for accident reduction and safe operations.
- Establishing a modified duty program that returns injured employees to work quickly.
- Increasing safety awareness through training, competitions, and employee seminars.
- Establishing specific safety-related activities as performance criteria for advancement or management promotion.
- Training, retraining, and training again in safe operations and safety procedures.

The thrust of a safety program must be actual safety, not records or statistics. A good safety program is designed to make sure that all guests and employees leave the property in at least the same condition in which they arrived. The key is prevention—not reaction to accidents. The facilities manager must play a constant game of "what if?" as he or she supervises the facilities activities for the property. Any accident that can be anticipated can be prevented. If the only point that the program emphasizes is reducing statistics, it will not be effective. Statistics can be improved by not reporting accidents and problems. As such, real safety is only enhanced by active thought and planning for prevention of accidents.

The implementation of a safety program does not guarantee safety improvement unless it is correctly managed. Properties that concentrate on the investigation of accidents and assigning blame or cause for problems will not improve their safety performance. Instead, such a practice will establish an accident cycle where periods of frequent accident occurrence are off set with periods of intense investigation and corrective action. The accidents don't stop, but actually just wait for the interest to relax so that they can strike again. Such properties are often called reactive properties.

Establishments referred to as plateau properties are similar to reactive properties, but they actually do reduce accident rates to a static level. They do this by stressing the statistics of the program. If the numbers are the driving force, it is very simple to keep them low. Accidents continue to occur but the employees will often hide them to keep the numbers low. The program is waiting for the accidents to occur before preventive measures or procedures are implemented. Therefore, the same accidents do not recur in the same way, but there is no anticipation of unsafe conditions so new types of accidents will replace them. Plateau properties cannot improve beyond a predictable level of safety success.

The safest properties are those that emphasize continuous improvement—not to reduce numbers or statistics, but to enhance safety by preventing accidents. Rather than being driven by the statistics, these properties anticipate problems and engage solutions before people are injured. Because they use planning and analysis rather than reaction and correction as primary tools in their safety programs, their statistics improve. The facilities manager must work to prevent accidents and unsafe operations instead of reacting to them.

LEGAL REQUIREMENTS FOR SAFETY

Most legal safety standards are established by local codes in the communities where the establishment exists. These local codes are based on professional standards and a few federal codes. Professional standards are published by organizations such as the National Fire Prevention Association (NFPA), which has created both Life Safety and Fire Prevention codes. It has also established codes for the installation of fire alarm systems and fire-suppression systems such as sprinklers. Local municipalities have adopted these standards and enforce them on hospitality establishments.

The Hotel and Motel Fire Safety Act of 1990 is the only federal legislation that has had a significant effect on lodging facilities. The law requires the installation of hard-wired smoke detectors in all guest rooms. It also mandates the installation of at least one sprinkler head in each guest room unless the existing building is less than three stories—existing buildings with less than three stories are not required to install sprinkler heads. Also, all newly constructed buildings must have a sprinkler head in every room on all floors. Current estimates indicate that approximately 95 percent of all high-rise motels and 45 percent of all hotels and motels are compliant with the Hotel and Motel Fire Safety Act.

Emergency procedures and planning are required for all businesses, including hospitality establishments, by the Occupational Safety and Health Administration. The facilities manager is usually the key manager in the composition of the emergency response plan required by this federal agency. This plan must be tailored to meet the needs of the specific property and address the following key elements:

- Pre-emergency planning and coordination with outside supporting or emergency services
- Employee roles, lines of authority during an emergency, employee training, and pre-planned communication systems
- Emergency recognition surveys and prevention inspections
- Established safe distances and designated places of refuge
- Building security procedures and control systems
- Planned evacuation routes and procedures
- Decontamination procedures
- Emergency medical treatment measures and first aid procedures
- Emergency notification and planned response procedures
- Prepositioned personal protective equipment (PPE) and emergency equipment
- Established procedures for the evaluation and follow-up corrective actions after an emergency incident

Unfortunately, most general managers are unaware of these requirements. The facilities manager is often called on not only to do the emergency planning and train the employees in their duties during an emergency for the property, but also to inform and train the general manager and other department managers to understand their emergency responsibilities. It is essential that all managers at every level understand their ethical obligation to protect the safety of their guests and employees. This includes the formation of preplanned emergency response teams using appropriate employees from all departments. These teams should be trained to respond to possible emergencies such as medical emergencies, power outages, floods, fires, or natural disasters. No matter what the anticipated emergency, the designated team must be trained to respond in an appropriate manner to protect the guests, employees, and property from preventable injury or damage.

The facilities manager must also plan for the recovery of the property after an emergency, especially one that damages the building or renders building systems inoperable. Immediate recovery activities in a lodging establishment include but are not limited to:

- Arranging for accommodations for guests after a fire, or other disaster that has damaged the building to a point that precludes safe occupation.
- Establishing agreements with outside contractors to secure and rebuild damaged facilities.
- Establishing agreements with cleaning specialists to recover from smoke or water damage.
- Establishing contact with insurance companies and bonding agencies.
- Completing required police and fire department investigations and reports.
- Arranging for any required additional security guards for the damaged building.
- Reporting conditions and recovering efforts to owners, department managers, and employees.
- Beginning plans to prevent future recurrences of the emergency or reduce injury or damage to guests, employees, and property.

FIRE SAFETY

The most commonly recognized major threat to safety in a building is fire. Most people are taught the basic points of fire safety in elementary school. Some of these procedures are very deeply ingrained, such as the procedures of "stop, drop, and roll" and "crawl out of a smoke-filled room." Fire safety in hospitality establishments, especially lodging enterprises, must go beyond this level of individual training. Facilities managers must implement fire prevention and fire safety programs aimed at ensuring the safety of large groups of untrained guests in unfamiliar surroundings. As with all other categories of safety, this responsibility is shared with all property employees, but the facilities manager must provide them with the equipment, tools, and training to perform their fire safety duties.

Fire safety factors have changed in recent years with better construction planned for evacuation and improved fire prevention, detection, and suppression systems. Many people remember being taught the three points of the "fire triangle"—heat, fuel, and oxygen. Because of synthetic construction materials and fabrics used in modern buildings, fire safety systems actually address the "fire tetrahedron," which includes the original three sides of heat, fuel, and oxygen and adds a fourth of chemical reaction. This fourth element not only makes fires more difficult to fight, it also increases fire risks if specific materials are used in the wrong combination or environment. The facilities manager must be aware of the increased fire risks from this factor and adjust fire safety programs to confront it.

The fire safety program in a building includes three categories of activities. There are those efforts that must be made to prevent fires from occurring, those that ensure detection and warning of fires, and those that suppress fires. At the facilities level, all of these stages emphasize occupant safety. Extinguishing a fire is the job of the professional firefighters. The facilities manager must develop the fire safety program to reduce the risk of fire and evacuate the building as quickly as possible to reduce injury during a fire emergency. All of the systems, equipment, and fire safety training of employees have this same objective. Prevention includes planning, training, and inspection to reduce the threats that can cause a fire. *Figure 15.1* is a sample checklist, based on criteria from the NFPA, that provides a basis for fire safety inspections. Each point of this checklist implies a detail of preparation or training that must be pursued by the facilities manager. Alarm systems must be installed and maintained, sprinkler systems must be installed and maintained, staff members must be taught to perform the required maintenance, and evacuation procedures and routes must be developed and published. The list of needed equipment is extensive, including fire pumps, door closers, alarm systems, emergency generators, stairwell pressurization systems, and fire extinguishers. All have to be properly selected for the property and its functions, correctly installed in appropriate locations for effective operation, and regularly inspected and maintained to ensure performance.

Figure 15.1 Sample Fire Safety Checklist , National Fire Protection Association

HOTEL FIRE SAFETY CHECKLIST
To be completed by the Facilities Manager/Designated Safety Officer:

1. Is there a fire alarm system to alert the occupants of a fire? What does it sound like?

     a. Bell   b. Horn   c. Slow Whoop   d. Other:_____

2. Are exit doors and routes to them indicated by illuminated EXIT signs?
3. Is there emergency lighting for the exit ways and exit stairs?
4. Are there any obstructions in corridors, exit doorways, exit stairs, and other routes that constitute exit ways for occupants?
5. Do exit doors from meeting, food service, or recreational areas swing out?
6. Are exit doors locked or secured in any way that would prevent ready use of the door?
7. Are doors which could be mistaken for an exit marked properly? At least: DO NOT EXIT.
8. Do doors to exit stairs close and latch automatically after use and remain properly closed?
9. Are you able to access the guestroom floors from the exit stairs?
10. Are instructions prominently displayed in each occupant's room, giving details of the fire alarm signal and indicating locations of the nearest exits?
11. Are occupants room doors self-closing and free of transoms or louvers that may permit penetration of smoke into the room?
12. Is there a sign clearly visible in each elevator lobby station that states, "Elevators are not to be used during a fire"?

13. Are there signs posted at the principal entrance to meeting and facility rooms, specifying maximum number of occupants?
14. Are the provided exits remote from each other so that occupants are able to use alternatives if one exit becomes unusable in an emergency?
15. Are folding partitions or air walls arranged so as not to obstruct access to required exits?
16. Are there mirrored surfaces near exits that create confusion for occupants attempting to evacuate the building?
17. Do meeting rooms have sufficient exits to allow the number of occupants to leave readily, based on the following schedule?

> More than 1,000------------4 exits (minimum)
> 300-1,000--------------------3 exits
> 50-300----------------------2 exits

18. Are all corridors, stairways, and aisles free of temporary or permanent storage, including laundry, chairs, tables, room service trays, and trash?
19. Is there a designated senior staff person responsible for on-site fire-safety inspections?
20. Are you subject to a fire code? If so, which one?
21. Are any violations related to fire safety inspections outstanding or uncorrected? If so, please list.
22. Does your facility have an established operating emergency procedure in case of fire? Please include a copy with this completed checklist.
23. Is your facility sprinklered? If no, indicate where sprinklers are located.

> a. Meeting Rooms   b. Corridors   c. Public Lobbies
> d. Guestrooms   e. Public Restrooms   f. Other_____.

24. Are smoke detectors located in all areas of the facility? If no, indicate smoke detector locations.

> a. Meeting Rooms   b. Corridors   c. Public Lobbies
> d. Guestrooms   e. Public Restrooms   f. Other_____.

25. Are all smoke detectors hard-wired into a central signaling system or directly to the fire department? If no, which are not?

> Name:_____Title:_____
> Date:_____

Employees must be trained to react to fire risks in effective and efficient actions to ensure the safety of building occupants. When the building is burning it is too late to tell people what they need to do. They must know what actions are needed to protect themselves and their guests. This can be as simple as a desk clerk being taught to call 911 when a fire alarm is heard, or a waiter being responsible to direct guests to the closest exit. Or it may be more complex, such as training electricians and information technicians to maintain electronic fire detection equipment or teaching a plumber to properly service and inspect an emergency fire pump. The plan for the employees' reaction to fire risks and actual fire emergencies must be developed by the facilities manager specifically for his or her property, and staff members have to be trained to execute that plan.

GUEST ROOM SAFETY

Unfortunately, the building occupants who are most vulnerable to unsafe conditions in a hotel are the guests. They are in unfamiliar surroundings with little knowledge of the threats that endanger their safety, and the facilities manager cannot provide the training to prepare them for an emergency. When they are in their guest rooms, they cannot even be supervised by a trained employee. Therefore, the facilities manager must do everything possible to remove dangers from the guest rooms. This begins with proper construction, using good materials to ensure that the structure is sound. Wiring and plumbing must be installed according to established safety codes, and equipment and appliances must be selected that have been certified for safe operation. HVAC and lighting systems must be properly maintained and the guest rooms cleaned and sanitized for safe occupancy.

The area of a guest room that presents the greatest risk to guest safety is the bathroom. Guests have fallen, been electrocuted, been scalded, and subjected to unsanitary conditions by faulty appliances and construction. Most of these accidents were preventable.

Hot water is both a luxury and a risk in a guest bathroom. For the typical adult, scalding begins with water at approximately 130 degrees Fahrenheit. Therefore, water heaters supplying the guest rooms should be set at 120 degrees Fahrenheit to produce water of 110 degrees at the tap. Unfortunately, many older hotels have remotely located water heaters, so guests must waste large amounts of water to obtain the right temperature, if at all, and spurring complaints if the water is not as hot as they desire. In some cases these hotels have increased the temperature settings of their equipment to compensate for outdated systems. This has created a scalding and liability risk that the facilities manager could prevent with the installation of recirculating pumps or supplementary water-heating appliances. In some hotels the domestic hot water systems also support the food service and laundry operations. These activities also are required by law to use much higher temperature water to sanitize dishes or sheets. Such systems also present an injury risk to guests. The facilities manager must ensure that these three heating levels are isolated into separate systems. The installation of modern low-flow shower heads and temperature-controlling smart valves on showers and sinks can also reduce the risk of scalding injuries if temperature fluctuations occur.

Electric razors and hair dryers in guest bathrooms introduce the risk of electrocution. The installation of ground fault circuit isolator (GFCI) outlets greatly reduces this threat. The standard domestic circuit in the United States provides 110–120 volt electrical service with a 20 amp current. This level of service can produce a significant shock, which can prove fatal to some people. The GFCI reduces the current to a much safer level of 3 amps, which is sufficient for a hair dryer or electric razor, but does not present the same risk.

By insisting on the installation of the correct materials in the guest bathroom, the facilities manager can greatly reduce potential injury. Water-resistant sheetrock sealed with moisture-resistant paints or waterproof vinyl paneling will resist the formation of mold and retain structural strength for a longer period. Slip-resistant vinyl floor coverings are more easily cleaned and sanitized than wood or carpet, and help prevent slipping and falls. The use of tempered or shatterproof glass is also much safer than common window glass in bathroom applications.

GROWING THREATS TO SAFETY

In recent years, bomb threats, terrorist attacks, violent demonstrations, and similar activities have become more frequent occurrences for hospitality properties. There are several reasons for this increase, but no matter the reason, a hospitality establishment is extremely vulnerable because of the nature of its function. Hotels and restaurants are open and relatively unprotected from entry by anyone, including domestic and foreign visitors. In fact, they advertise and radiate easy entrance and invitation to use their properties. It would be counterproductive to harden a hospitality establishment to limit access, because clients and customers would be discouraged from doing business through increased screening, personal searches, or similar security measures. The facilities manager, however, must still be aware of and attempt to protect his or her property from the threat of terrorism.

There are a few physical changes that the facilities manager can incorporate to increase property security. Vehicle barriers, landscaping features such as fountains and statues, or curbs and driveways can be designed and installed to control the approaches to the building. This can make it more difficult to damage a building with a vehicle. Secondary doors can be equipped with automatic locks that require the use of a guest room key to secure entrance to the building, and unused doors can be equipped with alarms. Security cameras or security personnel can be used to observe activity in areas that are not visible to employees. Windows and vents on lower floors can be secured and protected with metal screens, bars, or alarms. The facilities manager has direct responsibility for these physical improvements.

The most effective security approach available to the hospitality industry in protecting itself from attack is to train staff members to be vigilant and aware of their environment and surroundings. Employees should be taught to recognize and immediately report to management any suspicious behavior or appearance. A man in a business suit who is wearing shower thongs is not necessarily a threat to the property, but his appearance may be unusual enough to warrant that his activities be monitored. Or a housekeeper should report if a guest has refused to allow his or her room to be cleaned for several days, or who has not left a room that is marked with a "Do Not Disturb" tag for a long period. A vehicle parked outside a building without activity for a number of days, or parked too close to the building, should be investigated. Employees should be trained and encouraged to notice unusual or abnormal situations or behavior on a regular basis. This training should be repetitive and mandatory for all employees

CHAPTER SUMMARY

The facilities manager has primary responsibility for the maintenance and well-being of the physical structure and systems of a hospitality property, and therefore plays a central and critical role in the safety of the occupants. This includes planning for the prevention of loss or injury to guests, employees, or the property owners, as well as responding to emergency situations and accidents. This is not only a professional but also an ethical obligation for the facilities manager. Although recent years have shown a marked reduction in losses and accidents in the hospitality industry, improvement is possible in every category of risk. The facilities manager shares responsibility for safety with all other employees of the property through training programs, employee safety committees, and operational safety instruction. He or she is often designated by upper management as the key coordinator and planner of formal safety programs. Safety is not a system of statistics and policies, but rather the prevention and reduction of injuries and loss through the application of management emphasis and leadership.

GLOSSARY OF TERMS

Reactive properties
Properties that do not engage in accident prevention but only approach safety from the point of reacting to accidents and assigning blame or cause for the accident. These properties will show very little improvement in safety.

Plateau properties
Properties that are limited in safety improvement because they emphasize the improvement of statistics. They are more concerned with reducing the numbers of accidents than reducing the threat of unsafe conditions. They correct activities that have already caused accidents.

Fire tetrahedron
The modernized model of fire risk. It includes four elements or sides: heat, fuel, oxygen, and chemical reaction.

STUDY QUESTIONS

1. Who is responsible for safety at a hospitality establishment?
2. Explain the ethical obligation of the facilities manager to maintain a safe property.
3. Explain the legal requirements of the facilities manager to maintain a safe property.

4. Refer to questions 1 and 2 above. What is the difference between ethical and legal requirements for safety? Explain your answer.
5. Why is the facilities manager a key management position in the safety program of a hospitality establishment?
6. What is the fire tetrahedron? Explain.
7. Who is responsible for establishing a safety program?
8. For a safety program to be effective, what particular management position must support it?
9. What is the primary tool used to prevent terrorist attacks in a hospitality enterprise?

APPENDIX ONE

ELECTRICITY

Electricity is the most commonly used source of energy in modern buildings and structures. In the hospitality industry, electricity represents 80 percent of the energy used in lodging and food service establishments. Most consumers are well aware of the utility of electrical energy, because of its convenience, ease of distribution, and relatively clean use. But few people really understand its properties and nature. This often results in wasted energy resources. It also, at times, produces extreme hazards to personal and public safety. This appendix provides a discussion of the basic electrical facts, and the factors that facilities managers should be aware of.

SOURCES OF ELECTRICITY

There are only two sources for electricity. A property either has to install and maintain the equipment to generate its own power, or it must be purchased from the distribution system of the local utility company. Establishments in remote areas, such as golf courses or resorts, might generate their own electricity because the cost of obtaining service from a local utility company would be prohibitive. Other properties may produce their own power because they have specialized needs that exceed the capability of the local provider, or they use such an enormous amount of power that they can reduce their costs by installing their own generators. Amusement parks or water parks sometimes fall into this category. Even those buildings that use local utilities can install generation equipment, to provide redundancy and meet emergency requirements if their primary source should fail.

Most hospitality establishments purchase electricity from local utility companies. The utility company is responsible for providing sufficient amounts of power of the correct specifications to meet the needs of the facility. The actual consumption of electricity for the building is measured by an electric meter, with the information gathered, used to establish the amount of the electrical bill for the contracted billing period.

ELECTRICAL TERMS AND DEFINITIONS

Electric power is produce by the forced flow of electrons through a conductor. Scientific study over the last three centuries has established the existence of these electrons, though no one has ever actually seen one. To aid in the visualization and definition of electrical terms and measurements, the most common illustration of electric flow, dimensions, and behavior is presented by comparing them with the behavior of the flow of water.

To understand the behavior of electron flow, one must visualize a wire conductor as a common garden hose. If the hose is filled with water, it has reached its maximum capacity, and this volume is expressed in terms of gallons of water. When more water is forced into the hose at one end, the water in the hose increases in pressure and an equal amount of water will be forced out of the hose at the opposite end. The increase in pressure is measured in pounds per square inch (PSI), and the resulting flow is measured in gallons per minute. If more water is forced into the hose than is released at the opposite end, the hose will be stressed and eventually rupture because its capacity has been exceeded. When a wire is full of electrons it has reached its maximum stable capacity. If additional electrons are forced into one end of the wire, the electric pressure or potential electron flow in the wire is increased and electrons will be pushed through the wire and will try to escape from the opposite end of the wire. The wire is said to be charged or energized and flow will occur if the wire is connected to another conductor. The increase in electric potential is measured in volts, and the resulting electron flow is called current and measured in amperes. If the electron flow or current exceeds the capacity of the wire, its temperature will begin to rise, and if the current is not reduced the wire will eventually melt or burn through from the increase in heat. In the United States, the standard household voltage is 110–120 volts. It actually arrives from the electric company at 220 or higher voltage, but is stepped down for safety by the use of power transformers. In many other countries electricity is provided with a standard of 220–240 volts. Because of this difference, equipment designed for a higher voltage will not have as much power if it is plugged into a lower voltage system, and equipment designed for a lower voltage will overload and burn up in a higher voltage system.

Electrical power for a building is divided into circuits by the distribution panels. In large buildings it may be supplied in voltages as high as 880 volts, or 440 volts for larger buildings, but as it is broken into feeders for different circuits, the power is channeled through step-down transformers for specific uses. In a residence, the air conditioning or the oven may require 220-volt power, but the standard wall receptacle or outlet will be powered at 110–120 volts, usually with only 20 amps of current. In commercial buildings, larger equipment may require higher voltage and heavier amperage to operate effectively. Electronic equipment such as computers and cash registers often have internal transformers that reduce the 110-volt input to even lower levels to keep their more sensitive components from overheating.

In an electrical system, current does not pass through a system unless a circuit is complete. This means that an energized wire or circuit will not allow electrons to flow unless the circuit is connected to a neutral wire, which allows the electrons to flow back to ground or earth. When this connection is made between the energized wire and the neutral wire, the circuit is complete. Each energized wire in a circuit is called a phase. Most circuits are either a single phase or a three-phase circuit.

Electricity is supplied either as a direct current (DC) or an alternating current (AC). In a DC circuit, the polarity of the charged wires does not change. This means that the positive wire is always positive, and the negative wire is always negative. DC is very useful in equipment such as elevators, because it simplifies the requirement that a motor change its direction of rotation. A DC motor will rotate in the opposite direction if the polarity is changed on the two feeder wires coming into it. DC systems are efficient, but they also present a greater danger of electrocution if an individual comes into contact with the charged wires. In an AC circuit, the positive and the negative wires exchange polarity at a constant frequency. This reduces the danger of electrocution, but it also means that AC motors can only rotate in one direction. In the United States, AC power is supplied with a frequency of 60 cycles per second. This means that the polarity of the two feeders changes sixty times every second. Other countries do not have the same standards and many provide AC power at 50 cycles per second. A motor that is designed to produce a specified number of revolutions per second in a 60-cycle system will turn more slowly in a 50-cycle system, and vice versa.

OHM'S LAW

Some conductors are more efficient than others, meaning that they have less resistance to the transfer of electrons. Less-efficient conductors have greater resistance. A conductor with greater resistance will begin to increase in temperature as current is passed through it. This resistance is measured in ohms. An ohm is approximately equal in energy value to a watt, but where the watt measures work output, the ohm is a measurement of electrical resistance.

All electrical equipment has some level of resistance or requirement for work output. The relationship in a circuit between work output measured in watts, resistance measured in ohms, electric potential measured in volts, and electric current measured in amperes, is similar to the relationship of volume, pressure, and hose capacity in the flow of water. Large pipes have large volume at low pressure whereas small pipes have low volume at low pressure, but larger volume at high pressure, and so on. For electricity, this relationship is expressed as an algebraic equation in Ohm's Law. Ohm's Law states:

Potential (volts) = Current (amps) X Resistance (ohms)

Electricians use Ohms's Law to analyze requirements and activity in electric circuits through simple formula manipulation using the basic rules of algebra:

If

volts = amps X ohms

then

amps = volts/ohms

and

ohms = volts/ amps

Similarly, since watts are approximately equal in energy value to ohms:

If

volts = amps X watts

then

amps = volts/watts

and

watts = volts/ amps

The electrician only needs to identify two of the factors of circuitry to calculate the third and determine the correct wiring and power levels to support any item of equipment or system.

PLUG CONFIGURATIONS

To keep equipment from being connected to the wrong power and being damaged, the outlets and plugs for each country, or level of power, are configured in different shapes or numbers of connectors. For example, in the United States, most clothes dryers require 220 volts to operate effectively. The power cord for such equipment will not fit a standard 110-volt outlet. Conversely, appliances designed for 110 volts of power cannot be plugged into a standard 220- volt outlet. Different plug configurations established in different countries protect travelers from damaging their appliances by plugging them into the wrong power. The power cords of equipment and appliances should never be changed by anyone except a licensed electrician, and even then they should be clearly tagged and marked so that the change is obvious and the equipment is not damaged with incorrect power.

WIRING

Most electrical wiring in the United States is now done with copper wire. But other materials may be used for specific applications, and wire selection is governed by local building codes based on the National Electric Code. Copper is the most common because it is very easy to work with and provides excellent conductivity when properly sized and installed. In the past, building codes were more lenient than current codes. Many older buildings are still wired with bare copper wire that travels through the walls and ceilings guided by ceramic or glass insulators. Less ancient buildings may still be equipped with cloth-insulated wires, which are safer than bare wire but still not as safe as modern wiring sheathed in vinyl insulation. As systems are maintained or modified, older wiring should be replaced with modern wiring to reduce fire and electrocution risks. A few buildings still exist that were originally constructed with aluminum wiring. Aluminum wiring is an excellent conductor when first installed, but over time the resistance to the passage of current increases in aluminum wiring. This means that the wires will begin to generate heat and present a fire risk. Aluminum wire should be replaced with copper or steel wire when it is found by maintenance personnel.

As buildings are rewired or newly constructed buildings are initially wired, current local codes require increased levels of protection for the wires. This can include rigid or flexible conduit or other types of shielding for safety. The more common types of wiring protection include:

- *Non-metallic sheathed cable* This is electric wiring that is sheathed or wrapped in plastic or vinyl. This is often used in residences or smaller buildings and is usually called Romex cable. Unprotected Romex is usually not permitted in larger structures.
- *Armored cable* This is wiring that is insulated and then wrapped with a steel tape. This is sometimes called flexible steel cable but more commonly referred to as BX cable.
- *Raceway* The term raceway applies to several different configurations of electrical piping or conduit. Wiring or bundles of cable are routed through this piping. The types of raceway include:
  - Rigid conduit or steel tubing running through walls, ceilings, or floors.
  - Flexible metal conduit, which is a segmented or wrapped armored sheath, sometimes coated with waterproof materials like vinyl. Such conduit is sometimes called "Greenfield" conduit.
  - Surface or floor raceways are long metal or durable plastic channels installed in ceilings, floors, or attached to the surface of walls to gather and protect bundles of wires and cables.

ELECTRIC CODES

Local counties, municipalities, and communities in the United States have developed legal standards or codes for the installation and management of electrical systems. These codes are based on the National Electric Code (NEC), which was developed and is maintained by the National Fire Prevention Association (NFPA). These codes must, as a minimum, meet the requirements established in the NEC, but they may be more stringent and, therefore, serve as the governing factor in all wiring designs and installations. They establish the minimum standards for wire size and type for specific uses, as well as the standards for circuit loading and minimum capacities for wiring systems. The NEC is updated and published every three years. Local codes are also subject to change, and electricians are required to study and be qualified in the most current published standards. All electrical repair, installation, and construction work must comply with the most recently published codes.

Buildings that were built under previously published codes do not have to be updated to meet the most current codes. Authorities will publish any mandated modifications to existing structures that are required to meet revised standards. Existing systems that are not specifically addressed do not have to be updated to meet new codes. But any new work that is done in older buildings must meet the current code standards. Further, when a building is renovated or restored, the entire structure must be updated to the new standards. Sometimes this is cost-prohibitive and can delay the modernization of existing structures.

Care must be exercised to ensure that such delays do not create an unacceptable safety hazard for building occupants.

The Occupational Safety and Health Agency (OSHA) also publishes requirements concerning the work of electric technicians. OSHA rules address both the safety of the structure and the safety of the workers operating or maintaining the electrical systems in a building. Their publications are concerned with:

- Safety of electrical systems' design and installation
- Safe work practices and procedures for workers
- Safe maintenance standards for equipment and systems
- Safe use of equipment tools and electric utilities used in completing work tasks

Using the current electrical code and approved procedures under the requirements of OSHA, the electrical systems and equipment in a building can be safely maintained. Other items that are needed to develop an effective electrical maintenance system are:

- Schematic and updated or "as-built" drawings of the electrical systems in the structure.
- Well-trained maintenance staff members who are knowledgeable of electrical procedures and safe practices.
- Electrical equipment and spaces that are clean and free of clutter to allow effective fault isolation and maintenance access.
- An effective preventive maintenance system that includes electrical systems and equipment.
- Maintenance procedures designed to ensure safe maintenance operations.

The most important safety procedure in any electrical maintenance system is called lock-out/tag-out. Many technicians and operators have been injured or killed by working on live systems. Many additional accidents have occurred because someone has activated the circuit that the electrician is working on. The only dependable system to prevent such accidents is the lock-out/tag-out system. In this system, each electrician or technician is equipped with padlocks that are used to lock circuit switches in the open or de-energized position. The technician retains the key to the lock so that no one else can close the switch to re-energize the circuit. The technician also attaches a paper tag to the switch that records when the switch was locked out and the reason for the lock-out. The tag should also indicate the name of the technician that locked-out the switch, and the time or date when the circuit will be re-energized.

In addition, an electrical maintenance system should include the following safety efforts:

- Electrical systems and spaces should be kept clean.
- Electrical spaces and equipment should be dry and well ventilated.
- Electrical equipment should be sized appropriately for the application and location of the system.
- Electrical systems should never be overloaded.
- Faults and malfunctions should be reported and corrected promptly.

- Maintenance procedures should be performed by qualified and/or certified technicians.
- Electrical spaces should never be used as storage areas for anything. This includes spare electrical parts or equipment. Materials and supplies should be kept in appropriate storage areas.

COMMON ELECTRICAL COMPONENTS

Common electrical components include such safety items as circuit breakers and fuses. Both of these items are designed to fail. Fuses are quite common in older buildings and systems. A fuse is a heat-sensitive link installed in a system to prevent dangerous overloads that could cause a circuit to overheat and cause a fire in the structure, or to pass excessive current that could damage equipment. Each fuse is designed to melt and break the circuit at a specific current level. A fuse will not permit current levels, beyond its designated capacity, to overload a circuit. These safety devices have been defeated by improper fuse management or intentional abuse. In some cases, operators have installed fuses with a capacity that exceeds the proper load for the specific circuit. This is often done when the proper fuse has failed. Instead of identifying the fault and correcting it, unqualified or untrained people will install a larger fuse to prevent the annoyance of a service interruption. Fuses have also been defeated with improper bypass wires, paper clips, coins, or other conducting materials placed in the fuse holders to complete the circuit. Oversized fuses and improper fuse bypasses result in overloaded circuits that sometimes overheat, which can damage the equipment being powered by the circuit, or even burn down the building. When a fuse fails, the problem that caused the failure must be indentified and corrected before the fuse is replaced with the correct size for the specific circuit. And fuses should never be bypassed in any circuit.

Circuit breakers serve the same purpose as fuses, with the exception that they are not burned out or destroyed while protecting the circuit or its equipment. A circuit breaker detects when current exceeds its rated capacity, and then opens or trips to remove current from the circuit. It can be reset by clicking its control switch all the way to the off position, and then returning it to the connected or on position. Before it is reset, the circuit should be inspected and whatever is causing the overload should be corrected. When the circuit breaker is reset, and if it immediately trips again, the fault still exists and further inspection and corrective action is indicated. It is more difficult to defeat a circuit breaker than to defeat a fuse, but it can be done. The control switches can be wedged into place with a piece of wood or other material to keep it from tripping, but the most common approach is to use duct tape to secure it in the closed position. When the circuit breaker cannot trip to the off position, the circuit is unprotected and the circuit can overload, overheat, and cause a fire or damage the equipment that it was supposed to protect.

The risk of electric shock in proximity to water sources is higher than in other areas. Therefore, most current electrical codes require that electrical outlets within six feet of a water source be protected with a Ground Fault Circuit Interrupter or isolator (GFCI). This includes kitchens, restrooms, utility closets, or any other area with a water source. A GFCI is a hypersensitive circuit breaker that is usually set into the outlet receptacle itself. The standard wall outlet in the United States is supplied with 20 amps of current. This level of electrical power could deliver a significant shock in surroundings of increased conductivity because of water. The GFCI reduces the maximum current that can be delivered by the outlet to only 3 amps. If an appliance requiring more current is attached to the outlet, or a short circuit should occur because of moisture, the GFCI reduces the level of potential shock from that outlet and greatly reduces the risk of injury. A GFCI outlet receptacle can be recognized by a red button on its face that is used to reset the GFCI included in the receptacle.

All circuits in a building originate with the distribution panels. Electricity comes into the building from the source through a single connection to the distribution panels. These panels then break up the single source into circuit feeders for the different circuits in the building. This is necessary to ensure that items of equipment and portions of the building are receiving the correct amount of electricity at the proper voltage and amperage for efficient operation. It also makes maintenance activities much less intrusive for building occupants, because the entire system does not have to be taken off-line to allow mainte-nance work in specific areas. Only the isolated circuits need to be de-energized for work to be done. Distribution panels do not normally require much care, but some preventive maintenance will ensure that they continue to function reliably. They sometimes develop loose connections because of the normal expansion and contraction of conductors and fastenings, which can cause overheating and fire risk. Items that should be inspected, cleaned, or adjusted include:

- Wiring connections should be checked for tightness (this is often done with infrared cameras that detect increased heat around loose connections).
- The current in each circuit should be verified to ensure proper levels for the function/ purpose for that circuit.
- Voltage levels for each circuit should be checked with the circuit operating under load.

Wiring systems should also be periodically inspected to identify developing problems. Symptoms that may indicate potential failures or safety concerns include:

- Abnormal heat levels in wires, motors, or other equipment. Normal operating tem-peratures for equipment can be found in the operation and maintenance manuals.
- Check the current flow in multiphase circuits to verify a balanced load on all legs of the circuit.

Electric motors of many varying sizes and power output are found throughout a modern building. Everything from the cooling fan in an overhead projector to HVAC equipment can include the use of an electric motor to make them function correctly. Appliances not built-in to the structure but used to care for the building or provide an operational func-tion—e.g., vacuum cleaners, floor polishers, food processors, and washing machines—all contain electric motors with specific requirements for electric power. These motors must be included in the preventive maintenance system for the building, not only to ensure that they are receiving the correct power but also to verify that they are functioning efficiently.

The intensity of this activity will vary with the size, value, and function of the particular motor. All motors should be cleaned regularly and inspected while in operation to verify such issues as operating temperature, voltage and current levels, and general condition, such as the presence of noise or vibration.

Electric motors need more initial voltage to start the turning cycle than to continue the spinning. Therefore, the system that powers an electric motor must include a motor-control device. Such a control can be manual, as seen on equipment that is equipped with a start switch as well as a run switch, or automatic. Motor controls may also be designed to respond to condition-sensing devices such as thermostats or programmable timers to vary the amount of power supplied to a motor during operation. They can start, stop, speed-up, or slow a motor to adjust its performance in response to predetermined conditions. This variable-speed capability often increases the efficiency of energy use by matching the power used to the effort required. Before the invention of variable speed-control devices, motors were often operating outside their most efficient levels, either drawing much more power than was needed or wearing out quickly because they were being taxed beyond their most efficient levels of operation. Electric motors are most efficient when operating at approximately 90 percent of their rated capacity for an established level of input energy (voltage, amperage). This level of output compared with input is called the power factor of the motor. In the past, motors were often oversized to ensure they were capable of handling maximum loads in their applied function. Unfortunately, this meant that most of them were operating well below their fixed power factor. When a motor drops below 65 percent of its power factor it begins to lose efficiency and will have a shortened serviceable life. Variable-speed motor controls prevent this situation.

Electronic equipment such as computers and other digitized or automated data processing equipment require very specific electric power sources and conditions, or quality of electric power. Power quality refers to a stable source of current at a specific voltage to avoid abnormal equipment behavior or distortion of digitized information. Most electronic equipment is equipped with internal protective devices that will sustain operation with minor variations, but major discrepancies or jumps in power will either shut down the equipment or disrupt its operation. There are several symptoms of unstable power sources, including:

- *Surges* Unexpected rises in voltage
- *Transients* Intense surges or bursts of power sometimes caused by lightning strikes or sudden changes in generation loads
- *Sags* Unexpected drops in voltage
- *Brownouts* Sustained sags that last for a noticeable period of time. Brownouts are classified as voltage drops of 5 percent or more.
- *Blackouts* Total loss of electric power for a noticeable period of time
- *Electric Noise* Presence of static or interference in electric circuits that affect the operation of electronic equipment

The sources of these power problems are unpredictable and include lightening strikes, maintenance interruptions, faulty circuits with loose connections, power generation variances, and power grid load changes. Recurring problems are often present because new electronic equipment is installed in buildings that were built prior to the equipment's introduction to the business world. The distribution systems and circuits in the older building were not designed to support such equipment, and as a result faults are revealed that were not noticed previously. One approach to preventing internal problems in the facility is to redesign and rewire the building to produce more stable or clean power. This is often cost-prohibitive. Rewiring the structure requires total service interruption for an extended period and often includes extensive demolition and reconstruction work. Such work is called the "wiring-intensive" approach to solving power quality problems. An alternative method is the "equipment-intensive" approach. This alternative requires the purchase of protective equipment such as transformers and surge-protectors that are installed between the power outlets of the building and the electronic equipment. These items are relatively inexpensive and provide clean power protection to the automated equipment and systems.

Many of the electric circuits in a property require a level of redundancy to protect the profit-making operations as well as the safety and security of the property and its occupants. Redundancy is provided by emergency power systems. The purpose of an emergency power capability is to meet minimal needs of key equipment or operations within the facility. These requirements do not usually include normal full operations for hospitality operations. Most redundant or emergency systems provide only enough electric power to allow safe evacuation of the property, protect essential data, and protect key operational assets such as frozen food during a power interruption. Some facilities require more redundancy than others. For example, a hospital requires a great deal more emergency power than a restaurant because it has many more essential or key operational circuits.

Emergency systems can be as simple as battery-powered lights to allow for safe evacuation from a building, to engine-driven generators, to Uninterruptible Power Supplies (UPS). A battery is simply stored electric power that will provide minimal power for a limited time. Most systems that incorporate battery power are connected to the regular power source through a charging system, which maintains the battery at a peak charge level and automatically switches the connected services to battery power when the regular source fails. Motor-driven generator systems also are connected to the power system through an automatic switching system. When regular power is interrupted, the motor generator must start and power its connected circuits within ten seconds, according to safety codes. Most respond faster.

With either the battery-supported or the motor-generator systems, a service interruption will produce a flicker or a break in power, and they are usually not large enough to power the entire facility and all of its operations. Therefore, they only support key emergency or operational equipment. A UPS system is designed to provide service to its dependent circuits with no flicker or loss of power when the primary power source goes off-line. It provides power from a battery for a specified period, or from a motor generator for an extended period or until the primary power source is restored. Power is provided to the UPS during normal periods from the primary system through a charger or rectifier that charges a battery bank. Power is drawn from the battery through an inverter to power the supported circuits. Because the supported circuits are powered by the battery all of the time, the powered equipment does not experience a power outage when the primary power is lost. But since it is drawing power from a battery, continued operations are limited to the life of the battery charge. A small UPS system of this type is often found in computer systems. If electrical service is interrupted, a flag box will appear on the screen, which states something like "Electrical power has been lost. You have 5 minutes to save your data and shut down this system to prevent data loss!" Larger UPS systems are often connected to an emergency motor generator through an automatic switching system. Like the smaller systems, the primary power source is providing power to a battery bank in the UPS through a charger or rectifier, and the supported circuits are receiving power from the batteries through an inverter. Because the circuits are being powered by the batteries, they do not experience any variation of power when the primary system is interrupted. But rather than being limited to the charge life of the batteries, the automatic switch in the UPS starts the motor generator and connects it to the charger to restore charging power to the batteries. Such a system is used to support such needs as those required by hospital operating rooms, where a power fluctuation could cause loss of a patient's life.

In the hospitality industry, the following systems or equipment are supported by a redundant or emergency power system:

- Safety systems such as evacuation lighting, alarm systems, fire pumps, ventilation systems, or other life-support systems
- Electronic locking systems
- Smart faucet or fixtures that control water temperatures and conserve water
- Elevators and other essential cargo or people-moving systems
- Cash registers or accounting computers
- Fuel Pumps and essential supply systems
- Refrigerated storage equipment
- Other systems that are critical elements of the property operations

Redundant or emergency electrical systems must receive regularly scheduled preventive maintenance support to ensure their reliability. Required maintenance activities include:

- Checking fluid levels in batteries and engine fluid levels for motor generators
- Testing the charge level in batteries
- Verifying proper performance of ventilation systems in emergency equipment rooms
- Cleaning and lubricating battery post connectors to prevent corrosion
- Testing motor generators under appropriate load
- Maintaining maintenance records on all equipment
- Testing of automatic switching systems

ELECTRICAL BILLING

If a property does not produce its own electricity, it will purchase needed power from a local utility company. Commercial properties normally pay a consumption charge and a demand charge when they purchase electricity. Power companies also sometimes add a rachet charge to an electric bill.

Consumption charges are reasonably straightforward. The power company meter reader records the current meter reading on a particular day. This represents the total electricity used by the property since the meter was installed. To determine consumption during the current billing period, the meter reading from the previous billing period is subtracted from the latest meter reading. The resulting difference, expressed as kilowatt hours (kWh), is the consumption for the property during the latest billing period. When this number is multiplied by the appropriate rate per kWh, and local taxes and standing service charges are added, the total is the consumption charge for the billing period. A modifying factor to this cost is the demand charge. The demand charge is based on the highest level of demand for power the property has entered during the last billing period, and is used to modify the rate per kWh. Low demand charges reduce the electric bill, and high demand charges increase the electric bill. Demand charges are established to allow electric companies to cover the cost of required generating equipment that is not needed for normal levels of electrical demand on the company power grid. Each electric company must be ready to supply maximum power for every customer property. This means that the supplier must have enough equipment available to bring on-line to support each subscriber property, with all of its electrical systems operating at maximum load with an energized appliance plugged into every outlet on the property. Further, it must have that amount of generation capability available to support all of its customers at maximum demand at the same time. Realistically, such an amount of power is seldom needed, but as the power grid load increases during an operating day, more generating equipment is added to meet the load, which in turn increases the operating costs of the electric company. To offset these additional costs, each customer property's individual demand is recorded, with their highest level used to establish their electric consumption rate for the billing period. The consumption charges and the demand charges are both determined from meter readings. The consumption meter is cumulative and continues to grow during the entire billing period, but the demand meter only records the highest level of demand reached at any time during the period. This high demand could be reached at noon on the first day and establish a higher rate for the entire remainder of the billing period.

As facilities and operations managers consider their operations and required electricity use, efforts should be made to spread use or consumption evenly through both the entire working day and the entire billing period to reduce the demand charge. Schedules can be established to ensure that all equipment is not activated simultaneously, or that power-using activities are staggered though the entire working day to reduce peak demand loads. Doing laundry at night or vacuuming hallways in the early morning rather than both occurring in the middle of a hot day, when all the air conditioners are needed, could reduce the peak demand level for a property. In addition, a technique known as peak-shaving or load-shedding could be employed. This technique involves management decisions to turn off equipment for established periods of time to reduce the overall demand for the property. For example, if a property has four air- conditioning units, a manager might elect to only run three simultaneously and establish a schedule to rotate which unit is shut down for a given period through the day to reduce overall demand. And every third, or every other, light in the hallways might be taken off-line. If sufficient light is obtained with the remaining two-third, or one-half, of the fixtures on-line, the overall load is reduced.

Some electric companies also use a charge known as the rachet clause or the leveling charge. This charge is based on the highest demand of the property over the last twelve months rather than just the most recent billing period. This prevents great deviations in billing for a property because of seasonal or operational changes. In an arid climate, a facility might use four or five times the electricity during the summer months in comparison with its winter consumption. To reduce stress on the customer and to allow a smooth revenue flow for its operations, the electric company will add a rachet charge to the low demand periods to reduce the larger consumption bills during periods of high demand. The same thing would occur in a more temperate climate but the differences might not be as extreme. The rachet or leveling charge ensures that customer properties do not default during heavy use months, by transferring some of that high-demand cost to lower-demand months.

Good managers will review their electricity consumption on a regular basis. Meter reading should not be left to the electric company. Properties can read their own meters on a regular basis to determine their own consumption and demand levels. This information can then be used to manage operations to hold consumption to efficient levels, and simultaneously to identify peak-demand problems. The load can then be scheduled and managed more effectively. Further, a daily record of meter readings can prove very helpful, as supporting material, if the electric bill for a specific billing period does not seem to coincide with the rate of consumption that the property manager expected.

DEREGULATION

As the power generation or electricity distribution industry developed, electric companies were allowed to develop monopolies in their service areas. This meant that most areas only had one electric company available, and, as such, properties could only buy power from a single source. Quite often, power consumption bills included charges to cover the cost of grid installation to supply the power. Electricity customers were being asked to pay for the wire that brought the electricity to them. As requests for a more competitive market began to be heard from consumers, governing bodies began to realize that the electric companies had been paid several times over a period of years for the distribution system, or power grid, in their area. The grids were declared to be public domain because the consumers had essentially purchased them from the power companies. Thus, they were deregulated. This meant that any power- generating company could put power onto the grid and create a competitive market.

The customer now has a choice in a deregulated locality, and can buy electric power from any supplier that can produce electricity and put it onto the power grid. This allows consumers to bargain with suppliers to obtain the most competitive price. Each supplier provides enough power to the grid to meet the needs of its own subscribers or customers. A single company no longer is forced to supply power for the entire customer base, so each company is free to reduce its rates to match the power demand for its own customers. This also has produced some reliability problems. In a deregulated area, if a single company should suffer a sag in its power output, its customers do not reduce their demand, which causes an overload not only for the sagging company but for all companies on the grid. This can cause fluctuations in grid power levels, and even total blackouts.

THE NEED FOR TECHNICAL EXPERTISE

Facilities managers are reminded that electricity is an expensive utility and must be carefully managed. Further, if electrical systems and equipment are mismanaged or improperly maintained, electricity can present a severe threat to the safety of a property and all of its occupants. Facilities managers must know when an electrical issue, concern, or problem has exceeded their own knowledge, and then to obtain assistance from qualified, certified technicians. The proper, efficient, and safe use of electricity is a management responsibility.

APPENDIX TWO

WATER SYSTEMS

Water is a basic requirement for life on Earth. People cannot survive without water, which means that the provision of water for a hospitality property is a primary utility system for the facility. Unfortunately, as water usage rates and demand for the resource have grown over the past two centuries, the supply of water that can be used by man has not increased. In fact, there are valid arguments that the amount of useable water has been reduced through waste and mismanagement. The increase in water consumption and the decreasing availability of water continues to increase the cost of water. The facilities manager must understand modern water systems and their components to reduce water wastage and conserve this precious resource while meeting the water demands and needs of his or her customers and guests.

WATER CONSUMPTION IN THE HOSPITALITY INDUSTRY

Generally, larger hospitality properties use water at a higher rate than smaller properties. Water consumption is not actually connected to size, but rather to services. Since larger properties tend to offer more services, they consume more water. The addition of laundry services, irrigated grounds, food services, swimming pools, and hot tubs all add to water consumption. When properties begin to add more recreational attractions that use water, such as fountains, ponds, displays, and water features in the landscape, consumption accelerates in its growth.

WATER SYSTEM STRUCTURE/FEATURES

Water systems have progressed immensely since the days of pitchers and basins on the bedroom dresser. Water is now used not only for drinking, cooking, and human hygiene, but also in facilities cleaning, HVAC systems, and recreational facilities. Some of the items found in plumbing systems have been used for decades, while other appliances or features are relatively new. It is important to note that the management of water consumption and active water structures is a significant factor of utility cost. In most locations, water is paid for twice—the water itself is purchased from the supplying agency, and then disposal of that same volume of water is usually paid for again in sewage fees. Cooling towers, irrigation systems, and swimming pools do not contribute to the sewage flow of a property, because the water these uses consume does not flow into sewers—it either evaporates into the air or is absorbed into the ground. The addition of a separate meter for each of these items will provide a measurement of usage that can be subtracted from sewage fees.

- *Cooling towers* An integral element of the HVAC system in most large buildings. Water is used as a medium in cooling systems to extract heat from a building. This water then expels the heat into the atmosphere by evaporation.

- *Irrigation systems* Irrigation systems use water to support landscape features on a property site. This water is absorbed into the soil of the property.

- *Swimming pools* Swimming pools, ponds, and fountains are examples of water used as entertainment. Such features do not return water to the sewage system, but do suffer some water loss through evaporation.

- *Grease traps* Cooking grease is a by-product of food service operations. If this grease is allowed to enter municipal sewers, it will congeal and eventually clog the system. Food service operations in most municipalities are required to have a grease trap installed in their waste water systems to capture grease so it can be removed without clogging the system.

- *Storm sewers* Storm sewers provide site drainage for the property. They are designed to carry rainwater and melting snow away from the building and the surrounding grounds.

- *Sanitary sewers* Sanitary sewers carry all wastewater, except rainwater, away from the property. Sanitary sewers are separate from storm sewers and prevent the over-flow of contaminated sewage onto the surface of the ground or back into the structure during periods of heavy rain.

- *Backflow preventers* When water has been distributed into a property or a system such as an irrigation sprinkler system, it may be contaminated by the condition of the piping or fixtures on that property. To prevent this contamination from flowing back into the municipal system during periods of low pressure, one-way valves, called backflow preventers, are installed between the property and the water supply system. This equipment is required for all public buildings and irrigation systems.

- *Domestic piping* Any tubes or conduit carrying water are part of the piping of the water system. Many materials have been used for piping, including lead, cast iron, steel, ceramic clay, and poly vinyl chloride (PVC). But the most popular and most widely used is copper. Copper is used because it does not react with water, and is easily bent and turned for simple installation. Unfortunately, because it also is very valuable as a recycled material, it must be protected from theft. Building sites and some existing structures have suffered significant damage from copper thieves. Cast iron is most often used in sewer systems or fire-suppression systems. It is brittle and will not sustain a large amount of stress, and it tends to put a little rust into the water, causing a yellowish color. Steel pipe is used in applications that require high-pressure water because it is stronger than copper and more malleable than cast iron. Lead pipes are not used as much as they were in previous years. Lead tends to be soft, so it is often used to vent sewer systems, or on drain lines in odd shapes. Most local codes do not permit the use of lead in water supply pipes. Ceramic tile pipe is used in buried sewer lines. Although brittle, it does not rust or rot underground and therefore has a very long life. PVC is commonly used in residential applications and occasionally in commercial structures. In the thin wall varieties, 20-40 schedule, PVC does not do well with high pressure or hot water applications. Thicker PVC, 60-80 schedule, is more durable, but the only advantage it has over copper or steel is ease of installation.

- *Insulation* Piping must be insulated. For hot water pipes, insulation retains heat and reduces the cost of heating water by reducing energy loss. In cold water pipes, insulation prevents the formation of condensation on the pipes, which often produces water damage to walls and ceilings.

- *Fire protection* Fire protection piping systems are separate from domestic water piping and include sprinkler systems, standpipes, and deluge systems. Sprinkler systems are categorized as either wet or dry. In heated buildings, wet systems are filled with water, which will be released when a sprinkler is triggered. Dry systems are filled with a pressurized inert gas that prevents water from entering the pipes until a sprinkler is triggered, releasing the pressure. The system then fills with water to suppress the fire. Dry systems are used in unheated building to prevent freezing in low temperatures. Stand pipes also come in wet and dry categories. Wet standpipes are filled with water and connected to the fire pumps in a building. They provide water outlets that allow firefighters to attach hoses and obtain water inside the building, freeing firefighters from having to pull several hundred feet of hose through a door and up the stairs of a building. The connectors are already in the building. Dry standpipes serve the same purpose but they are not actually connected to the water systems in the building. A dry standpipe has outlets available throughout the building for firefighters to connect to and an inlet located outside the building. A fire truck called a "pumper" will connect to a fire hydrant on the street outside the building, and then connect a hose to the dry standpipe inlet to pump water into the dry standpipes. This gives firefighters a source of water above the building supply capacity that is not dependent on the property fire pumps.

- *Gas traps* To prevent the invasion of sewer gases into a building, sewer drain lines are equipped with gas traps. These are simple but very important structures in the sewer system because, in addition to being odorous, sewer gases can be explosive and poisonous. Under every appliance connected to a drain line, there is a portion of the drain line that forms a pocket of water to block the invasion of sewer gases. These are most visible under a sink. They are the U-shaped sections that can be removed to retrieve small objects that have fallen into the sink. When installed correctly, they will retain water as a gas trap.

- *Sewer vents* To allow a sewer drain to flow, air must be allowed to enter the top of the system to prevent the formation of a vacuum in the system that would prevent drainage. These vents are usually found on the roof of a structure and connected to the drain systems within the building. They are installed on the roof to allow flow, and to disperse any escaping sewer gas into the atmosphere outside the building.

WATER PROBLEMS

Quality problems with water are divided into areas of potability and aesthetics. Water is considered potable if it is safe for human consumption. This means that ingestion of potable water will not make a person sick. Potable water is not necessarily clear nor does it have to taste good or be mineral free. Public safety codes require that the water in municipal supply systems be potable, and if it is not, the municipality is required to notify its residents of the problem. Occasionally, cities must put out notifications that residents should boil their tap water before using it for drinking or cooking because contamination has rendered it non-potable. If the water is safe to drink, it is potable, even if residents complain of the odor or taste of their tap water. These complaints refer to the aesthetics of water, which include odor, taste, color, clarity, mineral content, and acidity/alkalinity. Potability problems endanger your customers' health, whereas aesthetic problems offend their tastes. Both categories of problems are undesirable.

WATER HEATING

In the last century, hot running water has gone from luxury to expectation for most hospitality industry customers. In the case of health codes and standards, hot water has become a requirement for operations. There are two primary types of water heater in use today, with a few new supplemental heating sources being developed to increase energy efficiency.

- *Directly fired water heaters* Directly fired water heaters are the most common. They are made up of a tank to hold the water, and a heat source directly under or inside the tank. These water heaters are the most responsive to requirements in the immediate vicinity of their location.

- *Indirectly fired water heaters* Heaters usually found in larger buildings, and consist of a tank to hold the water and heat provided from a centralized heat source elsewhere in the building. The most common medium to carry the heat from the heat source to the water heater is steam. These water heaters are efficient because the single heat source is usually also providing heat to the building's central heating system, so the secondary use of steam to heat water is more cost-effective than directly fired water heaters.

- *Solar water heaters* Sunlight-powered or solar water heaters are becoming popular because of their reduced use of energy, but they are limited because they only heat water during daylight hours. But they can provide supplemental heating capability to other systems, and thereby reduce the overall energy use for the property.

- *Geothermal water heating* Geothermal heating systems use the first law of thermodynamics, which states: "... when a warm body and cool body come in contact, heat will be transferred from the warmer to the cooler body ..." to extract heat from the earth and use it to heat water. Such systems work very well in terms of efficiency but are not responsive to immediate demands, so they are usually employed as supplemental water heating sources to decrease energy use.

Regardless of the water-heating system used on a property, all must be properly installed and equipped with the proper safety equipment. Electric systems must be installed with appropriate circuit breakers or fusing, while natural gas or other fuel-burning systems require fire-extinguishing equipment such as deluge systems and appropriate heat or smoke alarms. All water heater tanks must be equipped with pressure-relief valves to prevent explosive ruptures, and temperatures must be thermostatically controlled for occupant safety.

Required temperature levels are not the same for all hot water applications. Domestic water heaters that support sinks, showers, and bath tubs should be set no higher than 120 degrees Fahrenheit to prevent scalding, but this is not hot enough for dishwashing or laundry. Dishes should be sanitized by rinsing them in water of 180 degrees Fahrenheit, and sheets should be sanitized with rinse water of 160 degrees Fahrenheit. This means that each of these systems should either be connected to different water heaters, or the dishwasher and the laundry should have supplemental heaters in their appliances. It is a clear safety hazard to have these three applications all working from the same water heater.

WATER SYSTEM MAINTENANCE

Water is a corrosive and reacts with the containers, equipment, and pipes that hold it in the water system. To prolong the life of equipment and pipes, and reduce the effect of corrosion or mineral deposits, water supplies are often treated with chemicals. For tap water, the chemicals used are designed to sanitize the water and remove harmful bacteria and other micro-organisms from the water supply. For water heaters or HVAC systems, the chemicals added not only kill unsafe organisms, but also remove or neutralize minerals that produce scale and deposits in pipes and heating elements. Some equipment, such as super-heated boilers, are so prone to scale formation that the minerals dissolved in their water supply must be removed by reverse osmosis or distillation.

Sacrificial anodes, made primarily of lead, are often installed in water-heating systems. These lead elements combine with minerals in the water to form nodules, or stones, that drop out of solution with the water and are deposited at the bottom of the tank instead of forming scale on the inner surfaces of pipes or on heating elements. As these anodes react with the minerals, they are destroyed, or "sacrificed," to protect the system. Sacrificial anodes should be replaced as part of the recurring preventive maintenance procedures for water heaters. In addition, over time the tanks of the water heaters will fill with the deposited nodules and will need to be replaced.

To remove foreign bodies from water supplies, most systems incorporate filters and strainers. As these appliances capture material, water flow is reduced as they become clogged. Filters and strainers should be cleaned regularly to prevent stoppages or reductions in water flow or water pressure.

Drips, seeps, or leaks in a water system represent significant loss of water and increased costs for a building. In addition, the water damage to surrounding structure components can be very costly. Leaks should be repaired as quickly as possible after they are discovered. Regular preventive maintenance inspections of water systems and appliances are essential to the early detection of leaks.

Leaks can also be prevented with proper caulking and sealing of systems and equipment in the building. Caulking keeps water out of areas that are vulnerable to water damage. It also precludes the formation of moist areas and spaces that are prone to the growth of algae, bacteria, mold, and insects.

Water supply systems should be inspected regularly as a part of the preventive maintenance program for a property, and wastewater systems must also be properly maintained. Filters, strainers, leaks, and caulking problems also occur in wastewater systems and can do significant damage to the property. Wastewater is also considered a hazardous material and should be disposed of properly by the appropriate sewer system. Some contaminants such as cooking grease and petroleum products must be separated from wastewater to prevent damage to the environment and dangerous contamination of sewer systems.

Rainwater and melting snow can cause major damage to structures, and the equipment installed to control the moisture must be maintained. Preventive maintenance programs must include activities to clean gutters, scuppers, and downspouts, ensuring that rainwater is effectively drained from structures. Clogs, debris, and leaks should be corrected immediately to prevent moisture damage to structural elements of the building. Landscaping and surrounding surfaces should be designed to provide good site draining for the property. Standing water can undermine foundations, damage pavement, and provide an inviting environment for mold, bacteria, and pestilent growth.

SWIMMING POOLS

Swimming pools have become an expected standard in hospitality facilities. They present a very visible water system maintenance problem. The pool itself presents the first level of concerns. Concrete pools should be drained every year and resurfaced or resealed to prevent cracking, and outdoor pools should be left empty during cold seasons to preclude freezing, whereas more modern vinyl pools should be left filled year-round so that they do not float out of the ground. Outdoor pools should be covered during periods when they are not used to keep trash and dirt from collecting in them, and to prevent the safety hazard of an open pool.

Local codes often require that pool areas be fenced with child-resistant latches, and that safety hooks, life-saving floats, ladders, and other safety equipment must be available and maintained in a serviceable condition. Supporting equipment such as strainers, pumps, filters, heaters, and chlorinators must be cleaned, serviced, maintained, and calibrated properly for safe and efficient operation.

Swimming pools must be cleaned daily for safe and healthy use by swimmers. The water must be skimmed to remove trash and blown-in debris from the surface. If this is not done, the filters and strainers will become clogged. The bottom of the pool must be vacuumed to remove settled or sunken debris and foreign objects that not only affect the cleanliness of the water, but can also present injury threats to bathers. Pool sides must be brushed and scrubbed to remove dirt and lime that has built up from surface evaporation of water in the pool, and to remove any algae or mold colonies before they can grow into a problem.

Swimming pool water that is properly maintained provides an inviting, refreshing, and healthy recreation asset for guests if properly treated and cleaned, but it can also present a significant health hazard if neglected. The water must be treated with chlorine or bromine to prevent bacterial infestation, and algaecides must be added to keep the water crystal clear and prevent skin infection and eye irritation for swimmers. Acidity and alkalinity tests should be conducted daily to ensure that proper levels are maintained. The acidity of the water should be maintained between pH 7.2 and 7.6.

A properly maintained pool is a great asset, but this particular water feature also presents a great threat to customer satisfaction if it is neglected.

WATER CONSERVATION

With increasing consumption rates and reduced availability of water, the cost of water is rising every day. Government regulations on water use also add to the value of water by further limiting availability for particular uses, and penalizing property owners for wasteful consumption. In ethical terms, establishments also have a social responsibility to reduce water waste to ensure sufficient supplies for future generations. Hospitality properties must develop water conservation techniques and strategies to reduce water use through conservation of this essential resource.

Engineers and environmentalists are working very hard to find approaches to conserve water. Many devices and appliances are available to the facilities manager as a result of those efforts. Such advances as low-flow fixtures, reduced water laundry systems, timed irrigation systems, and foot-operated hand-washing sinks can all contribute to conservation efforts. But the most effective approach is management interest coupled with an active preventive maintenance system. Detecting and correcting problems while training employees to use water resources efficiently is the responsibility of the facilities manager.

APPENDIX THREE

HEATING

The purpose of heating, ventilation, and air conditioning (HVAC) is to provide a comfortable environment for building occupants. Heating is the most basic element of an HVAC system. To efficiently manage heating equipment and appliances, the facilities manager must understand the basic nature of heat. Heat is the radiant energy that is expelled by substances based on the activity and movement of their molecules. As energy is injected into something, the molecules become agitated and begin to rub and bounce off of each other. This movement produces heat because of the friction between the molecules. As the movement subsides, the material begins to cool and radiates less energy.

FACTORS THAT INFLUENCE HEAT AND COMFORT

The presence or absence of radiant energy heat has a direct effect on the comfort of building occupants. Heat and its relationship to human comfort involves several factors:

- *Sensible heat* Heat that a human being can feel. It is measured with a thermometer, and is also called dry-bulb heat. Sensible heat does not acknowledge any effect of humidity.

- *Dry bulb temperature* Dry-bulb temperature is what most people think of as the temperature. It is read directly from a dry thermometer.

- *Wet bulb temperature* The measured temperature from a thermometer with the bulb covered with a damp cloth. It indicates the effect of relative humidity on human comfort. The temperature reading of a wet bulb will be lower because of the cooling effect of evaporation from the damp cloth on the thermometer. If the relative humidity is high, then less evaporation will occur. This indicates that less cooling or comfort can be obtained by the evaporation of perspiration from human skin.

- *Wet bulb depression* Reflects the number of degrees difference between a dry-bulb temperature and a wet-bulb temperature. The wet-bulb reading has depressed the dry-bulb temperature by the value of the wet-bulb depression.

- *Relative humidity* A percentage comparison of the amount of moisture suspended in the air in comparison to the maximum amount of moisture that could be held at a given temperature. Warmer air can hold a greater amount of moisture than cooler air. But at any specified temperature, the amount that is actually suspended compared to the maximum capacity at that temperature is the measured relative humidity. When the maximum amount of moisture that can be held by the air is reached, the air is considered saturated with moisture.

- *Dew point* The temperature at which air exceeds saturation and can no longer hold moisture. The moisture will begin to condense out of the atmosphere. As saturated warm air is cooled to its dew point, moisture condenses out of the air.

- *Evaporation* A cooling process. When a material evaporates it releases moisture into the atmosphere, and the molecules of moisture that evaporate into the air take molecular energy with them. This removes heat energy from the surface of the evaporating material. The cooling effect of perspiration is a result of evaporation.

- *Convection* A cooling process caused by the movement of air across a surface. The movement removes heat and encourages surface evaporation. Thus, a breeze can produce a cooling effect on a warm day with no change in temperature.

- *Latent heat* Sensible heat with the added effect of relative humidity. It is measured by the wet-bulb temperature to produce wet-bulb depression. This indicates the amount of cooling that is felt by the evaporation of perspiration. Hence, the old saying: "... I don't mind the heat. It's the humidity that I don't like."

- *Radiant heat* The transfer of heat energy from one body to another. Direct contact transfers radiant heat by conduction, but radiant heat can also be projected or radiated from a warmer body to a cooler body through the air. Heat is energy or molecular movement, and cool is the absence of energy or molecular movement. The first law of thermodynamics states that energy can be transferred, but the absence of energy cannot. In simple words, the first law of thermodynamics states: "When two bodies come in contact, heat will be passed from the warmer body to the cooler body."

HEATING LOADS

Any activity, process, or object that reduces sensible heat is considered an element of heating load. As the heating load increases, it reduces the latent heat of the building and eventually produces sensible heat levels below the comfort level of occupants. It is the function of the heating system in the building to counteract the effect of the heating loads and keep the building occupants comfortable. Any actions than can be taken to reduce heating loads will increase the efficiency of the heating system.

- *Internal heating loads* There are not many internal heating loads inside a building. Very few appliances or objects normally found in buildings actually absorb heat energy to increase the heating load. If cooling equipment, such as a refrigerator or freezer, were left open the heating load would increase over time. In some food service operations, thawing activities for frozen food items may increase the heating load for the food preparation areas.

- *External heating loads* The primary heating load for a structure comes from outside the building. Outside temperatures during cooler seasons of the year will extract heat from the building, increasing the heating load. This is further affected by the relative humidity of the outside air. The roof and walls of the building must be insulated to reduce the heat loss, and windows should be double- or triple-glazed to reduce heat loss by radiation to the cooler external environment.

- *Infiltration* The actual transfer of heated air from inside the building, and cooler air from outside the building, will also add to the heating load. This infiltration of air will occur through any unsealed opening in the building envelope. The opening of a door or window will increase infiltration and heat loss. Revolving doors, double-layer entrance doors, and sealed windows will contribute to heating efficiency by limiting or eliminating infiltration. With a revolving door, the interior of the building is never actually opened to the outside environment. Double-layer entrances require two sets of doors far enough apart so that the inside door and the outside door are never open at the same time. This creates an insulating area of dead air in the entrance way that reduces infiltration. In a similar fashion, well-sealed windows will assist in the prevention of infiltration and increase the efficiency of the heating systems.

HEATING SYSTEMS

There are several heating systems in common use in hospitality facilities, but most will include the distribution of heat from either a furnace or a boiler. Furnaces are used in small properties or small areas of a property. A furnace is any device that uses a heat source to heat air directly. The heated air is then distributed through the facility by fans and ductwork. Unfortunately, air does not retain heat well and cools rapidly even in insulated ductwork. This means that the heated air cannot be projected any great distance before it loses its heat. About 75 feet is the distribution limit for heated air. After 75 feet, the air returns to its original temperature. Large buildings would require a great number of furnaces spaced throughout the building to produce the desired results

Boilers heat another medium to carry heat into a building. Boilers heat water to produce hot water or steam that can be distributed through the structure. Because water retains heat much more efficiently than air, it can be pumped a greater distance and still retain its heat. Boilers provide a much more efficient way to provide heat to a large building. The hot water or steam is pumped throughout the building to radiators or heating coils where the heat is introduced into building spaces by blowing air through the coils with fans. The water or steam, in the form of condensation or water, is then returned to the boiler to be reheated. Larger coil and fan assemblies are called air handlers and serve large areas of buildings, thereby increasing efficiency by reducing the number of distribution fans using electricity.

The primary difference between heating appliances is their heat source. Several different sources can be used to heat either a furnace or a boiler:

- *Electricity* Electric resistance heating units are probably the most versatile sources of heat, because they can be used anywhere that wires can be strung to carry the current. Therefore, they do not require piping or fuel-storage equipment and installation is relatively easy. Electric resistance, however, is the most inefficient use of energy to produce heat. It uses a great deal of energy to produce relatively small quantities of heat. This makes it useful for small units in remote locations, but very expensive when used to heat large areas.

- *Natural Gas* A very good source of heat and does not produce much pollution when it burns. It is also relatively inexpensive when compared with other heat sources. Therefore, it is a very popular and used in many areas. Installation requires more work than electricity because of the requirement to install a pipe to carry natural gas into the building. It also produces some increased safety risk because the gas itself is a suffocant and also flammable, so it must be carefully controlled and contained to prevent leaks within the building.

- *Liquefied petroleum gas (LPG)* A flammable gas gathered in oil refineries as a by-product of the refining process. It most often is marketed as butane or propane. It provides many of the benefits of natural gas such as being relatively clean burning and providing excellent heat production, but it also is a suffocant and very flammable, so it produces the same safety risk. LPG is usually distributed as a packaged or bottled product for small quantities or delivered by truck to an on-site storage tank. It most often is used in properties that want the efficiency of gas but are remotely located from a natural gas supply line.

- *Heating fuel oil* Smaller properties in areas remote from natural gas supplies often use heating fuel oil as their heat source. It is an efficient source of heat but requires more effort to deliver and manage on-site. It is delivered by oil-transport vehicles to on-site storage equipment. This equipment is not as complicated as that required for LPG, because fuel oil is not pressurized. It is, however, much more difficult to handle because of the risk of contamination if it is spilled or leaks. It is generally considered a dirty fuel system. Because of the large volume of fuel that would be needed for on-site storage, very few large properties use heating fuel oil.

- *Steam* In some cities, steam can be purchased from a central steam plant in the same manner as electricity or natural gas. This steam is then distributed through the building and the condensation is returned to the central system for reheating. If this is available, purchased steam is a very popular heat source for large buildings. It removes the requirement for building owners to maintain and support their own furnace or boiler. This reduces overhead cost, and also removes from the property fire and safety risks that are generated by internal heat sources.

DECENTRALIZED HEATING

Any building that has individual heating units for separate rooms is a decentralized system. The decision on installing a centralized or decentralized heating system is usually made during the initial design of the building prior to construction. In a decentralized system, the decision is usually driven by initial construction costs. Decentralized systems are much less expensive to install and design. They do not require large amounts of ducting and control wiring nor do they take a great deal of specialized training to install and operate. Each unit provides locally controlled service to a very limited area. This gives occupants the ability to adjust their individual area to their own comfort levels. It also allows them to forget to turn their units off when they are not needed, providing an opportunity to waste energy. Replacement of decentralized units is much easier because they are simply disconnected from the required utilities—usually electricity—then removed and replaced with a new unit, and reconnected. Decentralized systems allow for less initial capital investment, but do not have as long an anticipated service life as centralized units. As such, they will be replaced more often.

The package terminal air conditioning (PTAC) that is often found under the windows of hotel rooms is an example of decentralized heating systems. These units are completely self-contained with both heating and cooling systems installed in the same unit. They are usually powered entirely with electricity, making them very simple to remove and replace. The initial cost is low, and when the hotel is not full some savings in energy use may be realized if the units in unoccupied rooms are turned off. But when all rooms are in service, the energy use will be relatively high. Larger PTAC units are used in many buildings where the initial construction cost is of higher priority than the expected system life or efficient energy use. The final advantage of PTAC units is that they do not need to be maintained by specifically trained and licensed operators.

CENTRALIZED HEATING

Centralized heating systems use boilers to heat water or produce steam that is then piped through the building to distribute heat to the occupants. Older buildings are often heated by steam boilers, sending steam through a series of valves and pipes to radiators in the occupied spaces. Most new buildings use hot water as the medium to distribute heat. Steam is very effective, but also very hard to control, because the only real control is a valve to limit the amount of steam passing through the radiator. This has very limited effect and the result is that the occupant must choose between on and hot, or off and cold. Steam is also a high-pressure system and presents a higher safety risk to the building from explosions and steam leaks. Hot water boilers can be adjusted to produce varying temperature levels of water, and also provide more flexibility to the comfort settings for the occupants. A hot water-heating system sends the hot water through baseboard heating coils or fan coils in the occupied spaces. The fan coils are more common in large buildings. These coils allow the hot water to pass through a grid of small tubes and a fan blows air across or through the grid. This heated air is injected into the occupied space. This type of heating provides more flexibility to the occupant, who can use valves to adjust the rate of water flow or allow a thermostat to adjust the speed of the fan and alter the volume of air being heated. Further, because the hot water is not under the increased pressure of steam, it is less likely to leak or rupture a pipe or coil.

Steam and hot water-heating systems can also be incorporated into large areas using air handlers. An air handler is a large fan assembly that blows air through a heating coil and then distributes it through areas of the building, using ductwork to heat occupied areas. The heated air is introduced to the space, and return ducts remove air from the space and carry it back to the air handler for reheating. Some of these units are very large, with most constructed on site to fit the design of the building. Air handlers can provide conditioned air to large areas of a building, and they can be combined with a cooling system to use a hot coil and a cold coil to maximize the flexibility of the system in maintaining occupant comfort.

- *Two-pipe systems* Air handlers can be equipped with a single coil, making them a two- pipe system. In a two-pipe system, there is a supply pipe to bring steam or hot water from the boiler to the coil in the air handler, and a return pipe to take the cooled water or condensed steam back from the coil to the boiler for reheating. This is a very effective system, but in the same manner as the radiator, it is either hot or cold and provides very little adjustment capability for occupant comfort.

- *Three-pipe systems* A second variation of the air handler is the three-pipe system. In this air handler there are two supply pipes connected to the coil. One comes from the boiler to supply hot water, and the second comes from a chiller to supply cold water. The coil has a third pipe that returns the mixed water to the heating and cooling plant, where it is separated to be reheated and recooled. By adjusting the flow on either the hot or the cold supply pipe, the temperature of the mixed water in the coil can be controlled. This gives the occupant the flexibility to control the room temperature to keep it within the comfort level. But because the mixed water is returned to the boiler and the chiller by the common return line, they will need to work much harder to bring the water back up to, or back down to, the required supply temperatures. This has a significant influence on energy use and reduces the efficiency of the operation.

- *Four-pipe systems* This is an air handler that comes with two coils, also known as decks. The hot deck has a supply pipe from the boiler providing either steam or hot water, and the cold deck has a second supply line from a chiller providing cold water. Each deck has its own return line that sends the water back to the boiler or chiller without allowing it to mix. In between the two decks is a variable air vane that responds to the temperature setting on a thermostat, adjusting the volume of air being passed through each deck. This allows the air to be mixed to a specific temperature and provides flexibility to the occupant to adjust the air temperature within the appropriate comfort zone. The water never mixes so the return water does not require as much energy to reheat or recool as the three-pipe system. With the reduced energy use, the efficiency of the four-pipe system is greatly improved.

- *Control systems* Heating systems are controlled by thermostats. A thermostat is a control device that senses the temperature in a controlled space and provides instruction to the heating system to return the temperature to the comfort zone. There are two common thermostat types in use. The mechanical thermostat uses a bimetal strip to open and close an electrical contact. A bimetal strip is constructed of two strips of two different metals that are laminated together. The two metals contract and expand at different rates in response to the surrounding temperature, causing the composite strip to bend toward or away from a fixed contact. A variation of this design has a sealed glass tube mounted on the strip. In the glass tube there is a drop of mercury, which is a metal that is a liquid at room temperature. In one end of the glass tube are two electrodes connected to an electric circuit. As the bimetal tube bends or straightens, the mercury either rolls down to cover the electrodes and close the circuit, or rolls away from the electrodes to open the circuit.

The second type of thermostat is a digital thermostat. Within the digital thermostat is a device called a thermistor, which produces an electrical charge as the surrounding temperature rises. This electrical charge activates the off/on circuit of the heating system. The advantage of the digital thermostat is that it can be programmed to react to varying temperature levels for different time periods. A programmable digital thermostat allows a system to be programmed to change comfort settings according to operating hours, hours of darkness, or time of day, producing much more efficient energy use for the heating system.

HEATING SYSTEM ISSUES

There are two major concerns with heating systems. The one that is most often discussed is the efficiency of the system. This is the ratio of energy required to heat that is produced by the system. Efficiency is increased with less energy consumed, producing more comfort for occupants per dollar of energy expense. Energy prices have been rising for all heat sources in recent years, and there is no reason to think that this trend will stop in the future. Therefore, engineers and facilities managers continue to search for systems that operate at the highest possible level of efficiency.

The second major concern with heating systems is safety. Every heating system projects increased safety risk into a building. The first concern is fire risk, because of the presence of an artificial heat source. Electrical heating systems must be protected by circuit breakers or fuses, and flame-related heat sources must be guarded by smoke detectors and fire-extinguishing systems. They also require ventilation for the safe dispersion of poisonous exhaust gases and fumes. Heating systems using steam or water as a distribution medium require the installation of pressure-relief valves to prevent explosions. All heating systems must be installed by certified technicians who are well trained in the safe installation and operation of the specific equipment being used. Also, all building heating systems must be operated by trained personnel who understand the dangers involved and the correct procedures for their use. In some cases, such as steam boilers, the operator must be certified and licensed by appropriate agencies to safely operate the system.

All heating systems must be maintained in accordance with the manufacturer's specifications and instructions, and safety code requirements. The application of formal preventive maintenance systems and schedules is essential to ensure efficient and safe operation of these systems. They must be cleaned and serviced properly to provide a safe and comfortable environment for building occupants.

IMPROVING HEATING EFFICIENCY

There are several measures available to facilities managers to improve the efficient operation of heating systems. The following possibilities allow for the improvement of a profitable operation with reduced energy costs, but without comfort loss for building occupants.

- *Insulation* Installing insulation into roofs and walls will reduce heat transfer from the building to the outside environment, and reduce heating requirements.

- *Sealing/weather stripping* Closing leaks around windows, doors, and other penetrations through walls will reduce heat loss to the outside of the building.

- *Door closers* Automatic door closers will reduce heat transfer through external doors being left open.

- *Double-barrier doors* Two banks of doors for entrances will reduce heat loss if they are far enough apart to prevent unobstructed openings in the building envelope. If both doors cannot be opened at the same time, an airlock of dead air stops the loss of heat to the outside environment.

- *Revolving doors* Properly designed and installed revolving doors allow access to the building, but never actually present an unobstructed breach in the building envelope, thereby preventing heat loss from the building.

- *Window glazing* Double- and triple-glazing in windows create layers of dead air that restrict the loss of radiant energy through the window. They do not obstruct the passage of light or reduce visibility, but energy savings are realized with the reduced energy transfer to the outside environment.

- *Ceiling fans* Ceiling fans can improve comfort for occupants by creating a more even distribution of heat with air movement. The increased comfort reduces the demand for additional heating and reduces energy use.

- *Programmable thermostats* Automatic adjustments of heating demands for periods of reduced requirements, such as times of low occupancy, can have a very beneficial effect on energy use.

HEATING ■ 199

- *Solar exposure* Careful design of buildings to take advantage of sunlight to support heating needs can supplement heating requirements and reduce energy use.

- *Solar systems* Heating systems using solar energy to heat water can provide a medium to save and distribute solar heat through a structure. These systems will not usually meet all the heating needs of a large building, but they can reduce energy requirements to maintain comfort zones.

SUMMARY

The only purpose of a heating system is to provide an environment that meets the needs of human comfort. The two main concerns in any heating system are efficiency and safety. The facilities manager is responsible for ensuring that the needs are met and safety is protected with appropriate heating systems that are properly installed, operated, and maintained.

APPENDIX FOUR
COOLING

The purpose of heating, ventilation, and air conditioning (HVAC) is to provide a comfortable environment for building occupants. Cooling is a major concern for an HVAC system. The concept of cold or cool is generally misunderstood. The problem is that people have a sensation of feeling cold, which is in reality the result of heat being extracted from their bodies. Where heat is the radiant energy that is expelled by substances based on the activity and movement of their molecules, cooling is the reduction of molecular activity or the absence of heat. Heat energy can be induced or injected into a material but cold cannot. Cold is produced by the extraction of heat. As energy is extracted, the molecules slow down and molecular friction is reduced. Because of the first law of thermodynamics—which states that when two bodies are in contact, heat will move from the warmer body to the cooler body—the molecular activity of a body is gradually reduced until the body becomes colder than the environment around it. At that point the body ceases to radiate heat and begins to absorb heat from the environment. This simple principle is the key to understanding cooling systems used in modern buildings.

FACTORS THAT INFLUENCE COOLING AND COMFORT

The normal temperature of the human body averages 98.6 degrees Fahrenheit. This heat is maintained by a metabolism based on exothermic processes. Simply stated, the human body generates heat. Therefore, because we are subject to the requirements of the first law of thermodynamics just like any other substance, we radiate heat into our environment. The human body is comfortable when the heat that is being generated is radiated into the environment at a balanced rate to maintain our normal body temperature. When the environment is extracting heat from our body faster than we can generate it, we feel cold. Conversely, if the environment is warm enough that it does not accept the amount of heat that we generate, we start to overheat and feel uncomfortably hot. At that point, our bodies begin to perspire. Because we need to lose heat faster, the perspiration evaporating from our skin will increase the amount of energy that we lose to the environment as our bodies try to achieve that comfortable point at which we are losing heat at the balanced level that will maintain our body temperature.

Relative humidity is also a comfort factor. The term "relative humidity" refers to the percentage of water suspended in the air in comparison to the maximum amount that can be suspended. When relative humidity reaches 100 percent, the air is said to be saturated and cannot suspend any more moisture. Warmer air can hold more moisture than cooler air, so if the temperature of saturated air is lowered, water will begin to condense out of the atmosphere. The temperature at which this happens is called the dew point. If the temperature of saturated air is raised, its relative humidity is reduced and it can absorb more moisture. Relative humidity relates to human comfort by affecting the ability of perspiration to evaporate from the skin. As the relative humidity increases, less perspiration will evaporate and therefore the cooling effect is reduced. This is often expressed in the cliché, "It is not the heat that bothers me—it is the humidity."

Modern cooling systems maintain human comfort by ensuring that the environment of the building interior will accept the heat radiated by the bodies of the occupants at a balanced rate. In the process of reducing the temperature of the environment, they also reduce the relative humidity in the building. Both must be controlled. Systems that only cool the air produce a damp environment as moisture is released from the air, therefore the moisture must be extracted as well.

The capacity of cooling systems is measured in tons of cooling power. One ton of cooling power is defined as the amount of energy needed to melt one ton of ice in a twenty-four hour period. Most residential cooling systems are less than five tons in capacity but in commercial buildings it is not unusual to have cooling systems producing hundreds or thousands of tons of cooling capacity. These systems are actually extracting heat from the building. That heat is then expelled outside the building. In large buildings this heat is released into the atmosphere by the evaporation of water in large cooling towers, while smaller structures use direct-exchange systems that expel heat into the outside air by radiation.

COOLING LOAD

Any activity, process, or object that introduces or increases heat in a building is considered an element of cooling load. As the cooling load increases, it increases the latent heat of the building and will reduce the ability of occupants to radiate heat to their environment. Occupants will become uncomfortably warm. Any actions than can be taken to reduce cooling loads will increase the efficiency of the cooling system.

- Internal Cooling Loads. There are many internal cooling load sources inside a building. Most appliances or objects normally found in buildings produce heat energy that adds to the cooling load. Even cooling appliances such as refrigerators or freezers are radiating heat into the interior of the building that they have extracted from their own interiors. Light fixtures and data processing equipment radiate heat and are simultaneously very sensitive to overheating if the environment cannot accept the heat they give off. Every person in a building is actually a 98.6-degree heat source that is radiating heat for which the cooling system must compensate.

- External Heating Loads. Outside temperatures during warmer seasons of the year will inject heat into the building increasing the cooling load. The roof and walls of the building must be insulated to reduce the introduction of exterior heat energy and windows should be double or triple glazed to reduce heat gain by radiation to the cooler internal environment. Sunlight that is allowed into the building to reduce the need for artificial lighting increases the heat gain and cooling loads. The use of window curtains or blinds can reduce solar heat gain.

- Infiltration. The actual transfer of heated air from outside the building and cooler air from inside the building will also add to the cooling load. This infiltration of air will occur through any unsealed opening in the building envelope. The opening of a door or window will increase infiltration and heat gain. Revolving doors, double-layer entrance doors, and sealed windows will contribute to cooling efficiency by limiting infiltration. With a revolving door, the interior of the building is never actually opened to the outside environment. Double-layer entrances require two sets of doors far enough apart so that the inside door and the outside door are never open at the same time. This creates an insulating area of dead air in the entrance way that reduces infiltration. In a similar fashion, well-sealed windows will assist in the prevention of infiltration and increase the efficiency of the cooling systems.

THE REFRIGERATION CYCLE

Most modern buildings use refrigerated air to offset the effect of the cooling load. The refrigeration cycle is dependent on two very simple laws of physics, with the first being the first law of thermodynamics. The second is Boyle's law, which states, "At a constant temperature, the volume of a gas is inversely proportional to the pressure upon it." In simple terms, this means that a gas can be compressed into a smaller volume. The only other element that is needed for a refrigeration system to work is a medium to carry heat from one location to another. This is the refrigerant. Modern refrigerants are hydrofluorocarbons with a relatively low boiling point. The boiling point of a substance is the temperature at which it transforms from a liquid to a vapor or gas. Most modern refrigerants make this change at approximately 54 degrees Fahrenheit.

There are four required components of equipment in a refrigeration system:

- The *evaporator* absorbs heat inside the cooled area or compartment.

- The *compressor* reduces the refrigerant in a gaseous state into a smaller volume forcing it to become a liquid.

- The *condenser* exhausts heat outside the cooled area or compartment.

- The *expansion valve* allows the compressed liquid refrigerant to return to a gaseous state.

The basic operation of a refrigeration system is very simple. Refrigerant in a gaseous state in the evaporator is approximately 54 degrees Fahrenheit. If air of a higher temperature is blown across the evaporator, the first law of thermodynamics requires that the lower temperature refrigerant will extract heat from the air. The refrigerant is then sucked out of the evaporator by the compressor, which uses the principles of Boyle's law to compress

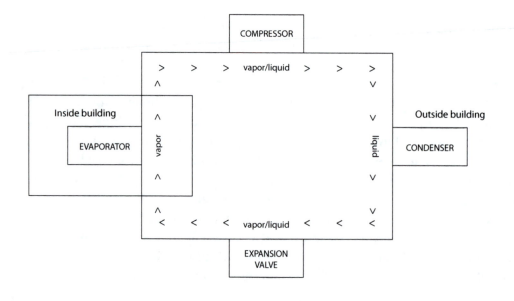

> = Refrigerant flow

Figure 4.1 Refrigeration cycle

the refrigerant into a liquid. With the additional heat energy that was extracted from the air inside the cooled space, the compressed refrigerant increases in heat and is transferred to the condenser outside of the cooled space. Because it has been compressed, the refrigerant inside the condenser is warmer than the air outside the cooled space and the first law of thermodynamics causes the outside air to absorb some of the heat that was captured by the refrigerant. The lower-temperature liquid refrigerant then moves to the expansion valve, which allows it to expand in volume and return to a gaseous state. In its original form as a gas, the gaseous refrigerant goes back to the starting temperature of approximately 54 degrees. It then moves into the evaporator inside the cooled space to extract more heat from the air and the cycle starts again. The refrigeration cycle will continue to remove heat from the interior of the cooled space and eject it to the exterior, as long as the refrigerant in the evaporator is a lower temperature than the air inside the cooled space and the refrigerant in the condenser is a higher temperature than the air outside the cooled space.

DECENTRALIZED SYSTEMS

Decentralized cooling units are very popular in milder climates because of their ease of installation and maintenance. They are also known as package thermal air conditioning units (PTAC) because the unit is complete as a single appliance. The decentralized cooling unit is installed on an outside wall of a room with the evaporator and condenser back to back. The evaporator is inside the room and the condenser is outside the room. Because the cooling unit extracts air from the space directly and transfers that heat to the outside air, it is also known as a direct exchange (DX) system. Decentralized units are very easily unplugged and replaced if they do not operate effectively. They also provide some advantage for periods of reduced occupancy because they may be turned off in empty rooms to reduce energy consumption. Unfortunately, the opposite is true during high occupancy. Because there are so many units operating in the building at the same time, they use much more energy than a centralized system.

CENTRALIZED CHILLED-WATER SYSTEMS

A direct exchange (DX) system can also be employed in a centralized configuration. The evaporator and the condenser do not have to be installed in the same location, as they are in a packaged thermal air conditioning Unit (PTAC). When the evaporator and the condenser are separated, the cooling system is called a split system. The split system is a common arrangement in many modern residences and small buildings. The evaporator is installed in a central location supporting the cooled spaces through a ductwork system. The condenser is located outside the structure and connected to the evaporator through extended refrigerant lines. Small capacity split systems are often used for single-residence structures, but they can also be large enough to support other structures. DX systems are limited in their application to really large properties because air does not retain temperature for very long, so split DX systems for larger buildings require multiple evaporator units connected to multiple condensers to cover large areas.

In large buildings or properties, the cool-air temperature-retention problem is resolved through the use of chilled water as a medium to extract heat from large areas at longer distances from the evaporator. Large centralized refrigeration units are called chillers. The evaporator in a chiller is used to cool water that is pumped to coils located throughout the structure. These chilled-water coils extract heat from the building spaces and the warmed water is returned to the chiller where the heat is removed by the evaporator. The heat that the evaporator removes from the chilled water is transferred to the condenser. The condenser is located in a container of water that accepts the transferred heat. This condenser water then moves to a cooling tower where the heat is expelled into the atmosphere by evaporation. The cooled condenser water is supplemented with make-up water, to replace evaporation losses, and returns to the chiller unit to extract more heat from the condenser. Using water as the medium, these systems can be very large, with capacities in thousands of tons of cooling power. They can also service cooled spaces at great distances from the chiller units. Some units supporting large groups of buildings from a central plant have chillers with a capacity of 6,000 to 7,000 tons or more and are located miles from their supported buildings. In some cities, central chilled water plants sell chilled water to buildings as a utility service similar to natural gas or electricity providers.

Large centralized units can provide cooling support to large buildings or a large number of buildings with significantly less energy expenditure than decentralized units. They are expensive to construct and install and require more maintenance than decentralized systems. Both decentralized and centralized systems require basic maintenance activities such as cleaning of coils and drain lines and repair of refrigerant leaks. However, large centralized units often require the attention of a licensed or certified technician. Because they are large pieces of machinery, using large amounts of refrigerant and extensive duct, piping, and control systems, they must be maintained correctly to ensure safe and efficient operation. Further, with their size and complexity, they cannot be simply unplugged and replaced in the way that a decentralized unit may be. They must be cared for with a carefully managed preventive maintenance program to ensure efficient operation. If discrepancies or faults are not repaired correctly, they present a significant safety hazard to building occupants and the structure of the building itself.

The care of drip pans and drain lines is of specific interest. Evaporators drip condensation that they remove from the cooled air into drip pans that are connected to drain lines to carry this moisture outside the building. If the drain lines become clogged, then the water that collects in the drip pan will stagnate and present a favorable environment for the growth of mold and bacteria. In humid climates the drip pans may even overflow and leak water onto the surrounding structure of the building. The water represents a potential for physical damage to the building and any mold or bacterial growth creates a potential respiratory health hazard. Drip pans and drain lines should be regularly inspected and maintained and the drip pans should be chemically treated to prevent mold growth.

CAPITAL BUDGETING ISSUES

The initial decision between using decentralized or centralized systems involves the cost of construction in consideration of the long term business plan of the property. Decentralized systems have lower construction and installation costs, but they also represent a shorter potential serviceable life time. Therefore, the repetitive replacement costs for decentralized equipment must be considered for the planned life of the property. The centralized systems are much more expensive to install so initial construction costs are much higher, but they have a much longer serviceable life if they are properly maintained. When customer satisfaction is considered, the decentralized system allows the guest to control the conditions in their individual room whereas the centralized system limits this capability. Even separate thermostats in each room do not give complete control to the occupant. Decentralized units are also noisy and do not produce even temperature distribution through the entire room. Centralized systems are quieter for the guest and the room is usually uniform in temperature without drafts or apparent air movement. These factors must be considered in the initial design process for the property.

In the centralized system, equipment size is a significant factor in system design. A property cooling requirement is usually developed based on the square footage of cooled space in the building. This number is expressed as a requirement of a number of tons of cooling requirement. For example, a building might be designed to require two hundred tons of cooling. With this information it would seem that installing a chiller with 200 tons of capacity would be the perfect fit but this is an error. If a two-hundred-ton unit were installed, it would be operating at maximum output 100 percent of the time. This is very similar to driving an automobile at maximum speed in that the car can perform at maximum output, but the miles per gallon or efficiency of fuel usage would be drastically lowered. Similarly, most cooling units operate most efficiently at around 80 percent of potential output. Instead of installing a two-hundred-ton unit, greater efficiency can be achieved by installing two separate one-hundred-fifty-ton units that operate at approximately 80 percent of their potential. Less energy will be used and the equipment will have a longer serviceable life.

Capital funding must also be considered in the replacement of cooling equipment. The centralized systems are complex and include piping and duct work throughout the building. The replacement of these systems is very expensive and may even require total restoration of the entire building. This may mean that the entire property must be shut down to allow the work to be completed, which eliminates all revenue flow. In some cases, the cost is so high and/or the amount of work is so extensive, the central cooling system cannot be economically replaced. The replacement of decentralized units is much easier and less costly. The unit affects only one room or area of the building so the entire operation is not interrupted and the unit can be very quickly removed and replaced with another unit usually in a matter of hours. The replacement of a single decentralized unit does not normally represent a large capital investment. If several units are replaced, the work can be phased over a scheduled operation that stops service only in small areas of the property at one time. This also allows for a scheduled expenditure of capital funds over the same period, which is often more manageable than the enormous cost of replacing a centralized system.

ENERGY CONSERVATION

Cooling systems require energy to drive the refrigeration units, but several measures are available to facilities managers to reduce the amount of energy used by cooling systems. The following possibilities will allow the improvement of profitable operation with reduced energy costs, without comfort loss for building occupants.

- *Insulation.* Installing insulation into roofs and walls will reduce heat transfer from the outside environment to the interior of the building and reduce the cooling load.

- *Sealing/Weather Stripping.* Closing leaks around windows, doors, and other penetrations through walls will reduce heat infiltration into the building.

- *Door Closers.* Automatic door closers will reduce heat infiltration through external doors.

- *Double Barrier Doors.* Two banks of doors for entrances will reduce heat infiltration if they are far enough apart to prevent unobstructed openings in the building envelope. If both doors cannot be opened at the same time, an airlock of dead air stops the infiltration of heat from the outside environment.

- *Revolving Doors.* Properly designed and installed revolving doors allow access to the building, but never actually present an unobstructed breach in the building envelope, preventing heat infiltration into the building.

- *Window Glazing.* Double and triple glazing in windows creates layers of dead air that restrict the transfer of radiant energy through the window. They do not obstruct the passage of light or reduce visibility, but energy savings are realized with the reduced cooling load caused by heat gain coming from outside the building.

- *Ceiling Fans*. Ceiling fans can improve comfort for occupants by creating a more even distribution of air. The increased comfort reduces the demand for additional cooling and reduces energy use.

- *Programmable Thermostats*. Automatic adjustments of cooling demands during periods of reduced requirements such as nighttime hours can have a very beneficial effect on energy use.

- *Air balancing*. Cooling loads can also be reduced by balancing the cooling system throughout the building so that the entire building receives the same amount of air flow to prevent hot spots.

SUMMARY

The only purpose of a cooling system is to provide an environment that meets the needs of human comfort. The facilities manager is responsible for ensuring that the needs are protected with appropriate cooling systems that are properly installed, operated, and maintained.

LIGHTING

L ight can be defined as electromagnetic radiation in wavelengths that are visible to the human eye. Light allows us to see things, but the light itself is invisible. In fact, if one attempts to look directly into a source of light, it is uncomfortable and can damage the eyes if the light is bright enough. What we really see is the illumination of light or the light that is reflected into our eye from the surface of objects. Light itself is a combination of radiant electromagnetic energy in wavelengths ranging from ultraviolet at one end of the visible scale to infrared at the other end. The combination of all the wavelengths between the two extremes into one source of light produces white light. The colors that are seen by the human eye are a result of reflected light. White light hits a surface and some of the wavelengths of energy are absorbed by that surface—the remaining wavelengths are reflected off the surface to produce a discernable color. The human eye is designed to react to sunlight. All measurements of artificial light are based on the characteristics of natural sunlight.

ARTIFICIAL LIGHTING

Any manmade source of light is artificial. The design and use of artificial light requires more than the provision of illumination to allow visibility inside a building. It can be used to affect the ambience or the mood of an occupied space and it can also be incorporated into the décor and furnishings of the building to produce a desired effect. General area lighting is used to change the ambience of an area, but most lighting systems are designed on the basis of task lighting.

Task lighting design principles coordinate the lighting system chosen to the specific activities that are being illuminated. The repair of a watch requires more intense lighting than the preparation of vegetables for a beef stew. The two tasks have different illumination requirements. The watchmaker must be able to see very tiny parts and work in a very small space and therefore needs a bright light. The cook does not need the same bright light but the kitchen should be equipped with enough illumination to be able to tell the difference between a carrot and a thumb. Similarly, the light required in a common hallway is not the same as that required for an office desk. In a restaurant, the kitchen needs enough light to work safely, but the dining room might not need the same intensity. In a fast food restaurant, the dining area will probably have lighting levels very close to those of the kitchen. The fast food atmosphere is supported by brighter lights so that customers can complete their meal quickly and leave to make room for the next customer. Whereas the fine dining facility would want less light in the dining room to provide a more relaxed atmosphere for customers to linger and enjoy their meal in a more leisurely manner, possibly staying for dessert or another cup of coffee. But the table top should have enough light so that the fine diner can see the plate in front of them, so each table may have its own candle or table lamp, and the wait staff service counter will need more light to ensure that the plates are presented correctly with the right salad dressings, etc. For example, the service counter should have light levels that allow the wait staff to tell the difference between Ranch and Bleu Cheese salad dressings.

Safety and furnishing requirements can also influence the task lighting design of a facility. Lights and light fixtures should be selected and installed to highlight strong points of the décor such as paintings or wall coverings. Lighting should also be provided to illuminate hazardous features of the building such as stairways or the edges of carpets in hallways or doorways. The color of artificial lighting must also be considered in the design of lighting systems. Not all light sources produce the same reflected colors as natural sunlight and this can have a detrimental effect on a facility. Broccoli that looked invitingly fresh and green in the kitchen could change in seconds to brown and wilted in the dining room if the wrong lighting is used. A lady's make up that looked very nice under the bathroom light may looked washed out or overdone in the ballroom under a different light source. A well-designed lighting system that uses good task lighting can highlight the favorable points of a room, enhance the presentation of a plate of food, or complement a lady's gown. A poorly designed lighting system in the same room can reveal the cracks in the walls, make the meal look unappetizing, and make the lady look overdressed and shabby.

LIGHTING TERMS

There are several terms that are used in the discussion of lighting systems that should be understood by the facilities manager:

- *Lamp:* A light bulb. The word "lamp" does not refer to the fixture. It is only the light bulb within the fixture.

- *Lamp Life:* The designated lamp life of a bulb is the approximate number of operational hours that the lamp can be expected to burn before failure. This is an average established by at least fifty percent of lamps of this design and manufacture.

- *Efficacy or Efficiency:* The efficiency of a light source or lamp is called efficacy. It is usually expressed in generated lumens per watt of electricity.

- *Fixture or Luminaire:* The appliance or fitting that holds a lamp is called a fixture or luminaire. It includes the socket for the lamp, reflective material to direct the light to the desired direction, and sometimes enclose the lamp behind a protective lens.

- *Coefficient of Utilization:* The efficacy rating of a light source refers to the efficiency of the lamp, but the amount of usable light emitted from a fixture is measured as the coefficient of utilization. A very efficient lamp can be installed in a poorly designed luminaire and have a low coefficient of utilization while a lamp of low efficiency that is mounted in a fixture that directs sufficient light to the desired illuminated surface would have a high coefficient of utilization.

- *Lumens:* Light output is measured at the source in lumens.

- *Footcandles:* Light on the illuminated surface is measured in footcandles.

- *Footlamberts:* Reflected illumination that reaches the eye is measured in footlamberts.

- *Color Rendering Index:* Color rendition is rated on a scale of 0 to 100. A lamp with a color rendering index rating of 100 is a perfect match to natural sunlight. The color rendering index is the rating of how closely a lamp approaches the color of sunlight.

- *Correlated Color Temperature:* The actual color of a light source is its correlated color temperature (CCT). This is best visualized in reference to an electric heating coil. When it is cold it is dark and has a low CCT. As the coil warms it changes to warmer colors or a higher CCT. As the coil continues to heat up it will go through orange to white and eventually to maximum CCT at violet.

AVAILABLE LAMPS

The most commonly used lamp or light bulb is the incandescent. An incandescent light build passes electric current through a metal filament coated with tungsten. The filament heats up and glows. This filament is contained within a vacuum bulb to prevent it from oxidizing rapidly. Incandescent bulbs are relatively cheap to manufacture and present a low initial purchase cost. The light from incandescent bulbs has a high color rendering index so they do not generally distort colors to an unacceptable level. A disadvantage for the incandescent lamp is that it is not very efficient and uses a large amount of energy for a relatively low amount of light. They also produce a high amount of heat, which adds to the cooling loads for the building. The final disadvantage of the incandescent light is that it has a relatively short life in comparison to other light sources. The average life of incandescent lights ranges from 800 to 1,000 hours of burn time. There are several types of incandescent lamps available:

- *Common:* The common incandescent light bulb is found in most homes and buildings.

- *Reflector:* An incandescent lamp can be made into a directional lamp by coating the glass bulb with reflective material. This application is especially useful for décor highlighting, hallway lighting, or entrance-way lighting where the light needs to be directed to a particular area without producing glare.

- *Heavy Duty/Vibration Resistant:* In some applications, such as an elevator or on an appliance or machinery, an incandescent lamp with a thicker filament will have a longer service light. These are called vibration resistant lamps.

- *Tungsten Halogen*: A modified incandescent lamp that produces very bright light. The tungsten halogen lamp uses a tungsten filament in a halogen gas–filled bulb or tube. They have excellent color rendition and are more efficient than common incandescent lamps, with a longer service life. The disadvantages to tungsten halogen lamps include a higher purchase cost than the common incandescent and they produce a large amount of heat and therefore can present a fire hazard if they break while lit. They also must be handled with gloves when being replaced, because the oil from our hands will boil on the surface of the glass and may cause it to break.

Electric Discharge lamps produce light by passing an electric charge through an inert gas inside a glass tube causing it to glow. Electric discharge lamps require a ballast in their circuit to make them operate. The gas needs more electric current to start glowing than it does to keep glowing. The ballast provides the initial required charge and then reduces the current when the lamp is energized. This process is often facilitated by a very small amount of mercury inside the tube to establish an electric arc in the gas. Most electric discharge lamps can be cataloged into two general categories: fluorescent and high-intensity discharge.

- *Fluorescent/Compact Fluorescent:* The most commonly used electric discharge lamp is the fluorescent and its recent offspring, the compact fluorescent. Fluorescent lamps come in a variety of sizes and shapes. They are more efficient than incandescent lighting and have their greatest application in area lighting. In the past, fluorescent lamps were known for their slow starting characteristic, sometimes taking as much as ten seconds to flicker to a lit condition. This delay is called strike time and all electric discharge lights are slower than incandescent to reach full light. In recent years fluorescents have been greatly improved and can start almost as quickly as incandescent lamps in some applications. Fluorescents were also known for their poor color rendition in the past, but this has also been improved in recent years. Their efficiency has also been improved as smaller tubes have been developed with smaller amounts of gas emitting equivalent lighting levels. The change from the older T-12 bulbs to the T-8 bulbs is an example of this improvement. The T-12 was 12 millimeters in diameter and the T-8 is only eight millimeters in diameter. T-5 bulbs were recently introduced and should become more common in a few years. The compact fluorescent was developed in the late 1990's and is gradually replacing many incandescent bulbs. The compact fluorescent lamp uses a small tube twisted into a small space. It is attached to a base with a standard screw connector and self-contained ballast, allowing it to replace an incandescent bulb without modifying the light fixture. Compact fluorescents can produce the same amount of light as the replaced incandescent while using much less electricity and providing a longer anticipated service life. The disadvantage of compact fluorescents is their higher initial purchase cost and some users have reported that the lamp life is not as long as was expected.

- *High Intensity Discharge:* These lamps are generally used for area lighting in large spaces such as parking lots, sports arenas, and large exhibition halls. They provide a great deal of illumination at a relatively low operating cost but they are notorious for poor quality color rendition.
    - *High Pressure Sodium* lamps give a yellowish light because the gas inside them is vaporized sodium. They are very energy efficient and are mostly used for street lights and parking lots.
    - *Low Pressure Sodium* lamps also have a yellowish glow but they have a shorter strike time because they have higher quantities of mercury mixed in the vaporized sodium gas. However, this higher level of mercury can pose health and environmental problems, so these lamps are gradually being replaced with other high intensity lighting.
    - *Metal Halide* lamps use a crystal arc with argon and mercury gases inside a glass bulb to produce very bright light. While not as efficient as the high-pressure sodium, they do have a better color rendition capability. They are used in large retail stores and other large indoor spaces.
    - *Mercury Vapor* lamps are not as common as they were a few years ago. They are being gradually taken out of service because of the health and environmental risks. They are the least efficient of the high-intensity electric-discharge lamps and have a very poor color rendition capability. The light that they produce has a bluish color. They are used mostly as streetlights and other outdoor applications because they have a very long serviceable life.

- *Light Emitting Diodes (LED):* A recently developed light source is the light emitting diode. It uses a semiconductor chip that produces light when subjected to an electric current. These chips or diodes have a very long life and produce a very bright light. They are small and have many applications for emergency lights and equipment instrument operating lights. Recent development has used clusters of these diodes to produce larger light sources. The color rendition of the light emitting diode is not very good as they often have a bluish tinge to the light they produce, but development is making progress in solving these problems. Light emitting diodes are beginning to appear in parking lots and street lights. Future development will bring light emitting diodes into more applications.

SELECTING THE LAMP AND FIXTURE TO USE

When designing a lighting system, both general lighting and task lighting requirements must be considered to achieve the desired results. In the hospitality industry, this requires an analysis of the business plan and operating requirements of the property. In a fast food setting, lighting levels are generally uniform throughout the establishment so bright general lighting might meet the requirements. The lamps and fixtures selected should provide even light to all areas and fluorescent lights probably will suffice for most considerations. In a family casual dining environment, fluorescents may produce a washed-out or uncomfortable effect if they are not supplemented with task lighting using either incandescent or tungsten-halogen to highlight points of the décor. The fine dining establishment might require a more subtle lighting effect with softer background lighting and highlighted but subdued lighting for the individual tables. In all three restaurants, the kitchen will require bright lighting to allow for safe operations and the service area will need sufficient lighting to allow for efficient service. If the décor requires specific color enhancements, the lamps selected should be carefully chosen to support those effects. In the lodging property, the lighting in the lobby will probably be different from the light required in the hallways. Further, the fixtures and the lamps in the rooms should provide a comfortable and welcoming effect. Meanwhile the light in the guest bathrooms must be bright, but not glaring, and color rendition over the mirrors can be very important.

In every hospitality property, a mixture of different light fixtures and lamps for different applications is the most effective approach. Once there is enough illumination in the building for safe operation, then the mixture of electric discharge and incandescent lights must be carefully used to present an ambience that matches the operation. In the process of developing this mixture, attention must also be given to using the most efficient lighting possible in every situation to reduce energy use. Fluorescents and compact fluorescents will greatly reduce energy use if they are used whenever possible, but they will not provide the correct lighting for every task.

The last consideration in the design of lighting systems is the maintenance requirements for the final system. Many different kinds of lamps and fixtures may provide an eclectic or artistic effect but every different lamp represents another item that must be stocked for replacement. A fixture can provide a wonderful ambience, but if it the bulbs cannot be replaced by the staff without special equipment, that ambience can present excessive maintenance costs. For example, a crystal Victorian chandelier can give a wonderful warm and luxurious feeling to a ballroom but the maid on the thirty-foot stepladder cleaning each prism will not appreciate it. When designing a lighting system, care must be taken to ensure that it can be economically maintained.

MAINTENANCE OF LIGHTING SYSTEMS

All lamps and fixtures attract dust, which reduces their efficiency. This is partly because they develop a static charge of electricity on the surface of the lamps while they are being used. If this dust is not cleaned off regularly, the lamp life will be shortened and quality of light emitted will be degraded. Lamps and fixtures should be carefully wiped clean with a damp rag and allowed to air dry. If they are dried or polished with a clean dry cloth, a static charge will be established on the outside of the lamps, which will attract dust more quickly. The proper maintenance of the HVAC system, including regular replacement of the filter materials in the air distribution systems, will also help keep lamps and fixtures clean for a longer period of time.

When ordering replacement lamps it is very tempting to order cheaper bulbs than the original design required. Often, this will change the effect of the lighting design and damage the ambience of the establishment. Poor choices in lamp replacements can even degrade the appearance of the food in some cases. Care must be taken to order the correct lamp replacements to maintain the design integrity of the lighting system.

In task lighting requirements, the most common approach to relamping is to replace burned-out lamps immediately. This is required because each lamp is selected for a particular task. A burned-out lamp may degrade or hamper that task or even produce an unsafe condition. In general, lighting requirements, such as area lights in hallways or large assembly areas, individual replacement of burned-out lamps may increase labor costs with no discernable improvement to the lighting. A single unserviceable fluorescent or incandescent lamp in a large ballroom that has 200 lamps in the ceiling is probably not even visible. Each single tube represents ten to fifteen minutes of labor to replace, including the time to set up and take down the ladder. The same ten to fifteen minutes of labor could replace eight or ten lamps. In large rooms, it is a common practice to allow as many as twenty percent of lamps to burn out before any are replaced and then to replace all of the lamps in the room at the same time. It is counterintuitive to throw away serviceable lamps as a way to save maintenance funds. In fact, throwing away lamps in the last quarter of their life may not be as costly as the labor needed to replace each of them individually. The facilities manager must establish relamping policies that address general and task lighting appropriately for each operation in the building.

CONSERVING ENERGY

Lighting is a significant energy requirement for hospitality operations and the increasing cost of energy has forced facilities managers to consider energy conservation in the management of their lighting systems. Many properties have realized a notable reduction in energy consumption by replacing incandescent lamps with fluorescent lamps in appropriate applications. The key to realizing a savings by changing to fluorescent lamps is to ensure the fluorescent provides the same customer satisfaction for the task being illuminated. If this can be done, then the savings can be significant.

Savings can also be realized through careful control of the operational use of lighting. Simply stated, lights that are not needed should not be burning. This can be manually managed by training the staff to be aware of energy use, but this requires continuous management attention. Several items of equipment are available to aid in the conservation of energy:

- *Occupancy Sensors.* There are two commonly used types of occupancy sensors, movement sensors and heat sensors. The movement sensor usually uses ultrasonic sensing to detect movement and will turn lights on when someone or something is moving around in a space. If someone is sitting still in the space then the lights will go out and the occupant will have to move to bring them back on. Such things as curtains blowing from an open window will also turn on the lights and as long as they keep moving the lights will stay on. The heat sensors use infrared beams to detect people in the space. As long as the beams detect body heat the lights will stay on, but they will go out shortly after the last person leaves the area.

- *Timers.* The simplest lighting control appliance is the timer. It can be set to turn lights on and off at preset times. They have the disadvantage of being inflexible. The timer will react to its setting regardless to local conditions. To operate on overcast days or to adjust for changing periods of daylight, they must be manually overridden or reset.

- *Programmable Lighting Control Systems.* A more sophisticated timer is the programmable lighting control system. The programmable system has a central processing unit that will accept control requirements to react to changing conditions. They can be set to bring on only some of the lamps in the system or to adjust dimmable units to match programmed requirements several times during the day or week. As these systems become more sophisticated in their capability, they also increase in purchase and installation costs. The programmable system also precludes the manual disruption of its system by unauthorized employees so that neither the designed lighting scheme nor the energy-saving measures can be damaged by inappropriate tampering.

- *Photocells.* An inexpensive way to control outdoor parking or landscape lights and security lights is with a photocell. Photocells are relatively inexpensive switches that react to changes from light to darkness. When the environment gets dark enough, the photocell will turn on the lights. They also conserve energy by preventing the lights from being activated during daylight hours. This is valuable during nighttime hours, but also provides lighting during storms and other disruptions of daylight conditions. Therefore, the photocell can reduce safety hazards because of unexpected visibility problems.

- *Photovoltaic Systems (PV).* The generation of electricity with solar cells can be used to support power requirements for interior lighting in some buildings. Photovoltaic systems are very expensive and will not generate enough power to support all requirements for most buildings, but they can provide significant supplementary power to reduce energy costs. Some applications will store electricity in battery banks, but such applications have very limited use and are very difficult to maintain.

- *Daylighting.* The design and construction of buildings to take advantage of natural sunlight to provide for interior lighting requirements is called daylighting. Although such construction can greatly reduce energy use during daylight hours, it is also very expensive to complete. Existing structures are very difficult to renovate or rebuild for effective daylighting so such designs are usually only available in new construction.

SUMMARY

Lighting systems must be designed, installed, and maintained to produce the required lighting to support hospitality operations. Modern lighting systems must incorporate energy-saving efforts without sacrificing customer satisfaction. Facilities managers are responsible to maintain the lighting systems on their properties to provide sufficient illumination for all activities with the most efficient possible energy use.

REFERENCES

1. Stipanuk, D.M. (2006). *Hospitality Facilities Management and Design, 3rd edition*. Lansing, MI: American Hotel and Lodging Association.

2. Brown, D.W. (1996). *Facility Maintenance: The Manager's Practical Guide and Handbook*. New York: American Management Association.

3. Dillow, R.O. (ed.). (1989). *Facilities Management: A Manual for Plant Administration, 2nd edition*. Alexandria, VA: APPA; The Association of Higher Education Facilities Officers.

4. Woods, R.H., and King, J.Z. (2010). *Leadership and Management in the Hospitality Industry, 3rd edition*. Lansing, MI: American Hotel and Lodging Association.

5. Jones, T., and Zemke, D. (2010). *Managing the Built Environment in the Hospitality Industry*. Upper Saddle River, NJ: Prentice Hall.

6. Murphy, E. (2000). *Energy Management and Controls*. Arnold, MD: BOMI Institute.

7. Vanderburg, L.W., Gotts, D.G., Falluchi, A., Fanelli, R., Leitz, E., Rondeau, E.P., Springer, T.J., Whitehair, R.L., and Wood, R.W. (1997). *Fundamentals of Facilities Management*. Arnold, MD: BOMI Institute.

8. Vanderburg, L.W., Fanelli, R.F., Getz. L.V., Kimmel, P.S., Leitz, E., & Ryburg, J. (1997). *Technologies for Facilities Management*. Arnold, MD: BOMI Institute.

9. Jaszay, C., and Dunk, P. (2005). *Ethical Decision Making in the Hospitality Industry*. Upper Saddle River, NJ: Prentice Hall.

CPSIA information can be obtained at www.ICGtesting.com
Printed in the USA
LVOW09s1610030715

444897LV00011B/249/P